AN ANGLO-WELSH TEACHING DYNASTY
The Adams Family from the 1840s to the 1930s

THE WOBURN EDUCATION SERIES
General Series Editor: Professor Peter Gordon

AN ANGLO-WELSH TEACHING DYNASTY

The Adams Family from the 1840s to the 1930s

WILLIAM E. MARSDEN

University of Liverpool

RoutledgeFalmer
Taylor & Francis Group

LONDON AND NEW YORK

First published in 1997 in Great Britain by
WOBURN PRESS
Reprinted 2004
by RoutledgeFalmer,
2 Park Square, Milton Park, Abingdon,
Oxon, OX14 4RN

Transferred to Digital Printing 2004

British Library Cataloguing in Publication Data

Marsden, W. E. (William Edward), 1932–
  An Anglo-Welsh teaching dynasty : the Adams family from the
  1840s to the 1930s. – (Woburn educational series)
  1. Adams (Family)   2. Teachers – Wales – Biography   3. Teachers
  – England – Biography   4. Education – Wales – History
  5. Education – England – History
  I. Title
  371.1′00922

  ISBN 0 7130 0203 4 (cloth)
  ISBN 0 7130 4031 9 (paper)

Library of Congress Cataloging in Publication Data

Marsden, William E.
  An Anglo-Welsh teaching dynasty : the Adams family from the 1840s
  to the 1930s / William E. Marsden.
    p.   cm. – (Woburn education series)
  Includes bibliographical references and index.
  ISBN 0-7130-0203-4 (cloth)
  ISBN 0-7130-4031-9 (paper)
  1. Teachers – England – Biography.   2. Teachers – Wales – Biography.
3. Adams family.   4. Education – England – History.   5. Education
– Wales – History.   I. Title.   II. Series.
LA2375.G7M37   1997
371.1′0092′242 – dc21
[B]   96–52689
                                                                      CIP

Typeset by Footnote Graphics, Warminster, Wilts

Contents

List of Illustrations

Abbreviations

BFSS	British and Foreign School Society
CC	Cross Commission
MCCE	Minutes of the Committee of Council on Education
OS	Ordnance Survey
PRO	Public Record Office
RCCE	Reports of the Committee of Council on Education
SBL	School Board for London Archives (in Greater London Record Office)
SSB	Swansea School Board
TSB	Tottenham School Board
1847 Reports	*Reports of the Commissioners on the State of Education in Wales, 1847* (Shannon: Irish University Press edn, 1969)

Acknowledgements

Among the many people to whom I am indebted for support and advice in the first place I must mention George Bartle who, in his time as Archivist of the British and Foreign School Society, brought together the correspondence of the various members of the family in an 'Adams file', the only materials resembling 'Adams papers' that exist. This file more than any other single feature convinced me that a book on the dynasty was possible. I also thank his successors at the BFSS for their help.

I am also grateful to the following, who in varying degrees have been extremely cooperative in the gathering of sources: in Wales, the staff of the Dyfed Record Offices at Carmarthen and Haverfordwest; Merthyr Tydfil Reference Library; Llanelli Reference Library; Tenby Museum; the West Glamorgan Record Office in Swansea; Swansea Reference Library; Swansea Museum; the Glamorgan Archive Service, Cardiff; Eluned Jones of Llanelli, and Wilfred Harrison of Tenby, authors of the histories of two schools associated with the Adams' family, and T.J. Williams of Cefn Coed Primary School, for supplying me with the relevant section of the school's log book relating to W.B. Adams' short stay there as headmaster.

In England, I am grateful for the help of staff at St. Catherine's House; Somerset House; the British Newspaper Library, Colindale; the British Library; the Public Record Office; the Greater London Record Office and Photographic Library; the Imperial War Museum; Islington Reference Library; Barnet Local History Library, Hendon; Bruce Castle Museum, Tottenham; the City of Westminster Archives Centre; the United Oxford and Cambridge University Club; the British School of Osteopathy; Hampshire Record Office, Winchester; Dorset County Council Library Service; Southampton Reference Library; Christchurch Museum; and Tonbridge Reference Library. Thanks are due to Miss Ruth Carpenter, and Mr and Mrs D. Watkins of Christchurch, whose help established the contacts with Miss Muriel Gossling and

Mrs R.J. Topp. My interview with Miss Gossling was particularly fascinating.

More locally, I have benefited from the help of Miss Victoria De Lara, a Lecturer in the Liverpool Hispanic Studies Department in the early 1930s, for information about provision for teachers of Spanish at that time, and confirmation that she knew of the work of J.W.B. Adams at Christchurch; to my colleague, Dr Robin Betts, for continuing to supply many useful leads; to the librarians of the Department of Education at the University of Liverpool, John Vaughan and his successor, Wendy Spalton; and to the Special Collections section of the Sydney Jones Library, University of Liverpool, for making accessible illustrations.

Once again I acknowledge with gratitude the support of a Nuffield Foundation, in this case from its Small Grants for Social Science Research scheme, which was most helpful in financing travel to so many libraries and record offices. I am equally grateful to the University of Liverpool's Centre for Community and Educational Policy Studies for providing financial support towards the actual costs of this publication.

As ever, I must thank Peter Gordon for his editorial skills; Norma Marson for seeing this book through to press; Vera Marsden and David Marsden for the drawing of many of the maps and assistance with the index.

More formally, I wish to acknowledge the permission of the following for the reproduction of illustrations:
Figure 1.10: Malcolm Seaborne; Figures 1.9, 6.1, 7.4, 9.5: the British Library; Figures 2.1, 7.1: Swansea Museum; Figure 2.2: University of Liverpool Sydney Jones Library (Special Collections); Figures 2.3, 2.5, 7.3: West Glamorgan Record Office; Figures 3.2, 3.6, 7.2, 9.1, 9.4: Aerofilms; Figure 3.7: London Borough of Barnet Local History Library; Figure 3.10: Greater London Record Office; Figures 8.3, 8.4, 8.5 and 8.6: W.J. Harrison.

Preface

The research leading up to this book has developed through three stages. The first was mostly involved with collecting case study materials for a number of publications on what might loosely be termed the historical geography of urban education in the nineteenth century. This culminated in the first of my books for The Woburn Press, *Unequal Educational Provision in England and Wales*, published in 1987. As this work was in progress, it became clear that there was sufficient documentation to produce a biography of Fleet Road Board School, Hampstead. In the second stage, therefore, additional material on this was collected, which resulted in another book for The Woburn Press, *Educating the Respectable: a Study of Fleet Road Board School, Hampstead, 1879-1903*, published in 1991.

Thirdly, in the course of the research on Fleet Road I became increasingly interested in biographical approaches to the history of education, an interest stimulated by the range of the materials available on two charismatic headteachers, William Bateman Adams of Fleet Road's Senior Mixed Department, and Louisa Walker of the Infant Department. Adams emerged as a member of a remarkable teaching dynasty, whose professional activity through three generations spanned a key century in the history of education in England and Wales, from the 1840s to the 1930s. The cache of Adams' letters at the British and Foreign School Society's Archives Centre at Isleworth provided an invaluable starting point. Apart from normal first hand sources, including log books and other school records, school board minutes, official reports and public records, local newspaper materials were particularly important in filling in the many gaps. There were also valuable sources of evidence in journals such as the *School Board Chronicle* and *The Schoolmaster*.

The members of the teaching dynasty, beginning with John Adams in the 1840s, are shown on the family tree overleaf.

Not included in the dynasty is John Adams' eldest son, Henry Adams, a mysterious figure, who emigrated to the United States in

THE ADAMS TEACHING DYNASTY: FAMILY TREE.

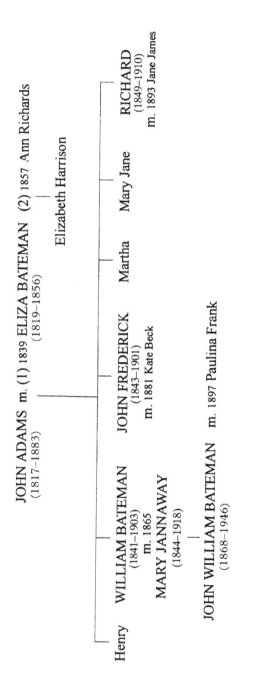

JOHN ADAMS m. (1) 1839 ELIZA BATEMAN (2) 1857 Ann Richards
(1817–1883)   (1819–1856)

Elizabeth Harrison

Henry | WILLIAM BATEMAN (1841–1903) m. 1865 MARY JANNAWAY (1844–1918) | JOHN FREDERICK (1843–1901) m. 1881 Kate Beck | Martha | Mary Jane | RICHARD (1849–1910) m. 1893 Jane James

JOHN WILLIAM BATEMAN m. 1897 Paulina Frank
(1868–1946)

NOTE: Names of members of the teaching dynasty are in capitals the 1860s, and reputedly died in London during the Edwardian period. Nor has any record been found of John Adams' elder daughter, Martha, who, perhaps surprisingly, does not appear to have made teaching a career. A second daughter, Mary Jane, did not survive infancy. John Adams' other daughter, Elizabeth, born in 1859 to his second wife, died young in 1881.

The biographical and educational focus of this third book is placed in the context not only of the Adams family's professional arena, but also of their geographical territory and social action space. Such an approach fits in well with the use of biographical material, out of which individual experiences and feelings emerge. The teachers engaged in nineteenth- and early twentieth-century education in England and Wales were not mere victims of circumstance or exploitation. Though life was tough, they were individual human agents, active in thought and in making decisions, fighting for their careers and the well-being of their families, overcoming setbacks, and refusing to be overwhelmed by external forces.

What is apparent, too, is that Victorian meritocratic advance could hardly be better embodied than in the career-based employment structure offered by Victorian educational expansion, especially after 1870, and especially in the large towns and cities. In addition to the opportunities provided by this social trend, teachers benefited from an enriched culture of educational support in a wide variety of journals and methodological texts; in economic terms from the growth of associations and, at least in the second half of the nineteenth century, from the demand for teachers exceeding the supply; and in social terms from a burgeoning of leisure activities.

It was an Adams family trait to keep itself in the public eye. So they live on in the official reports, national journals, and local newspapers, as well as in the letters they wrote and in the logbook entries they completed. At times the record remains frustratingly uneven, and there are gaps in the story that have not been filled. These relate mostly to the subsidiary detail, and do not appear to subvert the main thrust of the account. How widely generalisations can be made from this account of one teaching family is a matter of argument and conjecture. Though the Adams dynasty was clearly more successful and lived on longer than most, its achievement was not unique. What I hope the study offers is a living realisation of the impact on people of elements both of continuity and change over a century of educational development in England and Wales. If it helps to counter the dismissive and attenuated stereotypes of the teaching experience found in many of the more theoretical discussions, an important purpose will have been served.

Part 1
THE FIRST GENERATION
(1840s–1880s)

1

John and Eliza Adams in Pembrokeshire

THE WELSH FACTOR

Celtic Iron Age tribes gave their names to two periods of the Palaeozoic era, the Ordovician and Silurian, geological divisions well represented in Wales. Their associated rocks outcrop widely in north Pembrokeshire. In the south of the county, however, the dominant strata are later Old Red Sandstones and Carboniferous Limestones. The geological boundary running across the centre of the county roughly coincides with a linguistic boundary, between the Welsh-speaking area to the north, and the English-speaking area, the 'Little England beyond Wales', to the south. Norman settlement failed to penetrate north of this boundary. Southern areas were defended against Welsh incursions by impressive castles such as Pembroke. To the south, a feudal system was established, the church was organised on diocesan lines, and Anglo-Norman towns were built as English settlers and Flemish immigrants followed in the wake of the Norman lords. Most of the castles had access to the sea. Their associated towns become flourishing trading centres. By contrast, the Welsh were not town-dwellers.

The strength of the division between north and south can, of course, be overstressed. There was much intermarriage over the centuries between those on either side of the boundary. The distinction was less racial than linguistic. But from this language difference the dominant English culture enshrined a negative stereotype. Such was markedly present in the minds of the Commissioners who in 1847 reported on the 'State of Education in Wales'. By the late eighteenth century the Welsh-speaking parts of Pembrokeshire had been strongly influenced by religious revivalism. Nonconformity with its associated Sunday School system was well established. While some attempts were made to provide day schools in the Welsh-speaking areas, they were less apparent than those in the south of the county.

In 1846, the attention of the House of Commons was drawn to the state of education in Wales, and a resolution passed that an inquiry be made. The promoter of the inquiry was William Williams, MP for Coventry, a self-made Welshman, who later lost his seat, he claimed, as a result of his campaign. He was unrepentant, however, arguing that the evidence of the 1847 *Reports of the Commissioners on the State of Education in Wales* demonstrated the 'deplorably defective' state of schools in Wales, and the fact that the English language was 'vilely taught'. All sections of the population would benefit from a better-educated people, meaning those able to speak English.[1]

The team of Commissioners enquiring into Carmarthen, Glamorgan and Pembroke was led by Ralph Lingen. What it found was what had been predicted: 'Whether in the country, or among the furnaces, the Welsh element is never found at the top of the social scale....' The over-riding contention was that Welsh people were disadvantaged as a result of the language problem: '...his language keeps him under the hatches, being one in which he can neither acquire nor accumulate the necessary information. It is a language of old-fashioned agriculture, of theology, and of simple rustic life, while all the world about him is English....'[2]

Lingen claimed that this view was widely held by the Welsh themselves. Many parents wished their children to be taught English at school, while wishing to preserve Welsh as the language of family, social and religious life. He contended that the Welsh child faced great difficulties in reading English school books, for the two languages were 'dissimilar in genius and idiom'.[3] The hegemony of the Sunday school was blamed for stereotypical Welsh characteristics: impetuosity, volubility, eloquence, unreasoning prejudices, and even wild fanaticism and riotous disposition. The Report incensed the Welsh nation, most of all because it launched an attack on its manners and morals: 'a disregard of temperance ... of chastity, of veracity, and of fair dealing',[4] and 'of cleanliness and decency'.[5] Welsh-speaking districts were identified as lagging educationally behind English-speaking ones. One of the latter was, of course, south Pembrokeshire. Here the Castlemartin Hundred was described by Lingen as 'upon the whole the best educated district which I found in the counties assigned to me'. The English influence in the towns, such as Pembroke Dock and Tenby, helped 'to break through that feeling of isolation in which the lower orders of Welsh throughout remoter districts too complacently hug themselves'.[6]

THE RURAL ORIGINS OF A TEACHING DYNASTY

John Adams: The Early Experience

The Adams teaching dynasty emerged from this physical and social setting: a remote rural valley in south Pembrokeshire. Here a small stream flowing west had through ages past eroded through the Old Red Sandstone rocks to expose an inlier of Ordovician and Silurian rocks below. On the edge of this inlier, at about 150 feet above sea level, lay the tiny hamlet of Chapelhill. Along the sandstone ridge to the south of the valley was a line of churches, located on Figure 1.1. The parishes were tiny. At the 1851 religious census, Castlemartin had a population of 404; Warren 124; St. Twynnell's 210 (Figure 1.2) ; St. Petrox 86; and Stackpole Elidor 321 (Figure 1.3). John Adams was born at Chapelhill in St. Twynnell's Parish in 1817, the son of William Adams, an agricultural labourer. The 1838 Tithe Map showed Adams to have worked a holding of about 16 acres, some 'moor' in the valley floor, and two fields on the slopes above, together with house and garden. He paid tithes of two guineas to the landowner, Sir John Owen (Figure 1.4). Figure 1.5 shows that his land-holding is equally rural in its setting today.

In his early upbringing the young John Adams was said to have owed less to the influence of day school than to 'the intellectual awakening of the Welsh Sunday School'. He began as a Sunday School teacher at the age of 16. He walked four miles to the nearest town, presumably Pembroke, where lived 'a clever watchmaker and bandsman, able to help him with maths and music'.[7] He married Eliza Bateman, daughter of a miller, at Castlemartin Church in 1839, and worked as a miller himself. At the time of the 1841 census, he was living with his wife, his first-born son, Henry, and a 14-year-old servant, at Orielton Mill.

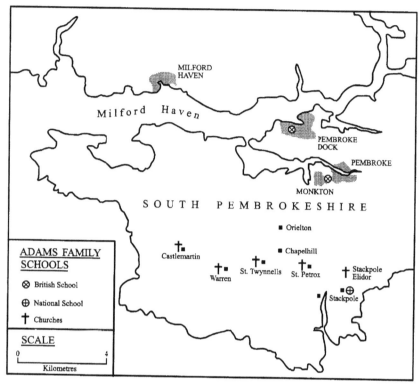

Figure 1.1.   Map: The Adams family in South Pembrokeshire

The Westminster Experience

In 1843, John Adams, aged 26, embarked on a six-month residential course for mature male students at the National Society's training department in Manchester Buildings, Westminster. The number of applicants far exceeded the supply of places.[8] The trainee teachers practised at the Boys' Central School at the Sanctuary, Westminster Abbey, the 'Model School' of the National Society.[9] The *33rd Report* of the Society indicated that the students were 'comfortably boarded and lodged, accustomed to regular and domestic habits, and instructed in religious and useful knowledge'.[10]

Candidates were carefully selected. Testimonials were demanded from local clergy and from three respected householders in their parish. Personal defect, chronic disease, or age over 40, precluded application. Information was required on situation in

Figure 1.2. St. Twynnell's Parish Church

Figure 1.3. Stackpole Elidor Parish Church

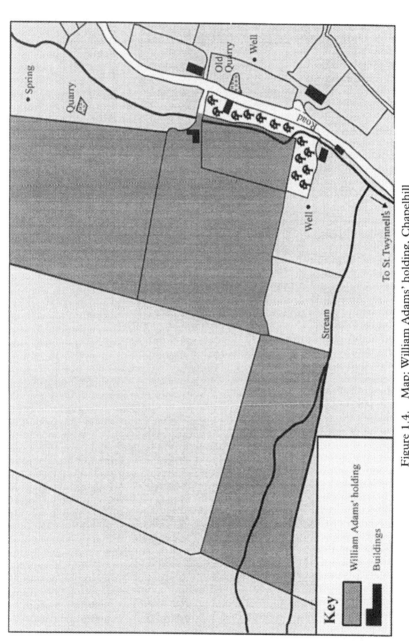

Figure 1.4.   Map: William Adams' holding, Chapelhill

Figure 1.5. The Chapelhill landscape today

life, family connections, education, employment, place of residence, moral habits and character, temper and disposition, especially with regard to children, whether fond of them, and accustomed to managing or teaching them, and whether a regular attendant at church and a communicant. Before admission, applicants were examined in knowledge of the Bible and prayer book, of sacred history and geography, and of the three Rs. These were regarded as the 'indispensable requisites'.

The students were trained to teach all the subjects followed in the Central School, including arithmetic, geography, history, music, drawing, writing and composition. Overall, the syllabus was pervaded by religious instruction, with catechetical teaching the key to the methodology. Lack of aptitude for teaching, as evidenced after a fair trial in the Central School, led to withdrawal. The student was expected to take each class in turn, starting, as a probationer, with the lowest. After demonstrating competence in managing and instructing the range of classes, he would be put forward as candidate for a post in a National School. He had to succeed both in the training institution and in practice at the school and, throughout, maintain good moral conduct. Following recommendation to a school, the new male teacher could expect a salary of over £50 per annum. In 1843, this West-minster crash-course provided 74 masters for National Schools, and in 1844 over 90.

The Stackpole Experience

Armed with his new skills, John Adams returned in 1843 to his native Pembrokeshire to begin his teaching career at Stackpole National School. Here he remained until 1848. During this period his third son, John Frederick, and two daughters, one of whom died in infancy, were born. The children, like Adams and his wife, were baptised. The school was maintained by the Earl and Countess of Cawdor, and was the only one in the parish of Stackpole Elidor (Figure 1.3). The 64 male and 36 female pupils in the day school represented respectively 32.8 and 18.8 per cent of the population. The 100 total on the books represented 25.9 per cent of the popu-lation overall, one of the highest percentages in Pembrokeshire.

The quality of Stackpole National School was noted in HMI John Allen's *Report* for 1845. He recorded that in the south of Pembrokeshire, where there were no difficulties with language, schools had been raised and teachers appointed 'that would be considered excellent in any part of England'.[11] At Stackpole the standards of reading a verse of the gospels with ease, of writing on slates and on paper, and of working of simple sums, were well ahead of other schools in the region. Allen observed:

School supported by the landowner. Arithmetic and writing very good; reading fair. Intelligence and knowledge of scripture good. Some knowledge of geography, grammar, and history of England. Discipline good. Master trained at Westminster; quiet and painstaking. Likely, as I hope, to improve year by year in his work. Needlework taught to the girls by his wife.[12]

The 1847 *Reports* reinforced this favourable early impression, indicating that the state of the school buildings was good, and the furniture and apparatus sufficient and in good repair. There were still 100 children on the books, of whom four were under five years of age, 54 between five and ten, and 42 over ten. Of these, 49 travelled over 1.5 miles each way to school. Thirty-four of the children had attended it for less than one year, and none for more than four years. The monitorial system was used, each class providing a monitor for the one below it. The school opened and

closed with a hymn and a prayer, and religious instruction was conducted by John Adams himself. Adams was also responsible, with
the Rector, for the running of the Sunday School, in which the language of instruction was English. This had 30 scholars under 15.
Here the scriptures and catechism were committed to memory. All
the children attended a place of worship. Adams was described as
'an active and intelligent man', who had been a corn dealer. His
salary was £30 per annum, and additional income of £22 derived
from school pence. He also had a substantial free house (Figure
1.6) and garden. The salary was better than that for most schools
in the area, where the average income was £22 10s per annum.

Adams 'spoke highly of the natural capacity of the children', and
considered it superior to that he had observed in the Central
School in Westminster. He had to contend with truancy at
harvest time, but attendance improved from after harvest to
December and from February to May. Expulsion was often
treated by parents with indifference, though most were anxious to
have their children educated. About twelve of the children prepared lessons in English grammar at home, to be repeated in school.
Geography was taught to some of the more advanced children

Figure 1.6.   Stackpole National School: the Master's House

through a book published by the Society for the Promotion of Christian Knowledge. They read from this with ease and answered in 'an animated and intelligent manner' when the master questioned them.[13] The Earl of Cawdor, it was later revealed, introduced a system of working allotments, encouraging the boys to cultivate small plots of garden, rewarding the most successful, as a contribution to training for later country work. [14]

The Borough Road College Experience

The Adams' stayed long enough at Stackpole both to gain a good reputation locally and consistently favourable reports at a national level. By 1847, however, they had resolved to leave the National system. In a letter from 'Stackpole Village' to the British and Foreign School Society (BFSS) dated 29 July 1847, John Adams wrote for advice about the 1846 Privy Council Minutes, which effectively established the pupil teacher system in England and Wales.[15] He appealed for guidance on the requirements of government, appearing to be under the impression that stiff questions would be put relating to his proficiency were he to seek pupil teacher support. He claimed to know his Bible well, to be a good arithmetician, tolerable at grammar and geography, and able to teach algebra. The implication of the letter was that he had been refused pupil-teacher support.

In a letter dated 12 December 1847 from the Pembroke Dock British School Committee to the BFSS, appealing for support to establish a new school, the Secretary referred to the possibility of John and Eliza Adams being appointed as Master and Mistress. Both were of 'excellent character' but had been working in a National School for the past five or six years. They wished to train for three months at Borough Road at their own expense. They would be willing to suffer any privation to accomplish their objective. A subsequent letter of 24 February 1848 thanked the Society for its help. It confirmed that the new Pembroke Dock British School would open in July 1848, with Adams and his wife in charge. John Adams was described as 'an intelligent worthy man' and his wife as someone who would 'suit us'. He could be in London in March to be interviewed. On appointment, the two would have a combined salary of £70 and a commodious house and garden.

A letter dated 21 February 1848 from John Adams to the BFSS

stated that he and his family would be arriving in London on 25 March to spend two or three months at Borough Road. He apologised for being troublesome, but noted that he had four young children. He appealed for cheap lodgings with a clean, honest and religious family, located near the College, as a walk night and morning might be too far for Mrs Adams. He thanked the Society for arranging for free dining at Borough Road. Adams was required to provide testimonials as to his religious character and that of his wife, one from the clergyman of the church he attended and one from the secretary of Pembroke Dock School.

The Borough Road Training Manual outlined in detail on the BFSS System's methods of instruction. Thus the ground space of the schoolroom had to be divided into three parts:

- An open space near the teacher's platform for draft work, in which the children were arranged in semi-circular standing groups for instruction from a monitor or pupil teacher. The divisions were measured out accurately on the floor. Each draft should have a blackboard and a strong box, functioning as storage for books and slates, and as a seat for the teacher.
- Fitted writing desks facing the platform, size and distance apart carefully specified.
- A gallery or galleries for collective lessons, again facing the platform, a gallery not accommodating more than 50 children at the same time, with 40 a preferable maximum for simultaneous instruction.

The Manual suggested that where there was one large schoolroom only, as provided for the monitorial system, for the new system there was the need to provide separate compartments to isolate each class and teacher from the rest to preserve them from interruption. It was advised that curtains be used for this purpose, so as not to jeopardise the master's powers of exercising general superintendence. It was urged that a large school should be divided into sections of not more than 50 pupils, each to be further divided into drafts of from ten to 15. The children in each section would continue to study until ready for promotion to the next, and would preferably remain in the same section for all studies. At the same time, the child need not be in the same draft for every study, but could move between pupil teachers or elder monitors. Precise details on the means of classifying children for different studies were given. In writing, children in the lower sections worked on slate, before the expense of paper was incurred. The trouble caused by pen, ink and copybook, it was maintained, was more than compensated thereafter by the improved method for training and the improvement they made possible.

Where the new system had come into operation, it was intended that each section of the school should be under a pupil teacher, who was expected to marshal the children in order before entering the schoolroom, and lead them quietly to their places. The pupil teacher kept the attendance register or roll-book for his section, and recorded their state of progress following regular examination. The master had to offer one and a half hours of instruction to pupil teachers daily. The pupil teachers had to give criticism lessons to drafts of children twice a week, which were subjected to 'friendly criticism and correction'. All lesson material had to be critically scrutinised by the master or mistress. Pupil teachers changed section every six months, to become acquainted during their apprenticeships with different age groups. The use of monitors was not abandoned, and it was argued that in conjunction with trained and pupil teachers they could still be valuable, ensuring closer surveillance of the whole range of pupils. Detailed guidance was given on their deployment.

While scriptural instruction appeared to loom less large than under the National System, it was made clear that more importance was attached to it than to any other branch of instruction, and that the scriptures should be made the *text book* of other subject instruction. Thus there would be Bible geography and Bible history, while reading would also be pervaded by religion. Work in these areas would often have a moral component. Advice was given on arrangement of playgrounds, which were designed for assembling before school and during hours of recreation. The playground should include conveniences with a good supply of fresh water, seats, flower beds and, for boys' playgrounds, apparatus for gymnastic exercises, to promote healthy muscular exertion.[16]

The Pembroke Dock British School Experience

At the time of the 1847 *Reports*, there were many more National than British Schools in Pembrokeshire.[17] Adams was fortunate in that he was able to make his move at the time when the BFSS was expanding its operations in South Wales. He also belonged to a teaching cohort in the forefront of effecting the transition from the old monitorial to the new pupil teacher system. Pembroke Dock British School was in the Pater district of the town. Lingen, though generally critical of the state of education in Pembroke Dock, noted that the 'condition of the population improves as they come within the influence of the dockyard'.[18] He indicated that if such a school were formed, it could establish a valuable connection with the dockyard school, where apprentices were trained.

The Adams family lived in a provided house (Figure 1.7), attached to the school building (Figure 1.8) in Meyrick Street, one of a series of parallel terraced streets climbing gradually from the dockyard (Figure 1.9). At the time of the 1851 census John

Figure 1.7. Pembroke Dock British School: Master's House, front elevation

An Anglo-Welsh Teaching Dynasty

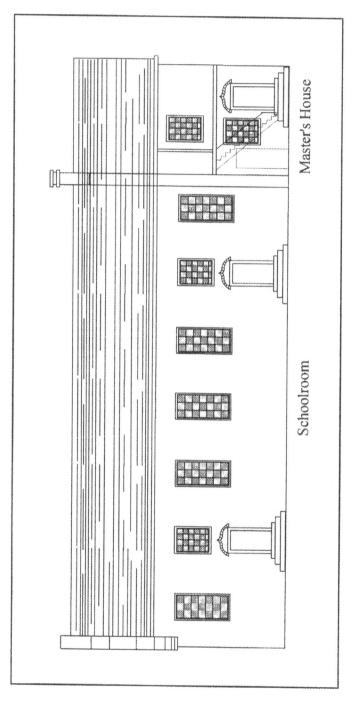

Figure 1.8. Pembroke Dock British School, side elevation

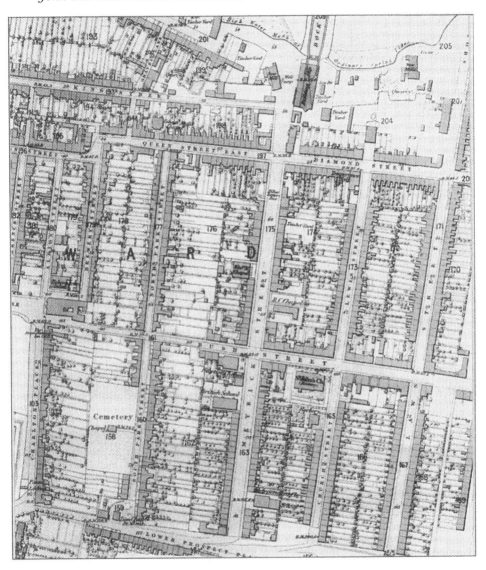

Figure 1.9. First Edition 25-inch Ordnance Survey map: Meyrick Street area, Pembroke Dock

Adams was 33 and his wife 32. They had four children living at home, three sons and a daughter, the eldest three recorded as scholars. The youngest boy, Richard, was born at Pembroke Dock. The family employed a female servant, aged 22, and had a pupil teacher as a lodger.

Adams and his wife continued to enjoy favourable Inspectors' reports. Of great importance for the future professional status of the dynasty were the influential judgements of, in the first place, Joseph Fletcher, Inspector of British Schools in South Wales. Thus for 1849 he reported no fewer than 300 scholars at Pembroke Dock British School present at the examination, 200 boys and 100 girls. He recorded four pupil teachers in the boys' school and two in the girls', though the plan of the schoolroom was based on the old monitorial system.

This is a double school, enjoying a full attendance and a vigorous organisation; the children in it are making a steady progress; and, in fact, although it has been at work for only 11 months, it is perhaps the most efficient school in this remote part of the principality, to which it presents a very valuable model; its tone and discipline being as satisfactory as its intelligence and industry.[19]

Fletcher's 1850 Report was even better. Numbers had increased to 185 boys and 140 girls, the girls having an additional pupil teacher.

. . . these are thoroughly well-organised schools, using the best methods with zeal and activity. . . . The progress in the ordinary branches of elementary education . . . is perfectly satisfactory throughout. . . . The next steps in advance will be by making the lessons in geography, grammar and common knowledge fall within a more 'training' effect upon the minds of *all* the children in the sections in which they are conveyed; to which end the augmenting abilities of the well-taught pupil-teachers of both schools will greatly contribute. These are among the best schools of the class existing anywhere in the principality.[20]

The 1851 Report was also approving, though with some reservations. John Adams was said to be an 'able and improving' master and his wife 'an excellent and intelligent matron'. Of the boys' school he remarked:

This school has made a fair year's progress, and merits the high character I gave it a year ago, though its room still wants upward ventilation, its middle sections a revision of their work in geography and grammar, which is too abstract and verbal, and its methods generally, a neater application, to ensure a yet more collective and vivid attention. With the addition of classrooms, it would thus become a model institution.

Of the girls' school he concluded: 'This school may be described in exactly the same terms as the boys, of which it is in most respects a counterpart, with an excellent tone of its own'.[21] Following Fletcher's death, Matthew Arnold took over as Inspector of British Schools in 1852. While expressing reservations about the need for another classroom at Pembroke Dock British School, Arnold described Adams as 'excellent as a master and fully adequate as a scholar', and his wife as 'a very respectable, good woman, with many excellent qualities as a teacher'. The two worked 'the institution in conjunction admirably'. About the boys' school he was particularly enthusiastic, and the accolade indeed sealed Adams' reputation as a head teacher.

This is on the whole the best school I have met with in South Wales; it is vigorously supported, and has a thoroughly effective master; all parts of the school feel the good effects of this. Out of the thirteen drafts, six write well from dictation. Arithmetic, which is peculiarly useful in such as place as this, is quite remarkably well taught. The more general branches of instruction are very fairly taught, except grammar, in which improvement is needed.

He was more qualified in his praise of the girls' school.

The performance of the school is altogether on a lower key than that of the boys' school but, this being premised, the same praise may be given to it. There is the same general character of a sound sensible instruction carried thoroughly through the school. The arithmetic is good; the grammar moderate as in the boys' school. History and geography, though tolerably taught at present, might with advantage be taught better.[22]

John Adams' son, William Bateman, in his later evidence to the Cross Commissioners, was to refer back nostalgically to the pre-Revised Code teaching in Pembroke Dock. He claimed that special attention was given to scholars in the upper standards to consult 'the peculiar bent' of their minds. He quoted the authority of Matthew Arnold for saying 'there were no classes equal to them, certainly not superior to them, in any part of Germany, or the best educated countries in the world.' The standard in mathematics had also to be high, in order to meet the demands for employment in the dockyard. Pupils had 'to work four books of Euclid and the first part of Colenso's algebra'.[23]

The school was fortunate in gaining a third respected and equally complimentary HMI, Joseph Bowstead, in 1853, when 195 boys were presented at the annual examination. The boys' school was organised in six sections and 13 drafts. Bowstead found discipline and methods good and the instruction excellent.

This is a first-rate school, and its superiority is not more manifest in the higher classes than it is in the very lowest. Every child has some elements of geography, grammar and mental arithmetic introduced to his notice; and the result is a tone of active intelligence throughout the classes which is very rarely met with. . . . The attainments of the most forward boys, especially in arithmetic, algebra and Euclid, are very striking. . . .

Bowstead was, however, more critical of the girls' school, and censorious about the accommodation, speaking of 'the continual noise and confusion, caused by the teaching of nearly 200 boys in a single, undivided, and not very well-formed room'. The inconvenience was increased by the fact that the boys' and girls' schools were divided only by a movable wooden partition.

These large and prosperous schools are more nearly self-supporting than any other British schools that I have seen, and this is effected without any degree excluding the children of the working classes. The circumstances of the population, whose chief employment is in the dockyards, are particularly favourable for such a result. It is very important that a class-room with a gallery should be provided for each school, and the erection of such an addition to the premises would claim their Lordship's liberal assistance.[24]

During the incumbency of the Adams, therefore, the accommodation of this new school far from matched the ideal, even in a relatively new and presumably purpose-built establishment. Bowstead's criticism of the accommodation was effective. An 1855 plan shows the adjusted accommodation provided. There was one large room, divided by a partition into boys' and girls' schools, measuring 36 by 38 feet and 36 by 30 feet respectively. Each department had spaces for drafts and desks in the approved Lancasterian manner, but the galleries were not at the back, rather on either side, seating respectively 26 boys and 24 girls. The interchange system was in operation, the twelve boys in each of the six reading drafts, for example, exchanging places with the 72 boys in the desks, or in the two galleries, fulfilling the axiom of 'relief by change of position' (Figure 1.10).[25] But around the time of these improvements, Adams left Pembroke Dock.

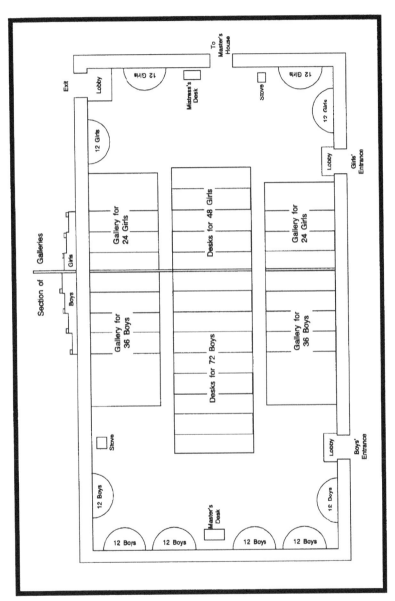

Figure 1.10. Plan: Pembroke Dock British School

The reputation of John Adams was thus established in the wider public domain on the basis of the consistently favourable reports of high-status inspectors. He also reinforced this esteem at the local level by, from the late 1840s, initiating public examinations of his pupils. In June 1849, for example, the local newspaper reported, with a hint of surprise, that a such an examination took place before 'a numerous and respectable audience'. The answers to the scripture questions indicated 'that considerable attention is given to this very important branch of juvenile instruction'. English history was a subject the children 'appeared to enter with great spirit, answering the questions with great promptness, and with a correctness which reflected great credit upon both teachers and pupils'. The British School secretary, Bonniwell, addressed the audience and asked Adams to allow his children 'to sing a few of their choice tunes, which elicited general applause'. Some of the visitors remained afterwards to inspect the needlework 'with which they expressed themselves highly gratified'.[26]

The *Carmarthen Journal* similarly attended a public examination in December 1852, which included an examination of scripture (Chapter 1, St. John's Gospel) by a local minister, of a boys' class in geometry, arithmetic and algebra, given by a pupil teacher, and of a junior boys' and girls' class on 'tea' and 'cotton' respectively by two female pupil teachers. Another led a session on naming places on a map of Ireland, while one on English history was offered by Adams and one of his pupil teachers. An English grammar test was conducted by Mr Wright, master of Milford British Schools. There was also an exhibition of knitting, crochet and plain needlework by the girls and of chalk drawings by the boys. Again the attendance of a 'numerous and respectable audience' won approving newspaper comment. It was pointed out that the schools had been in operation for five years and had 'surpassed the most sanguine expectations of the promoters'. They had now upwards of 300 boys and girls educated in them by Mr and Mrs Adams, assisted by four male and four female pupil teachers. Reference was made to Joseph Fletcher's favourable reports on the schools.[27]

The school opportunistically took advantage of the expansive mood of local people on the occasions of launches from the dockyard. Thus at that of the 31-gun frigate *Curacao* in April 1854, it was noted that there were outstanding orders for ten more naval vessels, all steamships. A bazaar was concurrently held at the British School, timed so that people could attend after the launching, to raise funds to pay off the school debt. Music was played by the Band of the Royal Dockyard Brigade. The reporter enthused about the occasion, noting the tables laid out, each attended by a lady and crowded 'with a most brilliant display of articles calculated by their attractions, elegance and tasteful arrangement to open the purse-strings of the most matter-of fact and remorseless old bachelor'. The room was decorated with floral arrangements, and 'the flags of Old England, her ensigns white and red, the Union Jack, and the Admiralty Anchor'.[28]

Adams was, however, to leave Pembroke Dock on a sourer note. It was a town in which Anglican influence was strong. The National School was well regarded and there was clearly some rivalry with the British establishment. In 1855 there was a proposal for a new National School. R. Bonniwell, secretary of the British School Committee, like Adams, was always keen to publicise the achievements of his school. He attacked the new proposal on the grounds that the evil of children being forced to learn the catechism in Church schools remained: 'Away, then, with such a system, and introduce one in which the children can be educated and instructed in Scriptural knowledge, without a fear of them being moulded and proselytised to a Church from which we, as parents, dissent.'[29]

These 'lucubrations' were scathingly renounced by another correspondent, under the pseudonym 'A Graduate of Honours, of Oxford'. He regarded British Schools as 'nurseries of Dissent and specious instruments in the hands of those … steeped in the grossest bigotry and intolerance'. He suggested that Bonniwell and others of his stamp would benefit if they were 'more actuated in their conduct by the excellent and incomparable teaching of this much abused Church Catechism'.[30] Returning to the attack, Bonniwell, who had advocated the need for a new British rather than a National School in the town, quoted the 1854 Report from Bowstead in which that HMI had suggested that the schools best suited to South Wales, a land of Dissenters, were those 'based on unsectarian, yet strictly scriptural principles of the British and Foreign School Society', as a means of commanding the confidence of people 'who hold nothing so precious as perfect religious freedom'.[31]

Another anonymous correspondent took up the cudgels, and commented that far from parents being put off by the catechism taught at the National School, they had been moving their children in large numbers away from the British School during the previous six months,[32] notwithstanding the 'zealous outcries' of Bonniwell. This intervention provoked a response from John Adams. He condemned the statement that over 100 children had left his institution for the National School as untrue and based on rumour. He agreed that children did change schools daily as a matter of parental caprice, but argued that a special factor in this case had been a change of staff at the National School. When the founding head, Mr Allen, had left, his 'unfortunate' and 'less popular' successor had caused an exodus. Many parents tried to transfer their children to the British School, who could not be admitted because of shortage of accommodation. When the new master of the school left and Allen returned, numbers picked up again. In general Adams' letter was intended to ameliorate. He agreed that the National School was not excessive in its promotion of the catechism, was a relatively fair school of its type, and that its parents were allowed to attend dissenting places of worship. This made the National School in Pembroke Dock less unpopular than other such schools.

His final paragraph, however, turned out to be more provocative. Adams concluded that he was leaving Pembroke Dock 'for a large field of usefulness elsewhere': 'but I doubt not that my successor – a man of considerable attainments, holding a higher certificate than any other public teacher in this part of the country – will, in his turn, make a draw of, of course, a hundred, or considerably more, from the National School'.[33]

This excited a sarcastic response and some personal abuse from the anonymous correspondent. In the first place he attacked Adams' syntax, complaining that a British schoolmaster ought to comprehend plain English. Secondly, he suggested that Adams' account of numbers indicated that he could not keep his registers with accuracy. There followed barbed comments about his once having been a National School master, who had not long ago applied, unsuccessfully, for a similar situation, 'no doubt considering it preferable to the one he held under Mr. Bonniwell's secretaryship'. He dismissed Adams' 'vain and silly ostentation' in announcing the approaching advent of a successor, and his 'boasting assumption' of that successor's superiority to Mr Allen.[34]

John Adams thus from an early stage initiated a family tradition not only of running an effective school, but also of ensuring that the wider public was made aware of it. The accompanying tendency towards self-promotion was later to result in the achievements of the dynasty being acknowledged in some quarters, but being subject to strong and possibly envious criticism in others.

REFERENCES AND NOTES

1. *Pembrokeshire Herald*, 22 Dec. 1848.
2. 1847 *Reports*, Vol.13, p.3.
3. Ibid., pp. 31–2.
4. Ibid., p. 6.
5. Ibid., p. 17.
6. Ibid., p. 389.
7. *Educational Record*, Vol.11 (1883), pp. 303–4.
8. National Society, *32nd Annual Report* (1843), pp. 10–11.
9. R.W. Rich, *The Training of Teachers in England and Wales during the Nineteenth Century* (Cambridge University Press, 1933), p. 31.
10. National Society, *33rd Annual Report* (1844), Appendix 5.
11. *MCCE* (1845–6), p. 107.
12. Ibid., p.115.
13. 1847 *Reports*, pp. 393–4.
14. CC, *2nd Report* (1887), p. 48. Reference made by John Adams' son, William Bateman Adams, in his evidence to the Commission..
15. Rich, op.cit. (1933), p. 118.
16. See BFSS, *A Handbook to the Borough Road Schools Explanatory of the Methods of Instruction Adopted by the British and Foreign School Society* (London, 1854).
17. See G. Bartle, 'The Role of the British and Foreign School Society in Welsh Elementary Education, 1840–1876', *Journal of Educational Administration and History*, Vol. 22 (1990), pp. 18–29; and also B.L. Davies, 'British Schools in South Wales', *National Library of Wales Journal*, Vol. 18 (1973–4), pp. 383–96.
18. 1847 *Reports*, p. 463.
19. *MCCE* (1849–50), p. 442.
20. *MCCE* (1850–1), pp. 758–9.
21. *MCCE* (1851–2), p. 901.
22. *MCCE* (1852–3), p. 698.
23. CC, *2nd Report* (1887), p.47. Again a reference from John Adams' son, W.B. Adams.
24. *MCCE* (1853–4), pp. 826–7.
25. M. Seaborne, *Schools in Wales 1500–1900: A Social and Architectural History* (Denbigh: Gee and Son, 1992), pp. 126–8.
26. *Pembrokeshire Herald*, 29 June 1849.
27. *Carmarthen Journal*, 31 Dec. 1852.
28. *Haverfordwest and Milford Haven Telegraph*, 12 April 1854.

29. Ibid., 5 June 1855.
30. *Pembrokeshire Herald*, 6 July 1855.
31. *Haverfordwest and Milford Haven Telegraph*, 18 July 1855.
32. *Pembrokeshire Herald*, 27 July 1855.
33. Ibid., 3 Aug. 1855.
34. Ibid., 10 Aug. 1855.

2

John Adams in Swansea

GOAT STREET BRITISH SCHOOL PRE-ADAMS

1806–1847

Goat Street School in Swansea was historically significant as one of the founding public elementary institutions in Wales. Following previous appeals for funds, the Swansea newspaper *The Cambrian*[1] made the case for a school for the education of poor children. In January 1806 the 'Swansea Society for the Education of the Poor' was formed. Its purpose was to establish a free school dedicated to the instruction of children who would not otherwise receive it because of the poverty of their parents.[2] The school opened in makeshift accommodation in June 1806. Organised on the Lancasterian system, it was claimed to be the first school in Wales of its type.[3] By the beginning of 1807, more than 100 boys were in attendance. Subscriptions were raised to build a new school house in Goat Street, opened in 1808, it was said by Joseph Lancaster himself. It provided day school instruction for 150 boys. *The Cambrian* recorded its gratification at the 'simplicity, order and regularity, with which instruction is communicated from the youngest to the eldest'.[4] The school building is sketched in to the left of the Wesleyan Chapel on College Street on this nineteenth-century painting (Figure 2.1).

The curriculum was restricted to the three Rs and to scriptural study. Thus in the 1816 Report[5] the state of progress of the nine classes was assessed. In writing, for example, ten of the 225 children were still using sand boxes. In the second class 21 children were writing on slates words of two letters. The fifth class were writing words of up to five letters. The sixth class was writing on slates words of two syllables, the seventh words of three, the eighth words of four and five, and beyond this there was the ninth or

Figure 2.1.   Old print of Wesleyan Chapel and Goat Street School, Swansea

'grammar class'. For reading practice, the children were directed to Biblical extracts.

Much later a former pupil reminisced about the work of the system:

> . . . the boys wrote on sand which was placed in a kind of box. The written letters were hung up on the walls in front of the scholars, and with their fingers they had to copy them on the sand . . . (classes) one and two were relegated to writing on sand, and when proficient they were allowed slates, and as the acme of proficiency the . . . upper class had the high honour of quill pens and paper, which proved the finishing stroke to their education. To be able to write on paper in those days was considered grand in the extreme for boys in a humble sphere of life.

The writer claimed that the first Master, Thomas Tomlinson, was noted for iron discipline, excessively harsh even by the standards of the time, which led to his dismissal for cruelty. He was succeeded in 1821 by James Hammett. He too was a martinet, old pupils retaining 'vivid memories of the severity of his punishments, by which the most perfect order was maintained'. The teaching of penmanship was his forte. His low voice regularly intoned: 'Boys beware of blots and bad writing.' If they transgressed, the response was a rap across the knuckles with 'a formidable pointer' or a blow under the ears with a clenched fist. The 'Old Scholar' suggested that if teachers of the 1880s had resorted to corporal punishment of Hammett's severity, they would have found themselves in prison. But scarcely a complaint was received during this earlier period. Among other ploys, Hammett bought three pairs of stocks, into which truants and late-comers were locked.[6]

Little time was spent on arithmetic and far more on handwriting, regarded by Hammett as of critical importance. Prizes were awarded for cleanliness. A barber was employed for 'the removal of superfluous hair', to ensure a high order of cleanliness among the poor boys. The will of the Committee was supreme, and no complaint from parents was even anticipated. Religious study was based largely on Bible reading. Funds were also expended on taking children on Sundays to the place of worship of their choice.[7] From 1835 fees were charged, ranging from 1d per week for poorer parents, to 6d for the children of shopkeepers and those designated as not belonging to the working classes. In 1838 there were 107 boys paying 1d per week, 66 paying 2d, and seven paying 6d.[8]

1847–55

The 1847 *Reports* indicated that the state of the building was good, though some of the furniture was in bad repair. There was accommodation for 310 and there were 240 boys on the books, and eight monitors. By this stage, Hammett's curriculum had broadened to include more arithmetic, and also grammar, geography, the history of England, and vocal music. The Master was 46, indicating that he had been only 20 when first appointed, having had no previous occupation. He had trained at Borough Road for four months in 1821 and one month in 1838.[9] The school was regarded in the region as a model of its type.[10]

Instruction was given entirely in English. The 1847 Commissioners approved the generally English-speaking nature of Swansea, and produced a long account of the instruction at Goat Street, particularly that in religion and geography. They were only partially impressed with Hammett. 'The master appeared rather a superior man. His school was under good discipline. I was surprised at not finding his scholars more proficient.'[11] HMI Joseph Fletcher's Report of the same year was more critical of Hammett's work. While acknowledging that he showed great energy in the management of the school and enjoyed a high local reputation, Fletcher complained that: '... his methods are not the most recent, and his plans generally are of the more mechanical character which belongs to schools of an early date'.[12]

The criticism would appear to have had some impact, for in 1849 Fletcher indicated that organisation and methods of reading and grammar had been revised and now were models for general imitation: '... the general tone as well as the vigour of the school render it one of the most valuable institutions of its kind in the principality'.[13] In 1850 he again praised the general industry and tone of Goat Street, making it one of the best of the old Lancasterian schools in Wales, but with the caveat that 'the bonds of old mechanical habit tend to restrict its progress...'.[14] By 1851, pupil teachers were being employed, though Fletcher judged that the best use was not being made of them. Hammett was continuing to find progress towards more modern methods difficult.[15] In 1853 Fletcher's successor Joseph Bowstead administered the *coup de grâce*, finding Hammett 'no longer in a condition to pursue his arduous labours with comfort to himself' owing to 'suffering health'. But he deserved a good pension. Bowstead concluded that Goat Street was still 'a very superior school ... and offers a fine field for the exertions of a first-rate teacher'.[16]

GOAT STREET AS ADAMS' SCHOOL

The Early Years

The first-rate teacher chosen to replace Hammett was John Adams. Swansea in 1855 was a more complex and congested urban environment than that he had experienced in Pembroke Dock. In the early part of the century, Swansea had aspired to become a fashionable seaside resort, but was soon to be overtaken by an industrialised landscape of coal mines, copper and tin-plate works, and potteries. The harbour was improved and extended, and port industries and trade grew (Figure 2.2).[17] The school was in the heart of this congested central area, hemmed in between the Wesleyan Chapel on College Street (Figure 2.1) and terraced housing, with the back entry of Banc-Caer restricting any expansion behind (Figure 2.3).

Figure 2.2. Daguerreotype of Swansea and its harbour, 1848

Adams quickly achieved his first objective: to restore numbers at Goat Street. They increased from 143 on the books when he took over in 1855 to 353 in the ensuing year. During the 1850s the school accommodation was extended, though at the expense of the already restricted playground (Figure 2.4). He revitalised the organisation of the school, splitting it into sections of 40 boys. These were further divided into classes of 12 to 14, each under a pupil teacher. Collective teaching was offered in a gallery, accommodating 40 boys. Reading, spelling and arithmetic were taught in smaller classes. From the start Adams introduced public examinations. An early example took place in June in 1856, presided over by the Mayor of Swansea. The pupils answered questions in scriptural history, geography, arithmetic and grammar, their answers reflecting credit on the industry of the master. *The Cambrian's* report concluded: 'the British school is now, *par excellence*, one of the best of its kind in the principality'.[18]

HMI Joseph Bowstead's Report of 1858 found the British School at Swansea as 'as efficient, in most respects, as any schools similarly situated that I inspect in England'.[19] That for 1859 covered

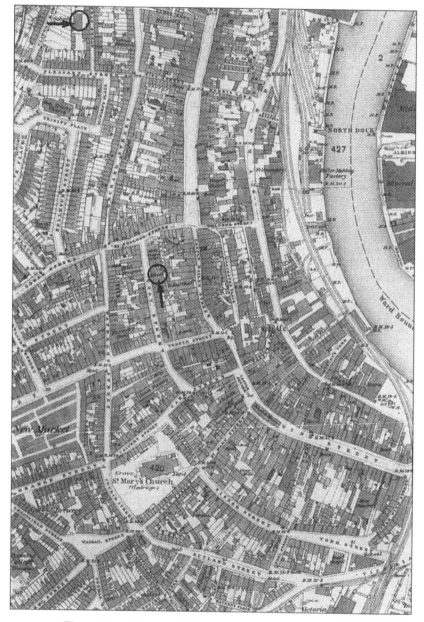

Figure 2.3.   OS map of Goat Street area of Swansea, 1878

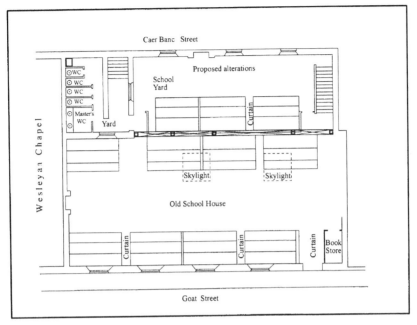

Figure 2.4.   Plan of projected alterations at Goat Street School, 1850s

British and other Nonconformist schools in Gloucestershire, Worcestershire, Monmouthshire, Glamorganshire, Carmarthenshire and Breconshire, and placed Goat Street among the best 22 in his area. A factor common to all these schools was that they were large, with 200 or more children. Every one employed pupil teachers in proportion to scholars – one to every 30–40. Bowstead regarded the presence of a number of pupil teachers at different stages in their development as of great help to the Head, allowing a large number of grades. At this time, Goat Street had six pupil teachers.[20]

Within months of the family's arrival in Swansea, Eliza Adams had died from chronic inflammation of the lungs, and less than 18 months later John Adams married the former matron of Bridgend Union House, Ann Richards. A daughter, Elizabeth, was born in 1859. At the time of the 1861 census his second son, William Bateman, was at Bangor. John Frederick was still living at home, working as a pupil teacher at Goat Street. The two younger children of the first marriage, Martha and Richard, were recorded as scholars. Margaret Long was their one servant. During the first five years in Swansea, the family was involved in four house moves, all within the central core of the town but within easy walking distance of Goat Street. These can be located on Figure 2.5, a late nineteenth-century Ordnance Survey map of part of central Swansea, to the west of Figure 2.3. Early residences were

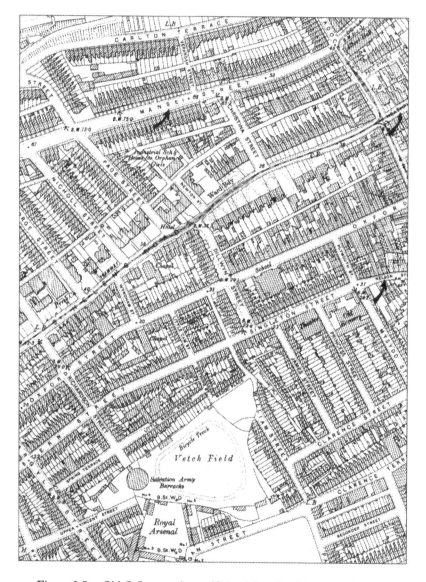

Figure 2.5.   Old O.S. map: Area of John Adams' residences in Swansea

in Nelson Street, on the east side of the map, followed by moves upslope to Heathfield Street, also on the eastern edge of the map marked by the tram route, and finally into Mansel Street, a major thoroughfare route on the north side of the map.

John Adams' continuing prestige locally was reflected in 1860 in his Presidency of the West Glamorgan and Carmarthenshire Teachers' Association, a regional group meeting quarterly to debate issues of professional interest, in this case at Goat Street. It was reported that tea was served up 'in excellent style' by the second Mrs. Adams, 'who ever does all in her power to make the teachers coming from a distance comfortable – she at this time, as on all other occasions, received their warmest thanks and approbation'.[21]

The Pupil Teacher Court Case

In 1860, however, Adams' professional reputation was jeopardised by his involvement in an serious court case, which reflected no credit on either himself or his pupil teacher sons.[22] It was brought by William Fulford, a boot and shoemaker of Goat Street, on behalf of his son William Edward Fulford, a pupil teacher at the school. The grounds were assault by Adams on the defendant; Fulford's wrongful dismissal as a pupil teacher; and the securing of his dismissal by the school committee by fraudulent means. Owing to a legal technicality, Adams was not formally charged on the last of these grounds, but the associated issue was brought up in court. The jury heard a case lasting five hours. The defendant's lawyer launched a blistering attack on Adams, contending that in a professional situation in which the master was engaged in a formal contract with a pupil teacher, and in one in which two of his sons were pupil teachers at the same school, parents would watch carefully to judge whether the master pushed his own sons at inspection to the prejudice of the others. But instead of dealing with the boys under his charge with 'firmness, kindness and attention, it would be found that a uniform system of passionate anger was persisted in by him … there had been a continued disposition on the part of the defendant to push his own children as pupil teachers, to the detriment and prejudice of the other youths'. He highlighted 'petty acts of tyranny' of the defendant's sons towards Fulford which had been ignored by the master.

Fulford had become a pupil teacher at Goat Street at the age of 13 in 1857. In January 1860 Adams was alleged to have sent his son, William Bateman, to the Fulfords' home, with a message that he had not learned his lessons. The young Fulford told Adams the following day to make his complaint to his father in person, and not through William Bateman. An irate John Adams told Fulford to leave, but he refused to obey. Adams then took him by the waist and physically propelled him to the school lobby where, after a struggle in the confined space, he threw him down the steps into Goat Street, causing him injury in the process. Witnesses, both in the school and in the street, confirmed the account. Fulford's father had subsequently complained to Adams. He found him in 'an excited state' and was told that he, Adams, would do the same thing again.

The following March, William Fulford returned home with a mark on his face, following a fight with William Bateman Adams. The defendant's version of the story was that, having divided his section into two drafts, he heard William Bateman telling the one he was not teaching to go home. Fulford protested, but the young Adams insisted on the boys leaving. A fight ensued, which continued for ten or fifteen minutes before another pupil teacher intervened. Fulford's mother came in and led him home. The next morning William Bateman further provoked his fellow-pupil teacher with the words 'You look well', referring to a scratch on his face. Fulford told him to cut his nails before he fought again, which excited the response 'I'll knock your b——— head off'. John Adams then entered, separated the two, and sent Fulford to the platform. Fulford demanded that Adams should hear his lessons, but the master refused, told him not to be impudent, and stated that he would not teach in the school again, summarily suspending him. The next day the unfortunate pupil teacher came before the Committee, where Adams threatened to flog him. He alleged that on a previous occasion Fulford had been the one to threaten his son. Fulford was dismissed from the school by the Committee. Adams also claimed that Fulford or his father had in the street been heard to taunt him with names such as 'old apple-woman' and 'there's a pretty schoolmaster'. The allegations were denied.

John Adams was also accused of conspiring the corrupt the course of justice in that he tried to persuade a pupil teacher,

William Lewis, who had been called to give evidence in the court case, not to do so, on the grounds that he was in weak health and would suffer if cross-examined in court. He advised him to get a medical certificate to avoid having to testify. Adams also was alleged to have more than hinted that he would sign a certificate for Lewis that would help him with the government inspector. Adams denied all these charges, apart from the one that he had ejected the boy from the school, arguing that in this matter he had used no more than reasonable force.

Adams' performance before the court was equivocal and un-impressive. A degree of negligence was revealed in his plea that he did not know about the fights, or the merits of the case, for his son had not given him particulars. He claimed he did not remember the details of his conversations with Lewis. Adams' lawyer pointed out that the case would not have been brought had Fulford not been dismissed, and that was done by the Committee and not by Adams. He made much of the argument that Fulford was an insolent youth. In showing his defiance in front of 300–400 pupils, Fulford had indeed agreed he had been impudent on occasions. Adams argued that he had been fully justified in ordering him out of the school. When Fulford would not comply, he had used legitimate force. It was the plaintiff's own struggles which led to his injuries. Adams' lawyer admitted, however, the impropriety of Adams' conversation with Lewis.

The judge, in summing up, concluded that some of the evidence presented was irrelevant. Although Adams' contact with Lewis was not part of the case being tried, the judge was still critical of it and suggested that Adams had not 'availed himself of imparting to Lewis the value of truth and integrity in every station of life'. He allowed that Adams was justified in asking Fulford to leave the room in the January incident, and in using some force when the plaintiff did not comply. The question at issue was purely whether Adams had employed unreasonable force. Following the five-hour hearing, the jury returned after a 'short consultation', unhesitatingly finding in Adams' favour.

The following week, the Goat Street School Committee met and, following completion of business, 'a cordial and unanimous vote of thanks was awarded to the headmaster for his zeal and attention to the duties of the school, the committee expressing their unabated confidence in Mr. Adams'.[23] The fact that he had conspired to pervert the course of justice and had certainly been guilty of unprofessional conduct in his dealings with pupil teacher Lewis, who bravely testified to the court, seems to have made less impression on the Committee than the feeling that Adams had dealt effectively with an act of insubordination, not to be tolerated in a pupil teacher.

Progress 1860–1875

Following the court case, the situation improved for Adams and Goat Street School, notwithstanding anxieties about the forthcoming Revised Code. The 1861 Government Report was very favourable, the school being described as 'remarkable for the extent to which good technical teaching is combined with a general development of intelligence.'[24] In a printed Report to its subscribers in 1863, the Goat Street Committee noted that 321 children were on the books, and 233 in average attendance. The Master's great efforts in ensuring regularity were meeting with greater success than previously. Regular attendance at places of worship was also encouraged, and favourable HMI reports were publicised. *The Educational Record* of the BFSS gave a detailed account of a public examination in December 1863, conducted by the Society's Inspector in South Wales, David Williams.

The pupils having sung a tune, the lower classes were examined in reading and spelling from their lesson-books in poetry and prose, when the attention that was paid to emphasis, pronunciation, and expression, together with the rapidity and accuracy of their replies to difficult questions in mental arithmetic, and elementary questions in geography, gave complete satisfaction. The upper class was next examined by Mr. John F. Adams (Adams' son) ... in reading, grammar and history, and it was manifest that they had been well grounded in these subjects. The Society's Inspector then proceeded to test their general intelligence by questions on the familiar topics of the day, the imports and exports of the country, the seats of the different manufactures, the Lancashire distress, the war in America, etc., with all of which they were well acquainted. They were then questioned in mental arithmetic, and their rapid and accurate replies astonished all present.... Mr. Williams said that their efficiency in the secular subjects was manifest to all; but that he now came to a subject of greater importance, a subject that had reference to this life and the life to come. He then proceeded to question the children, and the replies given must have convinced every one present that they were well acquainted with the Holy Scriptures.... Mr. Adams' ability and devoted attention to his duties were evidently manifest.[25]

The Cambrian commented that the public examinations had become important social events in Swansea. It noted that since Goat Street's founding, 10,000 Swansea boys had passed through the school, and claimed that none had appeared in a magistrate's court charged with a crime, a consequence of the attention paid to religious instruction.[26] Adams' own relatively recent appearance before the court was already either forgotten or ignored.

The impositions of the Revised Code did not divert Adams from offering his own version of what for its time was a broad and balanced curriculum. HMI Bowstead commented interestingly on how some schools avoided the worst excesses of the Code, arguing that it worked well in the best large schools he inspected, including Goat Street.

In these the Government applied its stimulus to the elementary subjects alone; but the schools are compelled by their own interests to devote quite as much attention as they ever did to that wider range of instruction which the people are sufficiently enlightened to require for their children. I have known cases in which these individual subjects were almost given up on the introduction of the New Code, and in which it was found absolutely necessary to re-introduce them in order to retain the children up to the age to which they had formerly stayed. This is a healthful symptom, and one that may be expected to extend itself year by year over a gradually expanding circle of schools.[27]

John Adams made no secret of his distaste for the Revised Code, as in the prophetic tones of a letter to the BFSS, dated 21 October 1862.

I fear the new fangled scheme is a death blow to the pupil teacher system. In large schools we may retain two or three of such youths: but in small schools it would be far better to employ paid monitors. I have been impressed for several years past that the market would one day be over-stocked with these young people, but I never could have believed that any Government in our country would have acted as Lowe and Co. have in ignoring stipulations and agreements. He seeks popularity; but I fancy his name will be, ever in future, amongst school people and many others, hated and repudiated.

At the time of the public examination in 1865, there were 383 pupils on the books and the average attendance was 318. A local newspaper gave a breakdown of the relative numbers belonging to the different religious denominations as: Church of England, 20 per cent; Calvinistic Methodists, 23 per cent; Baptists 21 per cent; Independents 20 per cent; Wesleyans 10 per cent and Presbyterians

6 per cent. It would seem there was no over-riding religious problem about the education of boys at Goat Street. 'It is clearly
understood that the children attend some place of worship and
Sunday School, the choice, of course, being that of the parents.
Your Committee think, from these items, they may fairly claim the
sympathy and support of all denominations.' The HMI Report
was quoted, which recorded that Adams 'continues to conduct
this school in a most efficient manner. It has passed a good examination under the Revised Code'. There was a heralding of dissatisfaction to come, however, in the comment that the premises
would be much improved if a playground, of however limited size,
could be found.[28] Adams had obviously managed to retain pupil
teachers despite the depredations of the Revised Code. In 1866
two of them came first and second in the first class in the Queen's
Scholarship examinations for Bangor Training College, a fact
'most honourable and respectable', according to *The Cambrian*,
reflecting well on the 'care and training' of Adams.[29]

By this stage Adams' own sons were in post as heads in British
Schools in South Wales and family contacts at a professional level
began. Thus father and sons helped with mock examinations at
each other's schools. Musical entertainments continued. A new
venture of the 1860s was the arrangement of sporting fixtures
between the boys, as in a cricket match between Goat Street and
J.F. Adams' Llanelly School, won convincingly by Llanelly.[30]
Interests in music and in sport were to become important facets of
the Adams dynasty's professional and social lives. The main
anxiety for Adams during this period seems to have been securing
regular attendance. Thus in 1868 a prize scheme was introduced
for children with over 400 out of a possible 470 attendances.[31]

The Cambrian's report on the public examination of 1869 was
prefaced by a tribute to Adams, who had 'ably conducted' the
school over 14 years: 'the managers are fortunate in possessing the
services of a master of such long experience, and of unquestioned
ability'. It noted that he held the highest Certificate awarded by
government. Sixteen of his pupil teachers had proceeded to Normal
Schools. He also received an accolade from David Williams, the
BFSS inspector, who noted that he could never pass through
Swansea without visiting Goat Street School, gaining pleasure in
witnessing the assiduity of John Adams, a pattern for pupil teachers which, if they followed, would bring success.[32] The range in

the curriculum tested had shown no diminution as a result of the Revised Code. The *Swansea and Glamorgan Herald* observed that the questions in geography were of a very practical nature, of particular relevance in that many of the boys were the sons of sailors, mechanics, etc. Intriguingly, Williams felt obliged to say that if anyone present felt the examination had not been a *bona fide* one, the boys would answer questions from any member of the audience.[33] The occasion was also reported in the *Educational Record* and was said to have reflected 'very creditably upon the ability and diligence of the master, Mr. John Adams'.[34] Thus the accolades were recorded both locally and nationally.

In 1870 there was high praise again from *The Cambrian*, placed in the context of the new Education Bill.

It is pleasing to find amidst all the changes of the educational system of the country, some schools steadily pursuing their work, doing good and maintaining a widespread popularity, heedless of the cavil that is being perpetually carried on about sectarianism, dogmas and catechisms. Amongst the first of these we would place the old established British School, Goat Street.

The editor applauded the high quality revealed in the public examination in spelling, mental arithmetic, Holy Scriptures and geography. In between the examinations school tunes were sung in very pleasing manner. Homilies to the boys and their parents were received from various local luminaries. *The Cambrian* noted that the Education Bill did not require alterations in this type of school as it was of the sort designed for use with the school boards, where children were all educated together without being taught the particular tenets of any sect.

Mr. Adams, the excellent head-master, by the creditable examination his boys have passed, has just given us a practical demonstration that this can be done consistently, with sound instruction in the Holy Scriptures, and therefore so far from being apprehensive we hail the advent of the spread of such institutions as one of the greatest blessings that could be conferred upon the country.... In conclusion, we must add a tribute of well-deserved praise to the Master, who has managed this school with such energy, ability and success for the past fifteen years. H.M. Inspectors have year by year expressed their high estimation of the training which the boys receive here; and the subscribers and committee are, we feel sure, doing much to elevate the condition of their poorer neighbours by providing the means of such a desirable education for upwards of 300 boys.[35]

During 1870 a major conference of South Wales schoolmasters was held in Swansea in particular to discuss the religious difficulty as related to the new Education Act, and also issues of compulsory attendance and superannuation. Adams spoke on the latter subject. He pointed out how much better the conditions had been for teachers when he had started over 20 years previously, with many inducements held out to attract them. He did not think he would have been a schoolmaster but for these. The government had broken faith with headteachers, and some were now getting £50 per annum less than before as a result, for example, of the decline in salaries for training pupil teachers. In his own case his Committee had generously indemnified him against loss. A pension for the teacher was indispensable. He claimed his ordinary salary was barely enough to keep himself and family decently and respectably. He could save nothing, and would have to rely on charity in his old age, or go to the workhouse, having expended his strength for his country. He proposed, and it was resolved, that a superannuation scheme would be a powerful means of securing and retaining efficient teachers.[36]

By 1871, the Adams had moved gradually to more desirable residential properties In that year they lived in Heathfield Street, on the edge of the town centre, and very close to Goat Street (Figure 2.5). By this time Adams was aged 53, and his wife was 51. She ran a Bible depository at the house. Richard Adams had returned home from college and was teaching at Goat Street, while his 12-year-old half-sister Elizabeth was a scholar. Margaret Long remained as the long-standing family servant. In the same year, Adams attended a meeting held to promote the opening of a new training college for schoolmistresses, an earlier venture having failed. Adams contributed one guinea to the fund.[37] He was to be on the Committee of the new college.

Under the Swansea School Board, 1875–81

By 1875 the Swansea School Board was well established. From the founding of the Board in November 1870 the religious difficulty surfaced, and the different denominations scrambled for places on the Board. But it quickly gained the reputation of being a progressive body, moving speedily to produce a census and an appraisal of existing public and private schools. It made Standard V the threshold for full exemption and III for half-time. It adopted compulsory powers as an antidote to the heedlessness of parents.[38] But local newspaper correspondents left it in no doubt that there was already ample school accommodation in Swansea, and that Board Schools were not required.[39] By the time of the School Board period, the Goat Street School accommodation was antiquated, and came increasingly under scrutiny because of its dilapidated condition. The extensions of the 1850s had removed the playground, and there was no room for expansion. The Education Department was informed that the managers were deliberating whether to close the building and move to another locality.[40] But the school continued to receive good government reports.[41]

As with so many other British Schools, however, the subscribers decided they did not have the funds to continue and improve the schools to current standards, and in 1874 requested the transfer of the Goat Street to the Swansea School Board.[42] *The Cambrian* was disturbed by this development. Under the heading 'The British School (Adams'), Goat Street' it gave its opinion that: 'The school boards of this country seem to be cutting at the roots of voluntary educational effort. As an example of this we may mention that Goat Street British School is about to be handed over to the Swansea School Board.'[43] The following week the newspaper confirmed the transfer, noting that the formation of Swansea School Board had made it impossible to keep up a good list of voluntary subscribers. It hoped the Board would retain the present able managers. It claimed that religious teaching had never been neglected at Goat Street but nothing sectarian was ever taught. It was the model British and Foreign Society School. *The Cambrian* demanded that the Board should run its schools on similar principles. 'It is a fact that the greatest harmony has ever existed in the management of this large school, and it is to be hoped that nothing may occur by the transfer of it to the School Board to mar its influence or efficiency....'[44]

Swansea School Board agreed to take over Goat Street School in 1875. It bought the desks, fittings, books and apparatus from the managers for £120, and agreed to appoint Adams at a salary of £170 plus one-fifth of the Goat Street government grant.[45] The school had accommodation for 350 boys. There were 308 on the books with 283 in average attendance. Irregular and fluctuating attendance was reported to be a continuing problem, with fifty fewer boys present in the afternoons than in the mornings. The staff included John Adams, his son Richard, and four pupil teachers. One hundred and six boys paid 4d fees, 123 paid 3d, 61 paid 2d and 18 were free. The Board enquired into why some were admitted free.[46]

It received a report from the new managing body of Goat Street suggesting that having no girls and infants on the same premises was a drawback. Boys were leaving to go to three-department board establishments where they could take charge of younger brothers and sisters on their way to and from school. There followed from Adams regular complaints in his log book that there was much ill-health among pupils and teachers because of the poor ventilation of the school.[47] The Board resolved to enquire why there were so many absences because of ill-health, registered almost daily. Examples were quoted:

… although I am pleased with the pupil teachers in their work in the school, I am far from being pleased with them in their home lessons – they appear languid. I fear bad air and smells in the school-room act upon them – they work well during the day, but are quite exhausted when school closes.… It is impossible for them to pass a good examination this year. They constantly complain of illness … found myself unwell this morning owing to the bad ventilation. I kept in the open air all the afternoon.[48]

The Board was suspicious because complaints about health had not been logged when the school was a voluntary institution, but began after school's transfer. The managers were asked why. Their reply stated that HMI had been complaining about the condition of the premises for many years, and that the Board must have been aware of this when they took the school over. The regular presence in the log book of complaints about ventilation and illness had been on the explicit instructions of the local government inspector. The fact that they were not made earlier was because they were communicated verbally at Committee meetings. The managers complained that the Board's remarks were 'somewhat unfriendly', seeming 'to imply a charge of want of candour on the part of the managers which they entirely disclaim'.[49]

The Clerk was asked to write to the managers in turn disclaiming any insinuation against them. But the debate was marked by unpleasant exchanges at the Swansea School Board in which pro- and anti-Adams lobbies surfaced. Among the latter, a member commented sarcastically that 'this was the wonderful school and the wonderful teacher who had been held forth as an example'.[50] *The Cambrian*, however, remained among Adams' supporters, criticising derogatory remarks that had been made about Goat Street and its declining intake, and 'as an act of justice' appended a report on the school which showed a recovery in numbers.[51] But Adams had already been presented in a somewhat negative light. It was clear that he was in for a rougher ride under the Swansea School Board than under the old voluntary procedures. Some members were consistently unimpressed by his performance. When a supporter claimed he was the 'model schoolmaster' and argued he was being paid too little, another countered that this was not the Board's general opinion, and that the Board's inspector had indicated that a much younger man in another Swansea school had produced much better results than Adams.[52] He achieved good government reports in 1876 and 1877, however, and a local newspaper recorded that he had the best results for children passing in the three Rs in Swansea.[53] The chairmen of the annual prize-givings continued to eulogise Adams work: always 'zealous to impart a godly education, and taking a deep interest in the spiritual welfare of the children'.[54]

In 1878 an excellent achievement was registered in the annual report of the Inspector employed by the Swansea School Board. Goat Street emerged very well on all his criteria. The Board gave prizes for regular attendance, good conduct and punctuality. Only five departments won a significant number of prizes, and Goat Street headed the list with 37. The Inspector had 'no hesitation in saying that the results in the subjoined tables may be taken as a measure of the efficiency of various schools ... it may be observed that the Goat Street school is the most efficient, having passed the highest percentage of the government and Mr. Cole's (his own) examinations, being the largest school and paying the greatest amount of revenue to the Board'. The figures were given as:

- 91.18 per cent passes in the government examination of 1877.
- 83.1 per cent in the examinations by Mr Cole in 1877, based on six visits (the lowest school achieving only 47.4 per cent).
- 31.9 per cent of children in Standards .IV,V and VI , the school nearest to Goat Street having only 22.3 per cent.
- Average attendance – Goat Street 253, the percentage not being given.

- Amount paid to Board in fees and grants £313 12s 1½d – the next largest being £302 4s 10½d.[55]

None the less, the Swansea School Board continued to be less than impressed with Adams. Early in 1879 he was severely criticised for spending an unauthorised week in London.[56] (Why he was there was not revealed, but this was about the time the Fleet Road Schools, under his son William Bateman, were opening in London.) The year 1879 was also stressful in that Adams' second wife Ann died from kidney failure, and about this time their daughter Elizabeth contracted what was to prove a terminal illness.

By 1881, John Adams had moved again to a more desirable residential thoroughfare, Mansel Street. It was described later, on the occasion of a National Union of Teachers conference in Swansea in 1897, held in the adjacent Albert Hall (Figure 2.5) as leading west to leafier suburbs, and lined by an avenue of trees.[57] The 1881 census recorded as resident at 44 Mansel Street John Adams and his faithful old servant, Margaret Long, the still unmarried Richard Adams, aged 31, and the unemployed daughter of his second marriage, Elizabeth, aged 22. Stricken by pneumonia, enteritis and tuberculosis, she died in May 1881. The stress of this period had already been heightened by the disruption of the move the previous month from Goat Street to Rutland Street, and in March by Adams' most serious confrontation with Swansea School Board, when the School Management Committee recommended that the Goat Street School should be required to reimburse the Board £10 as a part of the loss occasioned by Adams' unauthorised reduction of school fees. Adams' case was put by Rev. W. Williams, a member of the Board.

Mr. Adams had been instructed by the old committee that he should not turn any boy away, but take from the children what he could get, because it was felt that in every case in which a boy was sent away there would be a loss of fee and grant. And therefore the master was always under the impression that he could best promote the interests of the school by taking what fees he could get. Having lived for some time under the old dispensation, it was possibly difficult for him to comprehend that he was passing into a new dispensation. But there was another consideration. The Goat-street schoolroom had been in a deplorable condition for a long time, and the health of the children had been bad. As many as fifty or sixty had been absent with the fever, and some kept away for fear of infection. The master therefore got exceedingly anxious, thinking the school would go to nothing.

Williams accepted that Adams had been remiss, but moved an amendment to the effect that they pass over the case this time, but warn Adams as to his future responsibility.

The Board was unhappy with the amendment, insisting that the case was serious, calculating that it had lost £38 over the period of the remissions, and arguing that Adams should be setting a better example to younger teachers. The fine was small in relation to what the Board had lost. It had leniently taken into account Adams' age and anxiety over the issue, and had hesitated to demand the full amount of loss. The Report was adopted. Perhaps because the local editors were sensitive to Adams' other problems at this time, the case was given no coverage in the Swansea press, but was reported in the *School Board Chronicle*.[58]

RUTLAND STREET EPILOGUE, 1881–3

John Adams had one further radical change to negotiate: the final closure of Goat Street School and the transfer to Rutland Street. Richard Adams was appointed headmaster of the new Senior, while John Adams was made head of the Junior Department. In April 1881 over 300 boys met for the last time at Goat Street and were marched down to their lavish new building (see Figure 7.2). The *Swansea Journal* reminded its readers that though the school had been condemned by HMI, it stood first for efficiency among Swansea's educational institutions, a result of 'the ability and unremitting labour of the masters, whose names, in matters appertaining to education, have become local household words'.[59]

Unfortunately, in the following October, the Adams received a very unfavourable first report. They received an official warning to the effect that the '... attention of the teachers at Rutland Street be drawn to the unsatisfactory character of the Report, and that they be informed that a very different Report will be expected next year, otherwise the Committee will be compelled to consider their position very seriously'.[60] The Editor of the *Swansea and Glamorgan Herald* immediately sprang to the defence of the school, pointing out that it had only just opened with many poor scholars. An 'excellent defence' could be made against the Report, and a verdict should be based on years rather than months of operation.[61]

Similarly, a letter from an anonymous correspondent (W.L.) pointed out that the inspection had taken place a mere two and a half months after the school's opening. New pupils were mixed with the old Goat Street scholars, and two pupil teachers were working with classes of 60 rather than 30. Teachers had had to change classes and no fewer than 587 pupils were in attendance. Reports on Senior and Junior Departments were in some respects good. 'Perhaps those who have formed a hasty opinion, and may not think the Rutland Street schools are in an efficient state at the present time, will be generous enough to suspend their judgement until twelve months' work has been completed in the new buildings.' He hoped the same publicity would given to the Report then. He did not criticise School Board members, who were doing their duty, and did accept that the report was in certain respects 'somewhat unsatisfactory'.[62]

The editor of *The Cambrian's*, however, seized the opportunity to indict the work of the School Board, referring to these poor results.

The report of the last meeting of the Swansea and District School Board reveals something like a state of panic among the members. They had believed that everything was going along most prosperously. Into this belief they deluded themselves, and almost succeeded in deluding the town. Looking upon themselves as apostles of a new education, they have raised and expended no end of public money. As a matter of course, they have depreciated the work which their unostentatious predecessors did under the system of voluntaryism.... And now what do we hear? That the whole edifice of self-laudation is a make-believe, a sham.

He argued that the Board should take a stricter line with teachers, who should be disabused of the idea that they had a job for life. They deserved decent school houses, apparatus and staff 'but, on the other hand, a fairly high standard of results should be exacted from them under penalty of dismissal in case of failure'.[63]

In the following year the predicted improvement at Rutland Street was achieved. Prizegiving ceremonies were resumed. It was recorded that the behaviour of the children was admirable and that the schools were in 'a flourishing condition', with over 600 pupils in all the departments.[64] At a second prize distribution in 1882, the room was so crowded that some parents could not get in. Over 300 scholars, having successfully passed the government examination, were presented with illustrated certificates. It was noted that the government Report showed the school now to be in a very efficient state, and children were urged to attend regularly and punctually. Swansea's own inspector of schools congratulated the Rutland Street School on its recruitment, giving the lie to local prognostications that it would never be filled. Songs were sung and there was an exhibition of drill.[65]

In 1883 John Adams' health deteriorated. His final illness was a short one. During June and July he was confined by his doctor to bed. On return after the summer break on 20 August, the Rutland Street log book recorded: 'All teachers present with the exception of Mr. J. Adams whom [*sic*] I regret to say departed this life on Sunday morning last, shortly after one o'clock.' Like his second wife, he died from kidney failure. In his will, made a matter of days before his death, John Adams left a personal estate of £542 14s 1d, of which £30 was given to his 'faithful servant' Margaret Long, a gold watch to his grandson John, on condition he never sold or parted with the same, and the rest was divided equally between his children, William Bateman, John Frederick, Martha and Richard.

In its obituary the *Educational Record* described John Adams as

... an able schoolmaster, and a veteran and zealous promoter of education in the principality of Wales.... Not a few of the leading tradesmen
of Swansea sought the advantages of the British School for their children, and Clergymen and Dissenting Ministers of various denominations
joined in their approval of Mr. Adams' catholicity, comprehensive and
calm judgement, and thoroughly religious spirit.... The characteristics
of Mr. Adams' work as an educationist may be summed up in a few
words – thoroughness, practicality, adaptability, and power of simplifica-
tion. He was warmly opposed to the mechanical measuring of results,
and strenuous in endeavouring to subordinate the aiming at school dis-
tinctions, prizes, capitation and other grants, to the real education of the
pupils.[66]

The *Herald of Wales and Monmouthshire Recorder* noted that 'Adams's School' was a familiar name to many occupying posts of honour in Swansea and other towns, owing 'their position in no slight degree to the careful instruction received by them in their early days from the good old schoolmaster who passed away on Sunday last'.[67] *The Cambrian* deeply regretted the passing of 'an old and respected fellow townsman', master at Swansea for almost 30 years, a Sunday School teacher for 50 years, and an office bearer with Argyle Chapel. So successful was he at Pembroke

Dock British School, the newspaper revealed, that on the recommendation of Matthew Arnold, the Education Department had offered him a lucrative appointment under the government of South Australia, which he declined. It noted the number of head-teachers who had served with Adams as pupil teachers. They included the headmaster of Sale Grammar School, and heads in Pembroke Dock, Chatham, Poole and Sheffield.[68] The obituarists were at one in referring to the successes already achieved of his three teaching sons. John Adams had founded a teaching dynasty.

REFERENCES AND NOTES

1. *The Cambrian*, 18 Jan. 1806.
2. W.J. M. Gilchrist, 'A Study of Elementary Education in Glamorgan in the Nineteenth Century'. Unpublished University of Wales (Swansea) MEd Dissertation, 1980. See also *The Cambrian*, 4 March 1904.
3. *The Cambrian*, 28 June 1806.
4. Ibid., 22 Oct. 1808.
5. Ibid., 13 Jan. 1816.
6. Ibid., 21 Jan. 1887.
7. Ibid., 11 March 1887.
8. J.A. Weaver, 'The Development of Education in Swansea, 1846–1902'. Unpublished University of Wales (Swansea) MA Dissertation, 1957, p. 47.
9. 1847 *Reports*, pp. 86–9.
10. See L.W. Evans, *Education in Industrial Wales, 1700–1900* (Cardiff: Avalon Books, 1971), p.40.
11. 1847 *Reports*, pp. 373–4.
12. *MCCE* (1847–8), pp. 282–3.
13. *MCCE* (1849–50), p. 440.
14. *MCCE* (1850–1), Vol.1, p. 757.
15. *MCCE* (1851–2), p. 899.
16. *MCCE* (1853–4), Vol.2, p. 822.
17. See, for example, D.T. Williams, *The Economic Development of Swansea and of the Swansea District to 1921* (Swansea: University of Wales Press, 1940); and W.A. Beanland, *The History of the Royal Institution of South Wales, Swansea* (Swansea: Royal Institution, 1935), pp. 9–13.
18. *The Cambrian*, 27 June 1856.
19. *RCCE* (1858–9), pp. 156–7.
20. *RCCE* (1859–60), p. 167.
21. *The Cambrian*, 11 May 1860.
22. The account of the court case is based on newspaper reports in *The Cambrian*, 15 June 1860, the *Swansea Journal*, 16 June 1860, and the *Swansea and Glamorgan Herald*, 20 June 1860.
23. *The Cambrian*, 22 June 1860.
24. Ibid., 5 July 1861.
25. *Educational Record*, Vol. 6 (1864–6), pp. 59–60.
26. *The Cambrian*, 25 Dec. 1863.
27. *RCCE* (1866–7), pp.246–7.

28. *The Cambrian*, 5 May 1865.
29. Ibid., 26 Jan. 1866.
30. Ibid., 4 Oct. 1867.
31. *Swansea and Glamorgan Herald*, 26 Aug. 1868.
32. *The Cambrian*, 19 March 1869.
33. *Swansea and Glamorgan Herald*, 17 March 1869.
34. *Educational Record*, Vol. 8 (1869), p. 11.
35. *The Cambrian*, 14 Oct. 1870.
36. *Carmarthen Journal*, 27 May 1870.
37. *The Cambrian*, 17 Nov. 1871.
38. See Gilchrist, op.cit. (1980), p. 262.
39. *Swansea Journal*, 30 Nov. 1870.
40. PRO ED 16/395.
41. *RCCE* (1873–4), pp. 68–9.
42. *Swansea and Glamorgan Herald*, 18 Nov. 1874.
43. *The Cambrian*, 20 Nov. 1874.
44. Ibid., 27 Nov. 1874.
45. SSB *Minutes*, 3 Aug. 1875.
46. Ibid., 29 Sept. 1875.
47. Ibid., 23 Dec. 1875.
48. Ibid., 7 June 1876.
49. Ibid., 24 June 1876.
50. *The Cambrian*, 7 July 1876.
51. Ibid., 8 Sept. 1876.
52. *Swansea and Glamorgan Herald*, 14 June 1876.
53. Ibid., 3 Oct. 1877.
54. Ibid., 8 Oct. 1879.
55. *The Cambrian*, 1 March 1878.
56. SSB, School Management Committee *Minutes*, 13 Jan. 1879.
57. *The Practical Teacher*, Vol. 17 (1897), p. 554.
58. *School Board Chronicle*, 12 March 1881, p. 255.
59. *Swansea Journal*, 9 April 1881.
60. Ibid., 8 Oct. 1881.
61. *Swansea and Glamorgan Herald*, 12 Oct. 1881.
62. *The Cambrian*, 7 Oct. 1881.
63. Ibid., 14 Oct. 1881.
64. Ibid., 17 March 1882.
65. *Swansea and Glamorgan Herald*, 25 Oct. 1882.
66. *Educational Record*, Vol. 11 (1883), pp. 303–4.
67. *Herald of Wales and Monmouthshire Recorder*, 25 Aug. 1883.
68. *The Cambrian*, 24 Aug. 1883.

Part 2
THE SECOND GENERATION

3

William and Mary Adams: Before Fleet Road

WILLIAM AND MARY ADAMS IN SOUTH WALES

Henry Adams, the eldest son of John and Eliza Adams, was born at Orielton in south Pembrokeshire in 1840.[1] William Bateman Adams, also born at Orielton, on 20 September 1841, was the second son. His first educational experience was as a pupil at his father's Stackpole National School. Aged nine, he was recorded as a scholar at Pembroke Dock in 1851. By the time his father had moved to Swansea, in 1855, he was 14, and old enough to be apprenticed as a pupil teacher.

The first recorded evidence of William Bateman's aggressive disposition appears in the previously cited court case in 1860 (pp. 35–8), when John Adams' two sons, and specifically William Bateman, were accused of acting as 'petty tyrants'. It may be that he had gained an exaggerated sense of his own importance in his final year as the senior pupil teacher, asserting his authority over more junior peers. His evidence to the Royal Commission on Elementary Education, 1886–88 (the Cross Commission) many years later would corroborate this point. As part of a criticism of the system which operated before the Revised Code, Adams argued that pupil teachers then 'were really assistant masters' in their final year. The upper standards of schools were the focus of attention for the Inspectors and, as this was known in the schools, the master 'would spend the best part of his time in the upper part of the school ... there would be a natural tendency to neglect the systematic teaching in the lower classes'. These were left more or less under the control of senior pupil teachers.[2]

The Bangor Experience

In 1860 William Bateman Adams gained a Queen's Scholarship, Second Class, to study at Bangor Training College. In later years, again on in his evidence to the Cross Commission,[3] he was to remember as a cause of resentment the fact that he was not allowed to attend Carmarthen Training College, only 30 miles from Swansea, because he was not a member of the Church of England. Neither was he able to enrol at Borough Road College in London, for at this time young Welsh male recruits were compelled to attend the new Bangor Training College. HMI Joseph Bowstead was among those who campaigned against this arrangement. He indicated that Bangor was not accessible to students from South Wales, and its only advantage over Borough Road was from the 'sanitary point of view'. He argued that Welsh youths benefited greatly from the enlargement of their experience in the metropolis. Most young men also stated their strong preference for going to London.[4]

In 1861 there was no doubt even greater cause for frustration among Bangor students, for the College was not properly finished. It opened in 1858 in temporary accommodation, made up of two adjoining private houses. The new buildings had not been completed, as intended, by 1860, and Whitehall refused to allow the College to run a two-year course until they were. HMI W. Scoltock saw this as a disadvantage, for many of the students were young, and many Welsh-speaking, requiring a second year to gain maturity and improve their English.[5] The latter was not a problem for W.B. Adams, but possibly the former was, for he is recorded as having failed his course.[6]

It may be that the failure was on some technical ground, for Adams, who expunged other negative experiences of his early professional life from the family record, in later years referred to the Bangor experience as though it had been a fruitful one. He attended College reunions, and incorrectly asserted that he had had two successful years at Bangor, rather than one unsuccessful one. He also boasted that he was the only Bangor student who had ever swum across the Menai Strait.[7] Similarly, the Chairman at a prize-giving at Adams' school in 1900 told the audience that he had received a letter from Mr Price, Vice-Principal of the Bangor Normal College, that it had expected great things of Mr. Adams, 'but scarcely expected him to make such a name as he had done as the head of one of the best and most successful schools in the country'.[8] This too fits oddly with the official record of his failure.

But that was more than 30 years into the future. In the early 1860s, all was not lost, for William Bateman was taken back to his father's school as an unqualified assistant. He was quadruply fortunate. In the first place, not only had he Goat Street and his father to rescue him, but there was, in addition, a great shortage of teachers for British Schools in this period. Certificated teachers could not be found for many ordinary appointments, while trainees from English were not deemed as suitable as those from Welsh Normal Colleges for teaching in schools in Wales.[9] The third point was that officialdom seems not to have taken the training college experience and grading too seriously as a critical test of teaching competence. Quality had to be demonstrated in the classroom. The best that students in training could achieve at the time of the Revised Code was a fourth-class certificate. If this was in the lower division, they could not superintend pupil teachers. Thereafter they could improve their certificate status by success in the classroom, as attested by inspectors, and with the concurrence of the managers. His fourth advantage was that his father had already established an exemplary reputation and a wide-ranging connections in South Wales, in Swansea, Glamorgan and in Pembrokeshire. W.B. Adams' first major appointment was to be in the county of his birth.

The Pembroke Experience

It was not long, therefore, before William Bateman Adams had recouped his failure, if such it was. Early in 1863 he was appointed as headteacher at Pembroke British School, and recorded as having a certificate of the Third Division, Second Class. He began his duties at the beginning of May 1863. Again he had the experience of entering an institution recently established, and in temporary buildings. Pembroke British School was a long time in coming into being, for as early as the 1847 *Reports*[10] it was noted that such a development was planned in the town. Adams had the support of one pupil teacher and an uncertificated teacher of sewing. The school's first government Report was a good one, except in one respect, and that no fault of his. The

Pembroke Committee was warned that new school buildings must be available as soon as possible. The Inspector's comment on Adams found its way into *The Cambrian*: 'The present teacher, Mr. Adams, has been but a short time in charge, but he appears to have made a very good beginning. The children show unmistakable signs of skilful and careful teaching. If the teacher continues to exert himself I expect he will turn out an excellent school.'[11]

The school's annual government grant increased from 17s 6d in 1862 to £62 3s 6d in 1863. The initial success was followed up by another respectable Report less than a year later, which stated that the school had 'passed a fair examination under the Revised Code' and was doing as well under the restriction of temporary buildings as could be expected.[12] A similar Report followed in August 1865, when full grant was, however, to be made conditional on the completion of the new schools. The school's log book recorded lessons in geography, current affairs, which involved the reading of such newspapers as the *Cambrian Daily Leader,* and *The Times* in the sixth Standard, music, and plenty of history, a curricular range that suggests that Adams was not wholly preoccupied with the three Rs. Curiously, unlike his father who wrote scathingly about the Revised Code (see p. 39), William Bateman was retrospectively to give it some support, on grounds characteristic of those who were defending it in the 1860s, namely that it helped the less able pupil. In evidence to the later Cross Commission he stated that before the Code, 'the upper classes (of elementary schools) ... received a very large amount of attention from the head master, but the lower classes suffered. The advantage of the present system, speaking generally, is the vast levelling up of the instruction over large masses of children'.[13]

Despite perennial threats from the Education Department about loss of grant, the new building was far from being ready. As late as July 1865, the children of both Pembroke and Pembroke Dock British Schools, led by Adams, and accompanied by two bands, marched in procession to the new site.[14] The school was on the boundary between Pembroke and Monkton (see Figure 1.1). The site was awkwardly placed on a bend in the road. The plan of the school shows a large schoolroom and classroom off (Figure 3.1). The aerial photograph shows the school in the right foreground, with later extensions to the buildings (Figure 3.2).

The new building was finally opened in February 1866. Before

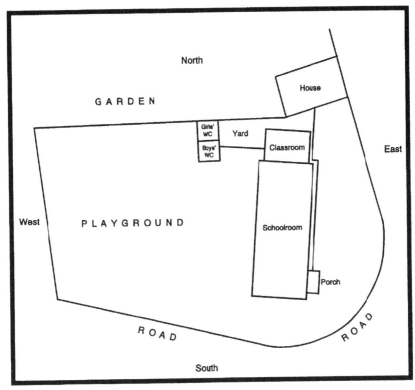

Figure 3.1.   Plan: Pembroke British School, 1860s

that storm damage had forced the scholars to move to temporary premises, in a house previously occupied by Pembroke Grammar School. On the opening day, William Bateman Adams' father John arrived from Swansea to conduct an examination of the children.[15] The *Haverfordwest and Milford Haven Telegraph* recorded that the children had passed a most satisfactory examination in geography, arithmetic, writing, and other subjects.[16] In the evening, a public meeting was held in the Town Hall, addressed by John Adams and prominent local individuals, at which the children, under the direction of their master, sang several pieces 'very creditably', in the cause of raising funds for the school.[17] By this time, however, Adams' days at the school were almost over. On 4 July 1866 he noted in his log book that he had been appointed to Mr Crawshay's schools in Merthyr Tydfil. His last entry on 3 August records that 167 children had been presented for the

Figure 3.2.   Aerial photograph showing later extensions to Pembroke
British School

annual examination, including 12 in Standard VI.[18] A previous
entry had noted: 'Mrs. Adams commenced her duties as sewing
mistress in the afternoon.' Her stay was a token one only.[19]

Adams' final HMI Report at Pembroke was again complimentary:

The general condition of this school is satisfactory and the children have
passed a fair examination. The numbers in attendance seem largely to
have increased since the new Schoolroom was opened.... Scholars are
attracted by the convenient cheerful premises and will be retained if ...
the school is maintained in a state of efficiency ... advancing with its
growth in number and popularity.[20]

One of the local newspapers congratulated Adams on his new
appointment 'which we understand is a very lucrative one'. It
claimed that during his period in Pembroke he had given 'much
satisfaction'. Attendance had doubled since the opening of the
new schoolroom.[21]

During his three and a half years in Pembroke, William Bateman Adams made himself known socially in the local community. His family upbringing had cultivated in him a love of music and the confidence to perform in public. At the 'Pembroke Penny Readings', for example, one of which was held in the Town Hall in February 1866, he sang the ballad 'Annie Lisle' 'very nicely', according to the *Haverfordwest and Milford Haven Telegraph*. Unfortunately, unlike the respectable Pembroke Dock audiences he had been accustomed to at school prize distributions while a boy there in the early 1850s, this one was attended by a vast and mixed audience drawn from all classes, and in which the roughs outnumbered the gentry. The former 'disported themselves in a most unseemly manner, hooting, swearing, and making all kinds of noises, to the infinite disgust of the respectable portion of the audience'. They stood on the benches and catcalled, preventing those behind from seeing. The room was filled to suffocation, the audience swayed alarmingly, and females fainted before some order was restored and the readings and songs began.[22] Future 'Readings' were ticket-only affairs, to ensure that the audiences comprised respectable citizens only. William Bateman regularly sang at these, his repertoire including the items 'Maid of Athens', 'Early in the Morning', 'Nil Desperandum' and 'Juanita'. His contributions were performed in 'a very pleasing manner ... well received by the audience'.[23]

Mary Adams, née Jannaway

Mary Jannaway was born in Brentford on 9 November 1844, daughter of a shoemaker. She became a pupil teacher at Brentford British School, which had been established in 1834. She gained a Queen's Scholarship, First Class, to the British Society's Stockwell Training College in 1863, qualifying in 1864. She was then appointed to Queen Street School, Swansea, the sister school of Goat Street. It can be located in the north-west corner of Figure 2.3. Queen Street dated back to 1821. By the time of the 1847 *Reports*, it was 'not in a flourishing condition'. The front elevation is shown on Figure 3.3. The spacious school-room, capable of accommodating more than 320 (Figure 3.4), was attended on the day of visitation by only 32 girls.[24] Fletcher's Report of 1850 found there was a young mistress, gentle and willing, but 'wanting

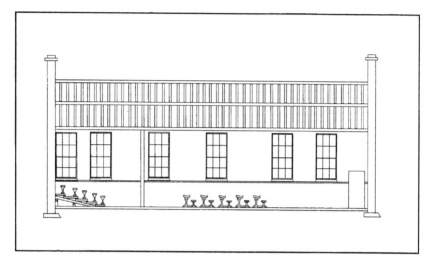

Figure 3.3.   Queen Street School, Swansea, side elevation

in the more concentrated energy which years would probably bring'.[25] In 1852, Arnold thought the mistress an intelligent woman, but had little to praise in the actual performance of the school, marked as it was by irregular attendance and defective discipline.[26] The following year Bowstead witnessed an 'amazing improvement', but feared that the mistress had had to work so hard that it had injured her health, and she was now convalescent.[27]

In 1858, the Committee upgraded the school, adding two new classrooms (Figure 3.3). In a letter dated 21 October 1862, John Adams, on behalf of the Ladies' Committee, wrote to the BFSS to ask if was possible for Constance Hammett, a Queen's Scholar at Stockwell and the daughter of his predecessor at Goat Street, to take over the girls' school. He knew her to be conscientious and steady and without false pride. He understood her suspect health had now improved.

In a subsequent letter dated 25 December 1864 Adams recounted the unfortunate history of headteachers at Queen Street since he had come to Swansea. Following her predecessor's resignation on health grounds, a Miss Fricker was appointed in 1855. Adams claimed that she had 'lacked energy'. Then Miss Cumming, though recommended to the school by the Principal of Bangor Training College, was, Adams indicated, 'always considered too juvenile in appearance and by far too inexperienced for

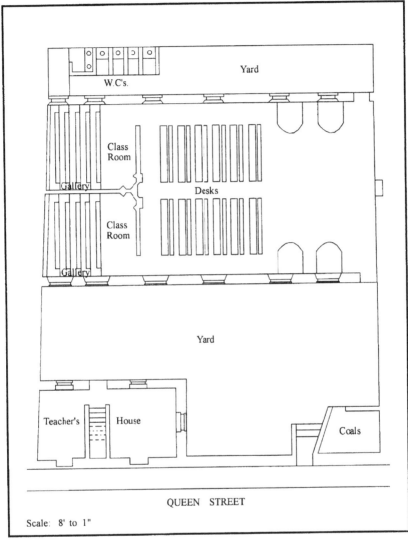

W.C's.

Yard

Class
Room

Gallery

Desks

Class
Room

Gallery

Yard

Teacher's   House

Coals

QUEEN   STREET

Scale: 8' to 1"

Figure 3.4.   Plan: Queen Street School

such an important school'. Following Cumming's resignation in the summer of 1864, Constance Hammett returned to Swansea to take charge of Queen Street. By this time numbers had fallen to an average of 80, in a school capable of taking 250–300. Adams' earlier opinion that her health was improved was over-optimistic, for Constance Hammett was taken ill soon after her appointment and eventually died, aged 20, 'after a very short illness' but 'full of Christian hope, and in a very happy state of mind'.

In this and in a letter written the following day, 26 December, Adams expressed the need of Queen Street School for a new headmistress, 'of energy and womanly appearance ... thoroughly steady and if possible of pious principles'. He did not imagine, however, that the Committee would like a Unitarian or a Baptist. He had to admit that the school was in a rough working-class district of Swansea, with 'the morals of the people near the school low'. He feared that if improvements were not made, the National School would take children away and Queen Street would have to close. The Society and the Committee clearly acted very quickly, for in the new year, he followed these letters up with another dated 2 January 1865.

The Ladies' Committee of our Girls' School (Queen Street) met this morning. They have decided upon engaging Miss Jannaway.... The ladies wish me to state they would prefer Miss J. to come here next Friday. She had better come by the first train so as to reach Swansea about 4. I have promised ... to meet her at the Station and take her to my home. Mrs. Adams will be kind to her, and is willing to aid her with all the sympathy in her power. She will have nice, comfortable apartments, and a kind old lady to wait upon her, who lives in the girls' school house.... I do hope this young person will fill the school. She will meet with every encouragement from me if she gives the school her undivided attention and be willing to take a kind hint or two. I am confident that she may in the course of 12 months make her salary £80: this with furnished apartments, fuel and lights, will be very good'.

At this time Mary Jannaway was living in Eton, possibly taking up a temporary appointment, and she made it clear she could not travel at the time requested but would do so the following week. She wrote to the BFSS on 4 January 1865 to thank it for 'procuring me an appointment so early'. It was therefore the unexpected death of Constance Hammett that provided Mary Jannaway with her opportunity. By May 1865 the Ladies' Committee was recording its satisfaction that numbers of pupils had reached 165. It trusted that under her superintendence the school would 'speedily resume its former position and influence'.[28]

Mary Jannaway was not to bring with her the hoped-for stability of staffing, however. In an obviously perturbed state, the BFSS's inspector in South Wales wrote to Headquarters on 17 November 1865, stating that he was trying to persuade Mary Jannaway to remain at Queen Street until she received her parchment. The problem was that she had quickly bonded with William Bateman Adams and was shortly to marry him. The impulsive William Bateman would not hear of her staying in Swansea and wished her to move to Pembroke straight after their marriage. In a similar letter to the Society dated 20 November 1865, marked 'Very Private', John Adams also indicated that Mary Jannaway was to marry his son at Christmas and then proceed to Pembroke. Mary thought she could obtain her certificate there, and that the College would not therefore lose grant for her training. He noted that she was a 'nice young person' who had become like one of the family. He added:

I am sure the two young people would be very unhappy if they knew the Society suffered anything by them. They are both very conscientious and beloved and respected by all who know them, and as a parent I should be sorry to mar their happiness especially as the match is approved by all the parties concerned.

One reason Adams gave for his son wishing his wife to move on to Pembroke immediately was that the new school building, though 'a beautiful structure', was for mixed purposes. No separate girls' school was intended. But he anticipated that one was inevitable. The local benefactor, Mr Meyrick, was very wealthy, and he and his wife intended to take a lot of interest in the school. His son therefore was anxious his intended wife would be there at the opening of the new buildings. A further hidden agenda was hinted at, Adams stating that Pembroke was purely an English town, and that church and Tory interests were strong there. The inference was presumably that William Bateman had to be careful not to offend.

In reply the British Society impressed upon Adams that if Mary Jannaway did not stay until 1 June 1866, the date of inspection when she would obtain her parchment, it would lose all the money for her training. On 23 November 1865 Adams wrote to say that he thought he could prevail on Mary Jannaway to remain until 1 June. He had consulted her mother about the matter and would press home its seriousness upon his son. In the event, Mary Jannaway wrote to the BFSS on 28 November, indicating that she had decided to remain at Queen Street until June, to obtain her parchment. On the same day John Adams wrote to confirm that his son was willing to accede to this arrangement. William Bateman

Adams and Mary Jannaway were, intriguingly for a pair associated
with the British Society, married in Swansea Parish Church on
20 December 1865. In May 1866 Mary Adams announced her
intention to leave Queen Street. She stated that her earnings were
£30 per annum, on top of which she received one-third of the
school pence, bringing her an additional £10–£12. She had raised
numbers to 130. On 21 June she left for Pembroke British School,
where she spent just over a month as sewing mistress.

William and Mary Adams in Cefn Coed

The Environs of Merthyr Tydfil

In the early nineteenth century, Merthyr Tydfil was the largest
town in Wales, and the 'iron capital of the world', with no fewer
than seven major ironworks.[29] These included the vast Dowlais
works, in association with which was founded one of the most
famous works schools in Wales, and Cyfarthfa. The Crawshays of
Cyfarthfa were one of Wales's most illustrious industrial families.[30]
At the time of the Adams' arrival in Merthyr in 1866, its population was over 50,000.[31] In 1839 Seymour Tremenheere, one of
the earliest HMI, had reported on the state of elementary education in the South Wales mining district, including Merthyr Tydfil,
a town already notorious as the most politically radical constituency in the country. He described the abused landscape of
north-eastern part of the coalfield.

Towards the head of these valleys most of the largest iron-works in South
Wales are collected.... The valleys ... are separated from each other by
tracts of cheerless moorland ... The surface of the soil around is frequently blackened with coal, or covered with high mounds of refuse
from the mines and the furnaces ... Volumes of smoke from the furnaces, the rolling-mills, and the coke hearths, are driven past, according
to the direction of the wind.[32]

Tremenheere deplored the deficiency of culture he found among
the working population. This, rather than poverty, he believed to
be the cause of their 'insensibility to the value of instruction'.[33]
The mass of the people belonged to dissenting religious groups. In
1839 Merthyr had two churches with Sunday schools, and 22
chapels and 17 Sunday schools of dissenting congregations.
Tremenheere was at least gratified to find the high measure of
attendance at the latter, adults joining children for instruction, in

Welsh and English, at the Sunday schools. But there seemed little hope of this being translated into an enthusiasm for day schools.[34]

Tremenheere's conclusions anticipated those of the 1847 *Reports*. The only schools 'of public institution' in 1847 in Merthyr Tydfil were the Dowlais works school and the National schools.[35] In response to questions from the Commission, the Rev. J. Campbell reflected on the Merthyr Tydfil district. He reckoned that seven out of ten working men understood English tolerably well, and one in five spoke it as their own language. He regretted that the influence of women, especially those who had been employed from a young age in the works, was not favourable.[36] His colleague H. White, responding about neighbouring Dowlais, concurred on many points. He regarded families as warm and affectionate, and attentive towards their children as regards food and clothing, but showing no interest otherwise than in getting them employed as soon as possible. He claimed that a third of the population spoke English fluently, a third indifferently, and a third not at all. The female part of the population were of good influence if they had been brought up in domestic service, but were 'ignorant of household duties, less careful of the wants of their husbands and children', if they had been employed from an early age in the works.[37]

The Minutes of the Committee of Council on Education of the 1850s continued to characterise Merthyr Tydfil as a 'town of a peculiar class', its people still showing, by 1854, little interest in schooling. Thus the recent Cyfarthfa school, with 107 pupils, included 95 who had been at school for less than one year, and only three for more than three years. HMI Longueville-Jones described the schoolmaster's task as 'almost hopeless'.[38] Improvement occurred in the late 1850s, however. The Newcastle Commission calculated that the percentage of scholars in Merthyr Tydfil had grown from 6.7 in 1851 to 9.0 in 1858, a particularly gratifying result in such a town, and bearing 'testimony to the activity of the agencies that have been engaged in educational provision'.[39] Even so, there remained much evidence of poor attendance. 'The slightest convenience to themselves is sufficient to induce parents to keep their children at home.'[40] The Commissioners sustained the basic premise of the 1847 *Reports* that 'it is in English that the Welshman must ultimately be instructed'. The influx of industrial workers they predicted would naturally establish English as the dominant language, but its time had not arrived.[41]

The educational problems of Merthyr Tydfil were part of the same nexus of disadvantage as health and housing. Infectious disease in Merthyr was endemic. In 1849 the town suffered a serious cholera epidemic, resulting in nearly 1,500 deaths. The 1854 outbreak accounted for 455. Between 1851 and 1865 there was an epidemic of typhus, smallpox, measles or scarlet fever in every year but two. Infantile mortality was very high. Many dwellings had no sanitation, while others were provided with a shared privy, located over a cesspit. Overflows and seepage from the cesspits, and water from the wasted landscape, polluted wells and streams, the source of drinking and washing water.[42]

The Cyfarthfa ironworks was at the peak of its prosperity in the first half of the nineteenth century. The coal seams came close to the surface in the Merthyr area, and the shallow workings and the nature of the iron mining maximised landscape damage, as did the huge amounts of waste from the iron furnaces, which were dumped on huge tips. Overlooking this devastated landscape, the Crawshays built their vast mock castle home in 1824. It was to be more than 20 years before they established their first ironworks school, in 1848, financed, like other works schools, from 'stoppages' from wages of half-pence, one penny or 2d per week. In 1850 the family sponsored a National School in the Georgetown area and, in 1860, a Works School in Cefn Coed (Figure 3.5).[43]

Cefn Coed was a satellite village to the north-west of Merthyr Tydfil. It was located on 'a barren and hilly tract upon which not a twig now grows ... raised in consequence of the neighbouring iron works at Merthyr ... built upon waste ... houses are seen starting up without attention to regularity or arrangement, the convenience of each other, or the preservation of health...'.[44] Though it was to have seven chapels and two churches, Cefn Coed was viewed locally as 'a notoriously wicked place, for here lived the chief pugilists, racers and gamblers of the whole district'.[45]

Cefn Coed Works School

It was to Cefn Coed Works School, run on British lines, that William and Mary Adams were appointed in 1866. The original buildings of the school are still present as a small part of the much larger school shown in the bottom right-hand corner of Figure 3.6. About this time, the striking viaduct which was to take the railway

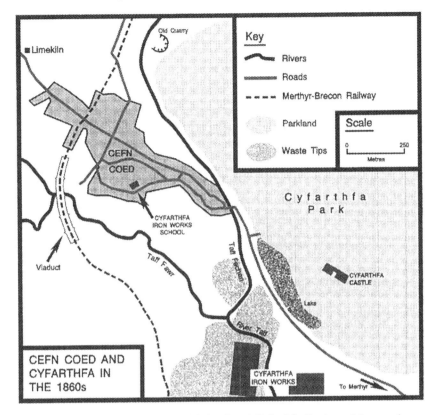

Figure 3.5. Map: Cefn Coed School and Cyfarthfa Castle and Ironworks

line to Brecon was being built. It would be surprising if the Adams' had been unaware of the negative stereotypes associated with the industrial environment of Merthyr Tydfil. It may be that the higher salary offered by the Crawshay family was the attraction. At all events, the decision was to prove an unhappy one.

William Bateman Adams' responses to the experience can be traced principally through his correspondence with the BFSS. On 29 August 1866 he informed the Society that he had been engaged by Richard Crawshay on the recommendation of HMI Joseph Bowstead, and in competition with numerous other applications. He and his wife had had to present their testimonials to Crawshay personally at Cyfarthfa Castle. There had clearly been some misunderstanding, for Adams apologised for not applying through the Society. In the absence of communication from Borough Road, he claimed, he had judged positions to be very scarce. He mentioned

Remnants of
Cyfarthfa works
school, Cefn
...d

Figure 3.6.   Aerial photograph of railway viaduct and schools, Cefn Coed

that they would both have preferred an appointment in England, 'as we do not understand the Welsh language'.

The most recent government report on the school had been uncomplimentary, the boys' school in 1866 having 'fallen off materially' while the girls' 'was in fair order but backward in attainment'.[46] In the early stages the curriculum was confined to the three Rs. Children had to bring their own copybooks, pen holders and pencils. They had all to belong to families associated with the Cyfarthfa works. Following the 1866 summer holidays, the children were required to pay school pence, presumably in place of the 'stoppage' system.[47] Adams' log book outlined the usual trials of schoolmasters of the time, particularly poor attendance, inefficient and unreliable monitors and pupil teachers, and un-supportive parents and, at least by implication, managers. He recorded visits of Mrs Crawshay to examine the children, and of failure to gain permission from the family to open an evening school. He tried to extend the curriculum beyond the basic demands of the Revised Code, not least in singing, but complained that 'the harsh rough voices of the boys present little encouragement for the introduction of music'.[48] At about the same time, his younger brother John Frederick came over to teach the school one morning. He tried also to persuade the managers to purchase a set of 'Arithmetical Cards', published by his father. During January 1867, there were constant complaints of the cold, this being one of the most bitter winters in living memory, and delays in the delivery of coal, an order made on the 5th not being delivered until 22 January, for example.

The autumn and winter of 1866 were indeed a bad time to be in Merthyr Tydfil. The cholera outbreak lasted from late August, just after the Adams had arrived, until the beginning of November. During this period over 2,700 in the area were infected and 229 died. Local newspapers were not slow to advance explanations which focused on the lack of 'cleanliness, self-denial and abstemiousness' of the working population.[49] Despite the fact that the outbreak spread from the slum to the more respectable areas of the district, Adams made less comment on the epidemic than on an attack of quinsy he suffered, merely noting in his log book early in November 1866 that the 'cholera has abated and the result has shewn itself in an increased and more punctual attendance'.[50] While the cholera, the winter freeze and the general quality of the environment can hardly have endeared Cefn Coed to the Adams, these were not the ostensible reasons they offered for their early departure. A lengthy correspondence with the BFSS in February and March 1867, contained notice of their early intention to leave after only eight months in the appointment.

It was apparently their cultural and social isolation rather than the physical environment that gave rise to their dissatisfaction, expressed in a letter from Adams to the BFSS dated 7 February 1867.

Since our appointment here we have found our ignorance of the Welsh language a great drawback to our complete success as teachers – in fact had we formed any idea of the drawbacks consequent on this, we should never have accepted the appointment. We are quite excluded from any converse with the parents, and have two miles to walk to an English place of worship.

On this account, I applied for the 'Aberdare British Schools', where English is not so prevalent; but the Committee, who were otherwise unanimous in my favour, rejected me because I did not possess a knowledge of Welsh ...

I have therefore decided on securing a permanent English appointment and trust, under the circumstances, you will feel no hesitation in entering our names on your 'memorandum book' ...

I am open at any time, either to a single, or double appointment – should much prefer London or the neighbourhood. I do not expect to commence with a large salary, but shall be happy to let any increase depend on my own exertions. I really do not wish to change for the sake of change, but I do wish to feel happy in my work.

Bolstered by an immediate response from Borough Road, Adams wrote back on 9 February, raising the stakes.

I am exceedingly obliged for yours of the 8th inst., the more especially as I have no claim on your assistance, not having trained at the 'Boro'. I am 26 years of age, and have connected myself with the 'Calvinistic Methodist denomination'. The minimum salary I would require would be £100 and house, or its equivalent – if a double appointment, £140 or £150. Should there be a chance of working a school up to my requirements, I should be glad to accept it.

If a 'mixed school' my wife would conduct the 'sewing' and give the girls extra lessons for a consideration. I have not given notice to leave, but will do so immediately on hearing definitely from you ...

Yes, the 'Drawing Certificate' is from the Society of Arts. The 'Music Certificate' was obtained at a 'Local Examination'. I have taught music with considerable success. When 'Assistant Master' at Swansea [i.e. uncertificated at his father's school] I had the entire management of this subject. The following remarks are from Mr. Joyce of the Council office who examined for Mr. Bowstead in 1863:

'The children under the direction of Mr. W.B. Adams, the assistant master, sang several airs, in admirable style'.

His new demands provoked a chilly reaction from the Society, and a follow-up letter of 12 February from Adams was characterised by significant backtracking. He assured the BFSS that he was obliged for its 'valuable hints' and 'saw the force' of its observations.

In a much underlined justification, he explained.

In fixing the salary named I stated that 'I should be willing to work it to my requirements'. In wishing to remove I am not in the remotest degree (doubly underlined) actuated by pecuniary motives (also doubly underlined), but am entirely guided by the reasons in my first letter ... they are ... so cogent that I have signified my intention of giving my notice to leave on the 25 March. Having the fullest confidence in your judgement, and being fully prepared to improve my position by hard work, I shall be glad to accept as a commencement what you consider a fair and reasonable remuneration ... for beginners in a new district. Once fairly settled in the district mentioned, I am determined to overcome every obstacle, and not risk my position for a change.

In a postscript he added somewhat cringingly: 'I cannot expect to engage above the salary usually given in such cases.'

He was soon offered a post at the new British Schools at Finchley, an expanding suburban area to the north of London. He wrote to the Society on 25 February accepting the salary named for the first year 'and subsequently to let any increase depend on the improvement of the schools'. He hoped to stay to await the visit of the Inspector at the end of April, and asked if the Finchley appointment could be delayed until May. This did not seem to find favour and W.B. Adams wrote again on 28 February to say the managers would have no objection to him leaving on 25 March. He indicated that his salary at Cefn Coed was £120 plus one-tenth of government grant and fuel at a nominal rate, in fact 2s 6d per ton. He added that he would be most glad of the change as 'the present place does not agree with my health'. Adams noted in his letter of 12 March 1867 that one of the Finchley Committee had come to Cefn Coed to examine their work, which he queried as 'rather an unusual course of procedure after your letter to them', adding 'but I don't think I have any reason to regret the ordeal'. In fact the school log book indicates he gave in his notice as late as 7 March, and was told by Crawshay on 11 March that he might leave on 1 April, if a suitable replacement could be found. He seems to have departed on reasonable terms, and was accorded the following testimonial: 'The Cefn Schools under your and Mrs. Adams's care have been conducted quite to Mr. Crawshay's satisfaction, and for myself I can only say I much regret you are about to leave'. The letter was signed by Crawshay's Manager, William Jones. In a previous letter to the British Society, dated 1 March 1867, asking for replacements, Jones indicated that Adams was obliged to leave 'on account of ill health'.

How far ill health was the true cause, and how far the Welsh language issue, is not one that can confidently be answered. The only evidence in the log book of illness was W.B.Adams' severe attack of quinsy.[51] He was clearly an ambitious man and saw no future in Merthyr Tydfil. That there was a Welsh language issue at

Cefn Coed would, however, seem to be evident from a log book entry of Adams' successor.

Unless there is a change of pupil teachers the school cannot be worked efficiently. This school in particular requires intelligent parents or friends, who as a rule speak English at home. The present staff always speak Welsh at home. Nearly all the scholars speak Welsh at home too, consequently, they need their reading lessons explained, which the present pupil teachers are unable to do.

The head claimed it was a difficult matter 'to get the children to speak grammatically, Cefn being much more Welshy than Merthyr'.[52]

When giving later public accounts of his professional history, William Bateman Adams obliterated any mention of the short time he spent at Cefn Coed. Thus in recounting his previous career to *The Practical Teacher* in 1894, he alleged that he stayed in the 'handsome new buildings' at Pembroke until appointed to Finchley.[53]

WILLIAM AND MARY ADAMS IN LONDON: BEFORE FLEET ROAD

The Finchley Experience

While the Adams were experiencing hard times in South Wales, the Finchley Committee of North End Congregational Chapel was seeking a man-and-wife pair to run its new school, opened in 1864. Problems had resulted from the illness of the current teacher, and the Committee was pressing the British Society to help find a satisfactory replacement. Clearly the BFSS had pointed them in the direction of the Adams. In a letter dated 16 February 1867, the Committee confirmed that it was in favour of Mr and Mrs Adams. The Society's help was requested in negotiating a salary, as was assurance that the Adams were 'presentable people', and details on whether they had a family, and about their past professional experience. A letter of 18 March 1867 informed the BFSS that a Finchley delegation had been sent to see them at work in Cefn Coed, and had come back with a very favourable report.

The school was newly built, on Dale Grove, not far from the Congregational Chapel in Nether Street (Figure 3.7). On moving

Figure 3.7.   Finchley British School, Dale Grove

to Finchley, William and Mary took up residence in Homan's Cottages, in the nearby village of Whetstone. Within a year, they had moved to a row of respectable terraced houses in Stanhope Road at Finchley North End, just across the main road from their school (Figure 3.8). The school is shown in the south-west corner of the map. On 11 June 1868 their only child, John William Bateman Adams was born.

Little evidence has survived as to either their private or professional life in Finchley, but it would seem that Adams was a success, grant for the same average attendance of 74 pupils rising from £15 8s 3d in 1868[54] to £24 10s 8d in 1870.[55] The schools had accommodation for 107, and the children paid 3d to 4d per week in school pence. Clearly the relatively high fees suggest that the school drew on a most respectable catchment population, of a different order from that of Cefn Coed.

On the evidence of a letter from Richard Adams to the BFSS dated 19 September 1869, W.B. Adams continued to suffer from quinsy. Richard sought permission to spend time away from Borough Road College to help out his sick brother, suggesting that Adams had no other teaching support, apart from his wife. His salary was £120 per annum, on top of which he earned in various

Figure 3.8.   Map: Finchley British School

ways, including a share of government grant, £40 more. The Committee also, after a year of service, found the Adams their house rent. On their resignation from Finchley, the local Committee, in a letter dated 28 October 1870, asked the Society for replacements. The Secretary indicated they had 'done good service'.

The West End Experience

Portland Street British School, to which William Bateman Adams was next appointed, was in the West End of London. Family information channels ensured that this prestige appointment was publicised back in Swansea, the *Swansea and Glamorgan Herald* reporting that the appointment had been in the face of stiff com-

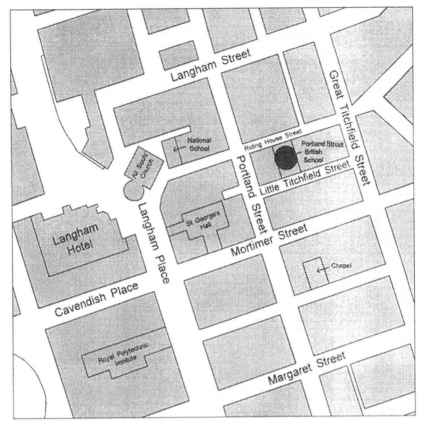

Figure 3.9. Map: Portland Street British School, London's West End

petition from between 50 and 60 candidates, 'many being first class London teachers of high attainment ... it is creditable to the energy, perseverance and ability of the son of our town' that he was to gain 'this distinguished preference'. Reference was also made to testimonials he had received from HMIs Arnold and Bowstead.[56]

Adams was later to confirm that his appointment at the school, as a non-Unitarian, was the result of the support of Arnold: 'To Matthew Arnold I owe much ... As scholar, as pupil teacher, as master, he knew me and noticed me, and helped me. Indeed he gave me my first big lift in London – the Headmastership of Portland British School ... then the biggest of its kind in the West End.'[57] In *The Practical Teacher* report on Adams of 1894, part of Matthew Arnold's reference to James Martineau was quoted: 'I

seldom interfere in the appointment of teachers, but Mr. Adams is
so efficient a teacher, that I cannot help writing to say that I think
him so. You need have no anxiety, as he is a certain success.'[58]

Portland Street School occupied a plot of land between Riding
House Street and Little Titchfield Street (Figure 3.9), and was
run on British School lines by the Unitarian congregation. The
original school of 1858 had been rehoused in a new building in
1866, provided without government financial aid. Portland Street
Chapel was a famous institution, led as it was by the charismatic
James Martineau. A Professor of Manchester New College, the
Unitarian training institution located from 1853 in London, Martineau was both a distinguished academic and a preacher. One
writer described the congregation, of a chapel which satisfied 'the
most austere demands for modesty and simplicity', as held by the
brilliance of thought which fell from the preacher's lips, writing
down in open notebooks that which 'they could not suffer to float
away into the air'.[59]

Another writer noted that if the congregation at Portland Street
Chapel was not large, it was of quality.

Drawn from all parts of London by interest in the preacher, came men of
law and letters, Members of Parliament ... women strong in heart and
head; nor were visitors from the country or from the United States lacking, in addition to the elder members for whom the quiet sanctuary had
been a tranquil home of devotion and faith.[60]

Martineau was the 'nourisher and guardian' of the Sunday and
Day Schools, and 'bestowed on them untiring care ... his sympathy and support were always ready for the teachers'. His office of
Secretary was pursued with 'scrupulous order ... the necessary
correspondence with the Education Department was performed
with unfailing accuracy'.[61] He was responsible for turning the
Sunday School into a day school as well, which under Adams was
to be regarded as one of the best of its type in London. The
auguries for Adams were therefore good. He was supported by
J.W. Grove, Headmaster of the nearby National School, who
played a leading part in the formation of the Marylebone Teachers' Association, and to whom Adams paid later tribute for his
'thoughtful kindness', which did much to 'smooth down and make
more endurable that specially unpleasant experience all strangers
undergo when they start life in this great wilderness called
London'.[62] The West End place of work and their residence in the

crowded streets near King's Cross were indeed radical environmental transformations for the Adams. The Portland Street area was socially differentiated, with some very well-to-do streets, mixed in with others in acute poverty, and with a varied land use mingling residence with small-scale commercial development.

About the time of Adams' appointment there were 190 boys in the school, paying fees of 3d, 97 girls, paying 3d and 6d, and 170 infants, paying 2d per week. By 1871 numbers had risen to 105 boys, paying 3d and 6d, and 120 girls, paying the same rates, with the same number of infants. On his appointment, Martineau had put Adams under some pressure to start at Portland Street as soon as possible, following the death of his predecessor, and the appointment of his assistant to a school in Exeter. In a letter dated 26 April 1870, he asked Adams to attend a parents' evening to introduce himself to the families of some of the scholars. The boys ranged in age from seven to over 13. Seventy-nine of the 211 boys in the school in 1871 were 11 years old and over. The school had one large schoolroom and two classrooms. There was also a night school, attended by 52 youths. All the children took the three Rs, religious instruction and vocal music. Other subjects taught were dictation and drawing and, to the senior section, 80 in number, history, geography and grammar. The school met five days a week for five and a half hours, 46 weeks each year. By this stage, Adams had achieved a Second Class certificate.[63]

During his time at Portland Street, the London School Board introduced its scholarship system, and it was here that Adams gained his first scholarship successes.[64] A Portland Street boy as early as 1872 won one of the Waterlow Prizes, a result of the 'liberality' of the Lord Mayor.[65] There was no attempt to proselytise Unitarian principles and the school was run on strict British lines. Scholars were not required to attend religious instruction nor a particular place of worship. The school day opened with a scriptural extract and closed with a hymn. Parents could exempt their children from the religious provision on request.[66]

Adams' professional success was exemplified not least by the appearance in 1872 of his textbook *Leading Events in English History*, 'adapted to the requirements of the 1871 Code'. It was very well reviewed in *The Schoolmaster*, which described it as, if wanting in originality, the work of 'a careful student and a practical teacher. Great judgment is shown in the selection of facts to be presented to the youthful learner, and the arrangement of the work throughout is excellent. Taken as an introductory textbook, it is about as good as any we have seen'. The short biographies included, in which Adams was said to have proved himself as 'a master of terse and vigorous English', were strongly commended as encouraging pupils to become 'intelligent and interested readers of their country's story'. The reviewer was uncertain whether its adaptation to the requirements of the Code could be regarded as a recommendation or not.[67]

Adams was again to meet with personal and professional frustration caused by a number of differences of opinion with his managers. One was over the way in which one of his pupil teachers had been treated, which he described as a 'monstrous piece of tyranny'. Adams reflected in a letter dated 29 September 1874 to the British Society that the 'Church Party' there was 'very strong', and 'would move heaven and earth to injure us'. The position worsened and the following year John Adams interceded on his son's behalf. In a letter to the BFSS dated 30 November 1875 he noted that his son had been a very efficient master at Portland Street for some years and that his qualities had been reflected in 'really first class reports' by HMIs Arnold and Alderson. Martineau had recently retired on the grounds of ill-health and Adams claimed that his successor

wishes all the teachers to be Unitarians and my son says he cannot submit to this. He and his wife are members of Dr. Parker's Church and congregation. The whole thing is plain. Mr. Alderson and Mr. Arnold know all about my son, and report on his school as being the best in Marylebone. He says he would like a Board School and if possible in Marylebone ... You see the case is very peculiar. My son's connections are evidently not Unitarian. He has been brought up with orthodox views. Can you possibly aid him in this matter? I am so sorry for him. He has worked very hard, has been very attentive and tried to please everyone. He is very intelligent and has splendid practice and good experience.

The Society would seem to have had some influence with the London School Board, for a letter from W.B. Adams dated 9 December 1875 thanked its Secretary for taking an interest his situation and stressed that anything that was 'kindly suggested' would be treated as 'strictly confidential'. By the following February the tense situation at Portland Street was still unresolved. Adams was helped in his campaign by a visit he had received from a senior Marylebone magistrate, accustomed to dealing with the children of inefficient ragged schools, who had been invited by the London School Board to ascertain what being an efficient school under the Code meant. So impressed was the family with the tribute, that they prevailed on the *Swansea and Glamorgan Herald* to print it, and of course informed the BFSS of the accolade. The magistrate's report was quoted:

I have been equally surprised and delighted with the progress of the children in the fundamental subjects. The examination passed by the senior division in geography and history was such as I should scarcely expect to have witnessed in a school of the highest type. It is simple justice to the managers and teachers of these efficient schools to say that the quickness, intelligence and proficiency of the children under their care were remarkable.[68]

Meanwhile, the London School Board had been suggesting new posts, though Adams was demanding consideration of his wife as well. One at its school in Buckhurst Hill was turned down, in a letter dated 25 February 1876, on the grounds that the salary was small and there was no opening for Mary Adams. Similarly, on 17 March 1876, another proposal was rejected on the grounds that his wife 'would not care to accept any appointment except as headmistress of a girls' school'. A further opening was refused on the grounds it was outside London. Adams wanted an appointment in a good board school in the metropolis. The prospect became a reality when in February 1878 he was appointed to a temporary establishment in Gospel Oak, in emergency use pending the completion of the new buildings for Fleet Road Board School, on the fringe of Hampstead. Adams received an excellent testimonial from James Martineau.

Mr. Adams' conspicuous success here during the last eight years has been due to his rare skill as an organiser, his untiring zeal and enthusiasm, and the stimulating power of his own quick intelligence among the scholars. His honourable ambition to equip his scholars for the front rank in the competitions of their life is sufficient alone to stamp him as a teacher of the first order. The anxiety with which the managers receive his resignation is the sincerest tribute they can render to the value of his services.[69]

Mary Adams in Slumland

The Nightingale Street Environment
Meanwhile Mary Adams had achieved her goal of obtaining the post of headmistress in a London Board School. In August 1877

she was appointed to Nightingale Street, a recently constructed Board School in the notorious Lisson Grove area of Marylebone. The appointment would appear to have made possible a decisive residential upgrading. In the early 1870s the Adams lived in the still respectable but socially declining Caledonian Road area near King's Cross, where the main road was classified by Booth as red, but behind which there were not only the purples of mixed comfort and poverty, but also the blues and blacks of distress. In 1877 they moved to Lorne Gardens, hard by Regent's Park and Lord's Cricket Ground. In a letter to the BFSS of 7 April 1877 Adams indicated he had just 'removed my residence to St. John's Wood'. Formerly Hanover Cottages, the houses in Lorne Gardens were less substantial than those of surrounding streets, though still classified as red by Booth. They adjoined an even more prestigious residential area, yellow in the same classification. The Adams were still living at Lorne Gardens at the time of the 1881 census, together with their son, John William Bateman, and Mary Adams' unmarried younger sister, Caroline Jannaway.

Geographically not far from Lorne Gardens, but socially an alien world, were Booth's blues and blacks of the dire poverty of the Portman Market area, with a small number of streets, like Nightingale Street, portrayed as black. Of this area Booth and his team spoke of the 'numerous' and 'glaring' indications of poverty, with visible street life of an 'unpleasant character'. Every public house had its 'contingent of loafers.... In street after street evil specimens of womankind shuffle along with head wrapped in a shawl, or lean out of windows, or stand gossiping at the open doors. Evil-looking, idle, hulking lads are not an uncommon sight; children who ought to be at school are playing about in the streets; and the houses look filthy without and within'.[70]

Local newspapers had long reinforced the negative stereotypes of this area. A typhus outbreak in 1881, for example, was blamed on the effects of the local Lisson Grove environment, 'in which there are peculiarities which render a fever so infectious peculiarly liable to spread. The chief favouring influence being the great populousness of the streets, the existence of a sort of open market, and a large admixture of the Irish element, among whom, as is natural, there is much fraternising and personal contact'.[71] Another newspaper editor claimed the Marylebone Vestry was only just waking up to the perils and needs of 'dens like Charles

Street. Imagine a family occupying a room the walls of which are saturated with water, and throwing off a continuous foul vapour, added to which was an accumulation of black poisonous matter under the flooring which sent forth a constant supply of poisonous gases'.[72] Before the 1870 Act, the only school in Nightingale Street had been a ragged school, with accommodation for 175 children. If the setting did not daunt Mary Adams, one of the final entries in the log book of her predecessor could not have been encouraging: 'The children of this school are thoroughly wicked. They have given no end of trouble this week.'[73]

The Lisson Grove area was symptomatic of those which most tested the energies of the London School Board in the first decade of its operation. There were large numbers of ragged or near-ragged children to be accommodated, about 3,000 in this general area, many not having been to school before. Three Board Schools were needed, of which Nightingale Street was one. The sites for such schools were very often in congested streets, difficult to find, and 'not favourable to economy'. In addition, there were some-times enough pre-existing voluntary schools for the religious bodies to complain that the Board was unnecessarily competing with them. On the other hand, the Nightingale Street area was not one in which the voluntary agencies were very active. The Board was defensive on matters of the financing of the school, with an estimated cost of £26 per head, against an average of £13. Apart from the expense of the site, the smallness of the ground area available demanded building high.

... owing to the peculiarity of the site (the school) is planned somewhat differently to the usual manner. The buildings form a hollow square having a small playground in the centre, while under the girls' school is a covered playground for the infants. Similar accommodation is provided for the boys and girls on the roof of the building, which is laid with a patent asphalt floor and protected by brick piers and a stout iron railing ... By this arrangement, separate and ample play and school space is provided for all the 829 children which the building is designed to accommodate.[74]

According to the Education Department calculations, the pre-liminary cost of Nightingale Street was over £25,000, with site costs (£14,400) greater than building (£10,000). The school was intended to accommodate 782 children – 253 boys, 253 girls, and 276 infants.[75] The school can just be seen in the right background of Figure 3.10, which vividly depicts the local environment and some of its people.

Mary Adams at Nightingale Street

Mary Adams began her work at Nightingale Street at a salary of £115 per annum. The problems she faced were predictable. One was unpunctuality. In the first month of her appointment she was complaining that punishing late-comers 'seems of little use'.[76] Parents came to the school to complain of their children loitering and begged her to punish them. The health of the children was poor. In the same month she recorded sore heads and ringworm as of epidemic proportions, and constantly put forward as pleas for absence.[77] During her time at Nightingale Street other infectious outbreaks were noted: of scarlet fever, endemic measles, bronchitis, whooping cough, smallpox and diarrhoea. Smallpox was the most feared of the diseases.

Mary Adams used the cane to punish girls late through playing in the street, and leading younger ones astray, among other offences she regarded as serious.[78] She sent for the mothers of

Figure 3.10.   Nightingale Street and School, Lisson Grove

children rude to her and the staff, but found their daughters under little maternal control. A particularly aggravating incident in her view was that of two girls entering the cloakroom and cutting the elastic of three or four dozen hats with scissors. One of the offenders was described by the mother as 'not quite right and subject to fits' and by Mary Adams as 'vicious and nearly an idiot', while the other she condemned as 'very wicked' with 'sisters in a reformatory'.[79] Another pupil was picked up for robbery, and was noted by Mary Adams as 'a very bad and vicious girl'.[80] She also refused to admit girls who could give no reason for leaving their previous school. Few girls stayed for long. In one entry she lamented that her last two Standard VI girls had left, being the eldest in their respective families and required at home.[81] In the 1878 scripture examination, 178 children were entered for Standard I, but this declined steeply to 58 in Standard II, 30 in Standard III, 14 in Standard IV, and only 4 in Standard V.[82] In the government examination later that year, 70 were entered for Standard I, 74 for Standard II, 45 for Standard III, 22 for Standard IV, and 9 for Standard V.[83] An 1879 entry notes reorganisation to allow 15 dunces to be accommodated in Standard I.[84]

Despite the problems, Mary Adams went beyond teaching the three Rs, recording in her log book the songs and recitations to be learned, and work in drawing, physical education, needlework, and physical exercises, while out-of-school trips were undertaken to the Zoological Gardens, and to Crystal Palace for scripture prize-givings. In common with the family tradition, her husband was invited over to examine the girls while, towards the end of her stay at Nightingale Street, she in turn gave two assistants leave of absence to visit her husband's Fleet Road School.[85] Mary Adams was clearly singled out by the London School Board as a promising headmistress. She was visited by Lyulph Stanley, an influential member of the Board . She received a very promising report from its Inspector in July 1878, the order and tone of the school being described as 'very creditable to the Headteacher and her assistants.... Mrs. Adams has not been in charge of this school for very long; she is evidently laying a foundation for its future success'.[86] The July 1879 Report recorded a great improvement again.

Her reports from government inspectors, even the first one of 1877 by HMI Charles Alderson, were also good. He commended both the discipline and instruction, though he pointed out that almost all the girls were presented in the first three standards But by the following year the numbers in the three higher standards had risen from 17 to 31. Alderson's 1878 Report was included in the log look:

This is not so large a proportion of the whole as one would wish to find, though, no doubt, as large as possible in the circumstances. Within the limits thus indicated, the girls have passed a good examination in the fundamental and extra subjects, and creditably, to the number of 15, in one specific subject, Domestic Economy. The discipline is satisfactory.

Numbers in the higher standards increased considerably in the following year, and the 1880 Report was also a favourable one, 'considering the class of girls attending'. The high point of Mary Adams' stay at Nightingale Street was no doubt receiving her parchment in January 1880, raised to First Class. On the basis of her good reports, her salary was increased to £121 in 1878 and to £127 in 1880. Apart from minor problems with pupil teachers, she seems to have been happy with her staff. In November 1880 she was presented with an elegant flower arrangement on her birthday. When she left in November 1881 she received a silver teapot and flower pot and stand, which she described as 'tokens of love and esteem'.[87]

That she experienced problems at Nightingale Street is reinforced by a comment made by her husband when interviewed by the Cross Commissioners in 1886. He pointed out that teachers in the Lisson Grove group of schools were sometimes of excellent quality but never obtained 'excellent grants'. He instanced one teacher he knew of (that is, his wife Mary Adams) who, on moving to 'a school in a better neighbourhood' in Kilburn, in the same inspectoral division, in the first year earned the 'Excellent' merit grant with ease.[88]

Mary Adams in the Suburbs

The Kilburn Environment

Mary Adams was appointed the first headmistress of the new London School Board Netherwood Street School in Kilburn, opened late in 1881 in an area described in the local press as 'a district on the extreme western boundary of Hampstead, and only just within the metropolitan area, which has been transformed in the last few years from fields into a neighbourhood closely re-sembling the thickly-populated portions of Kentish-town which bound the parish of Hampstead on its eastern side'.

This was the classic Booth mixture of pink comfortable territory, with a large number of purple streets in mixed comfort and poverty. It was an altogether more propitious situation than Nightingale Street. The advantage was reinforced by the school's proximity to Fleet Road, on the other side of the railway tunnels which cut through the heights of Hampstead, where her husband was by now well-established as headmaster. The local newspaper columnist piquantly described Hampstead as being on a hill, and 'very difficult to be got at by cabs or School Boards'. Board Schools were confined to the fringes. A school in the area was sorely needed. The chairman of the inaugural meeting observed that the London School Board had great difficulty in keeping up with the fast pace of population growth in its outlying areas. Even the local vicar congratulated the Board on its new 'palace' and agreed its necessity, as all the schools in the neighbourhood were more than full. There were about 1,500 children needing accommodation in the district, and only a school for 300–350 to serve them. The new schools were intended to accommodate 1,000 children, with departments of 300 each for boys and girls and 400 for infants.[89]

The London School Board had made arrangements for parents to visit the schools before the opening, and the *Kilburn Times* recorded that many of the visitors belonged 'to the poorer class which surrounds the schools, and from which the school children will be drawn'. The provision seen was said to have caused 'pleasurable surprise', ranging from the internal facilities to the 'spacious playgrounds, tar-paved and well-drained, each provided with swings'. Lyulph Stanley was present at the opening and 'pleasantly alluded' to the fact that this was the second Board School to be built in Hampstead, and that the new head of the girls' department, located on the top of the three floors, was Mrs Adams, wife of the 'respected headmaster of the Fleet Road schools'. The evening was concluded by the staff of Fleet Road providing a musical programme of part-songs and solos.[90]

Mary Adams at Netherwood Street Board School
Planned in typical London School Board architectural style, Nether-wood Street was a three-storey brick building with a spacious play-

ground. Mary Adams entered her duties on 15 November 1881. The admissions registers made clear the crying need for school places in Kilburn. Over 70 children entered the girls' department after having attended church schools, and over 120 from local private schools, which severely felt the draught from the School Board's intervention. Indeed, Mary Adams recorded still receiving scholars from two private schools during the first half of 1882. But by September both had closed. The vast majority of the children flooded in from the streets adjacent to the school: Netherwood Street itself, Palmerston Road, Lowfield Road, Loveridge Road and Iverson Road, all categorised on Booth's social maps as either pink or purple.

Within a week there were 150 girls on the books. Mary Adams classified the children, finding them very low in attainment. Only 78 had attained Standard I and only half had any notion of reading.[91] As late as the following June, none of the first schedule of girls was good enough to move into Standard II.[92] In January 1882 she recorded that two very respectable and well-dressed children aged 11 and 13 had presented themselves for admission, of whom the latter just knew her letters, and the former not even that.[93] She was less concerned about attracting pupils and more about losing them. The population was in a fluid state, changing house and school frequently. Of one early group of 140 scholars, 87 stayed for two years or less.

In the early stages she had problems of obtaining the staff she felt she needed, in January 1882 being left with over 100 children in Standard I, 'all dreadfully backward, on my hands', with only a candidate (in lieu of a qualified member of staff) to assist.[94] In the first quarter of the year she suffered from a pupil teacher candidate frequently being absent because of her mother's and her own illness, while Mary Adams herself suffered from colds and headaches. She seems to have been more harassed by complaining parents than during her years in the supposedly more difficult Lisson Grove area. For example, having given a girl 'two taps on the head with a pointer' for 'defiant disobedience' to a member of staff, she was confronted by the mother who came into the school and 'made a great fuss'.[95] Another mother complained of the treatment of her children whom Mrs Adams described as 'certainly the most defiant and obstinate in the school, and (who) have given trouble to every teacher who has had anything to do with them'.[96]

Another made 'impudent complaints' about the overworking of her children, and withdrew them after objecting to the 'Netherwood Street system'. Mary Adams described her as 'rudely claiming she could send them where she pleased'.[97]

Again she made good progress in improving standards, and once more imported her husband to examine the children in the three Rs[98] and then in the extra and specific subjects.[99] Among the November 1882 log book entries was the first and more than satisfactory HMI Report:

I am well satisfied with the progress made in this school since its opening. The two lower standards are abnormally large; but this is an unavoidable feature of the school in its present stage. In the coming year I hope it will be possible to advance clever girls two standards. Within its present limits, the school work shows thoroughness, and good quality, and I am very glad to be able to report the Needlework is already good.

Better was to come. By the 1883 examination there was a more appropriate spread with 80 entered for Standard I, 70 for II, 44 for III, 35 for IV, 38 for V and 4 for VI: 'The whole of the work in this Department is of good quality, the slate work of the first and second standards especially.... Needlework is very good and discipline is very good. I recommend a Merit Grant for the year at the rate of "Excellent"'. This London School Board Inspector's Report also noted the girls' department was 'in excellent order' having passed 'a very creditable examination'.[100] Following in the family tradition, Mary Adams went beyond the basics. In June 1883 the girls were given the opportunity to bring in plants with which to decorate the school. Fifty plants had been brought in 'with great glee' by girls of all classes, and some of them were 'quite choice'.[101]

In late October 1883 Mary Adams was summoned to a managers' meeting at Fleet Road for nomination for the headship of the junior mixed school there. On 2 November she attended a meeting at the London School Board offices. Clearly the Board thought carefully about whether to select her or not, for the appointment was at first postponed and only later confirmed. On 11 December her resignation was accepted.[102] Fleet Road called.

REFERENCES AND NOTES

1. Henry Adams was the only son of John Adams not to become a member of the teaching dynasty. He was not in residence at home on census day in

1851, nor in 1861. He disappears from the family record until 1898, when W.B. Adams, then Headmaster of Fleet Road School in Hampstead, stated in his log book that his elder brother and wife, of Boston, Massachusetts, had visited the school. He indicated that Henry had emigrated to the United States in the mid-1860s. In the obituary of the Adams' youngest son, Richard, in 1910, it was suggested that Henry had made a fortune in the United States, and had recently died in London.

2. CC, *2nd Report* (1887), p. 59.
3. Ibid., p. 57.
4. *RCCE* (1866–7), pp. 249–50.
5. *RCCE* (1861–2), p. 350.
6. *RCCE* (1862–3), p. 273.
7. *The Practical Teacher*, Vol.15 (1894), p.1.
8. *Hampstead Record*, 27 Oct. 1900.
9. *RCCE* (1864–5), pp. 156–7.
10. 1847 *Reports*, pp. 36–7.
11. *The Cambrian*, 5 Feb. 1864.
12. Pembroke British School Log Book, 23 Sept. 1864.
13. CC, *2nd Report* (1887), p. 45.
14. *Educational Record*, Vol. 6 (1865), pp. 224–5.
15. Pembroke British School Log Book, 15 Feb. 1866.
16. *Haverfordwest and Milford Haven Telegraph*, 21 Feb. 1866.
17. *Carmarthen Journal*, 23 Feb. 1866.
18. Pembroke British School Log Book, 3 Aug. 1866.
19. Ibid., 26 June 1866.
20. Ibid., 17 Aug. 1866.
21. *Haverfordwest and Milford Haven Telegraph*, 8 Aug. 1866.
22. Ibid., 14 Feb. 1866.
23. Ibid., 14 March 1866.
24. 1847 *Reports*, p. 375.
25. *MCCE* (1850–1), pp. 734–5.
26. *MCCE* (1852–3), p. 698.
27. *MCCE* (1853–4), p. 823.
28. *The Cambrian*, 5 May 1865.
29. 1847 *Reports*, p. 304.
30. See Evans, op.cit. (1971), Ch. 4.
31. Merthyr Teachers' Centre Group, *Merthyr Tydfil: A Valley Community* (Cowbridge: D. Brown and Sons, 1981), p. 378.
32. *MCCE* (1839–40), pp. 176–7.
33. Ibid., pp. 182–3.
34. Ibid., p. 192.
35. 1847 *Reports*, p. 305.
36. Ibid., p. 483 and p. 487.
37. Ibid., p. 484 and p. 488.
38. *MCCE* (1854–5), pp. 592–3.
39. Newcastle Commission, Vol.2, (1861) pp. 459–60.
40. Ibid., p. 488.
41. Ibid., pp. 451–2.
42. See, for example, R. Grant, *Water and Sanitation: the Struggle for Public Health in Merthyr Tydfil* (Cowbridge: D. Brown and Sons, 1993); and J. Lowe, *Welsh Industrial Workers' Housing 1775–1875* (Cardiff: UWIST, 1994 edition), pp. 3–4.

43. T.J. Harris and J. Evans, *School and Play in the Parish of Vaynor, South Wales, from 1850 to the Present Day* (Cowbridge: D. Brown and Sons, 1983), p. 11 and pp. 21–2.
44. Quoted in ibid., p. 19.
45. Quoted in E. Bowen, *Vaynor: A Study of the Welsh Countryside* (Merthyr Tydfil, 1992), p. 16.
46. Quoted in Harris and Evans, op.cit. (1983), p. 33.
47. Ibid., pp. 50–1.
48. Cefn Coed Works School Log Book, 8 Nov. 1866.
49. *Cardiff and Merthyr Guardian*, 31 Aug. 1866.
50. Cefn Coed Works School Log Book, 2 Nov. 1866.
51. Ibid., 29 Sept. 1866.
52. Quoted in Harris and Evans, op.cit.(1983), p. 54.
53. *The Practical Teacher*, Vol. 15 (1894), p. 1.
54. *RCCE* (1868–9) p. 569.
55. *RCCE* (1870–1), p. 496.
56. *Swansea and Glamorgan Herald*, 18 May 1870.
57. See C. Morley, *Studies in Board Schools* (London: Smith, Elder and Co., 1897), p. 105.
58. *The Practical Teacher*, Vol.15 (1894), p.1.
59. A. W. Jackson, *James Martineau: a Biography and Study* (London: Longmans, Green and Co., 1900), p. 94 and p. 160.
60. J.E. Carpenter, *James Martineau, Theologian and Teacher: a Study of his Life and Thought* (London: Philip Green, 1905), p. 409.
61. Ibid., p. 418.
62. *The Schoolmaster*, 30 Jan. 1892, p. 193.
63. PRO ED3/19.
64. See *Hampstead and Highgate Express*, 21 March 1903.
65. *Borough of Marylebone Newspaper*, 12 July 1872.
66. PRO ED3/19.
67. *The Schoolmaster*, 4 Oct. 1873, p. 170.
68. *Swansea and Glamorgan Herald*, 16 Jan. 1876.
69. Quoted in *The Practical Teacher*, Vol. 15 (1894), p.1.
70. C. Booth, *Life and Labour of the People in London: Third Series: Religious Influences*, Vol. 1 (London: Macmillan, 1902), pp. 199–200.
71. *Borough of Marylebone Mercury*, 22 Oct. 1881.
72. *The Indicator*, 29 Oct. 1881.
73. Nightingale Street Girls' School Log Book, 11 May 1877.
74. *Borough of Marylebone Mercury*, 29 April 1876.
75. PRO ED21/11890.
76. Nightingale Street Girls' School Log Book, 22 Aug. 1877.
77. Ibid., 30 Aug. 1877.
78. Ibid., 31 Aug. 1877.
79. Ibid., 6 March 1878.
80. Ibid., 14 April 1880.
81. Ibid., 25 March 1878.
82. Ibid., 4 Feb. 1878.
83. Ibid., 4 Nov. 1878.
84. Ibid., 4 April 1879.
85. Ibid., 15 June 1881.
86. SBL *Minutes*, EO/PS/12/96/3, July 1878.
87. Nightingale Street Girls' School Log Book, 9 Nov. 1881.

88. CC, *2nd Report* (1887), p. 48.
89. *Hampstead and Highgate Express*, 19 Nov. 1881.
90. *Kilburn Times and Western Post*, 18 Nov. 1881.
91. Netherwood Street Girls' School Log Book, 24 Nov. 1881.
92. Ibid., 12 June 1882.
93. Ibid., 16 Jan. 1882.
94. Ibid., 30 Jan. 1882.
95. Ibid., 9 May 1882.
96. Ibid., 25 April 1883.
97. Ibid., 28 May 1883.
98. Ibid., 1 Aug. 1882.
99. Ibid., 3 Aug. 1882.
100. SBL 1588, 1883.
101. Netherwood Street Girls' School Log Book, 12 June 1883.
102. Ibid., 11 Dec. 1883.

4

William and Mary Adams at Fleet Road, Hampstead

A more detailed study of Fleet Road Board School in the years of William Bateman Adams' headship can be found in the author's *Educating the Respectable*.[1]. This provides the context for what follows, which will focus less on the school and more on the ideas and work of William Bateman (Figure 4.1) and, so far as the record allows, Mary Adams, during their culminating professional experiences at Fleet Road Board School, Hampstead, dubbed by Charles Morley, author of *Studies in Board Schools*, as the 'Eton of the Board Schools'.

FLEET ROAD: THE SOCIAL GEOGRAPHY

In November 1877, the London School Board purchased a parcel of land adjoining Fleet Road, Hampstead, as the site of a mixed school. The school opened in temporary rooms in Lismore Road, in Gospel Oak, in February 1878, with 54 scholars, of what Adams later described as 'a somewhat rough type'.[2] Only eight were in the fourth Standard. They were taught by Adams and one assistant. They moved into the new Fleet Road buildings in 1878. Over 450 children enrolled on the first day. The accommodation was planned first for 800, but the voracious local appetite led to a rapid increase to 1,200, then, in 1884, 400 more, which required the erection of a junior mixed school. Together with the infants' department, Fleet Road ended the School Board era with accommodation for nearly 1,800 children. In 1900 there were 204 scholars in the ex-seventh Standard, and 800 in the fifth Standard and above.[3]

Fleet Road School was built to meet the urgent need for school places of families living in the working-class streets to the south in

Figure 4.1.   W. B. Adams, Headmaster of Fleet Road Schools

West Kentish Town, mostly coloured purple, signifying mixed poverty and comfort in Booth's classification, but with over 35 per cent of the population experiencing real poverty. Fortuitously, as it turned out, the school faced north on to land still to be built over, but soon to be covered by respectable lower middle-class residences, solidly 'pink' in Charles Booth's classification. Adams pivoted his catchment area in this direction, towards the parental cohort whose children achieved for Fleet Road its scholarship-winning reputation. He was committed to the improvement of public education. He rejected the view of the voluntary sector that school boards should devote their resources to the needs of poorer children. As a convinced meritocrat he had higher visions, and envisaged the day when 'waifs and strays' would become a thing of the past.[4]

Adams defended himself vigorously against allegations that he and his highly trained teachers found it more congenial to teach the higher branches of the code to the children of prosperous

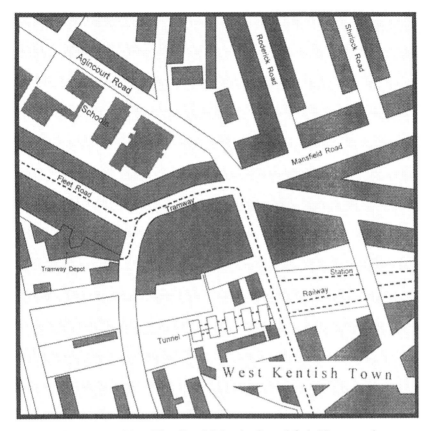

Figure 4.2.   Map: Fleet Road Schools, Gospel Oak, Hampstead

parents, and that he offloaded submissions for entry from poorer parents on to neighbouring voluntary schools. In his evidence before the Cross Commissioners in 1886, he described the nature of his catchment area.

The population is a very mixed one; we have the children of bricklayers and labourers; a considerable sprinkling of the parents of the children are employed on the Midland and North-western Railways. The great indus-try of the neighbourhood is pianoforte making ... and a great number of the parents of the children are employed there. Then we have a new neighbourhood of small villas, which are occupied by people engaged in City warehouses, and so on.[5]

In a later interview, Adams recalled that he had started with 'about forty scholars of a somewhat rough type' in the school,[6] but that there was 'no truancy, and no boots, clothes, nor free dinners need be given to the Fleet Road children'.[7] The *School Board Chronicle* probably judged the situation accurately in describing the school as 'not by any means extravagantly, but reasonably favourably' placed.[8]

As the school prospered, so did the Adams' financial circumstances. In the early 1880s they moved from Lorne Gardens to Willow Road in Hampstead. The housing here was of secure middle class status, meriting the red of Booth's classification, while falling short of the yellow of true wealth in nearby Belsize Park. Adams' starting salary at Fleet Road was £145, and rose to £155 in March 1880 on receipt of a good report. In each of his first five years he received a £10 increment for further good reports. By 1884, his fixed salary was £185 but a £223 share of grant gave him a total of £408. His financial position was also helped by increasing numbers. By 1886 there were 900 children in his department, of which nearly half were, remarkably, in Standards V, VI and VII/ex-VII. At the time of the 1891 census, John William Bateman was still with them, his occupation given as undergraduate at Oxford. They employed a 26-year-old cook and domestic servant, and a 16-year-old housemaid. They also had a lodger, a 36-year-old London School Board schoolmistress. It would seem that at least periodically the Adams enhanced the family income by taking in lodgers. Thus in 1902 the Honorary Secretary of London's Pembroke County Club, T.W. Ormiston, was recorded as residing at 10 Willow Road.[9]

THE GRADING OF SCHOOLS

Adams was a keen supporter of the London School Board's policy of grading elementary schools. This was less on social grounds than on professional. But he strongly urged that full support must be given to the Board's 'schools of special difficulty', and that the results of teachers in such areas should not be judged against those of schools in less difficult ones. It was for their moral excellence and training that such schools should largely be appraised. He suggested dividing schools into three groups. In the first, schools in poor districts, the three Rs and singing, drawing and drill should form the subjects of instruction. Here teachers should be paid higher salaries, and should be given government grants for doing good work under these difficulties. The second grade of schools he thought should be the general run of elementary schools, undertaking the current curriculum as laid down by the Codes, but without the specific subjects. The third group was that in which the children moved beyond Standard IV in large numbers, to form Standards V, VI and VII. Such would be likely only in large towns and cities.[10]

ORGANISING THE CURRICULUM

Soon after Fleet Road's opening, the *Swansea and Glamorgan Herald* despatched a correspondent to report on the school. He described it as conducted on the new or Prussian system, in buildings with one great central hall, and twelve side annexes of classrooms.

Each class room communicates with the hall by a door, which forms the only means of ingress and outgress for scholars and assistants; but the class rooms communicate with each other by means of private doors intended for the sole use of the head master in making his rounds. Every class room was really a separate school, well furnished with maps, diagrams, blackboards and other etceteras, where 60 scholars, under absolute control, were being taught under the supervision of one certificated teacher, responsible to the head teacher. This method we considered far more efficient, and far superior to the monitorial or pupil teacher system.[11]

Adams confirmed that Fleet Road was 'worked entirely on the Prussian system' which meant, among other things, that he used no pupil teachers in the Senior School.[12]

The Three Rs

Adams viewed the basic three Rs as very important, but as a means to an end. He was critical of the artificiality he discerned in HMI examination of spelling and arithmetic. He maintained that the children were liable to spend too much time learning the spellings of words not likely to be met in ordinary conversation or reading books. These included words taken from geographical readers, possibly containing Welsh or Scottish names which readily tripped up the children.[13] The same criticism applied to 'mechanically and practically useless',[14] that is 'Government arithmetic' in which, for example, a girl in the fourth standard was asked to

convert 123,456,789 inches into miles, when she should have
been taught through working out a washing or a grocery bill for a
week. More attention, he argued, should be paid to attaching
these subjects to 'the problems of everyday life'.[15]

In general Adams reacted strongly against the system of individual examination practised under the Codes, but he agreed at that
stage that it should be retained to ensure that each child was
properly instructed in the three Rs.[16] He appreciated more, however, the reforms brought by Kekewich in the 1890s, an administrator whom he regarded as in tune with schools and teachers,
having infused 'a new and vigorous life into every detail of school
work ... the whole system of mechanical drudgery and Code
grinding' had become a thing of the past. Now they were able 'to
study the bent of scholars' minds, the backward children were not
unduly pressed, and the bright children were no longer retarded in
their progress'.[17]

History and Literature

While trained as a generalist primary teacher, Adams turned himself into a history specialist. His commitment to the teaching of
history in the primary school was profound, and he lamented that
under the current Codes it was 'almost extinct' in elementary
schools. He recommended its study on both social and patriotic
grounds. 'I think that all our elder scholars ought to know how we
are governed, and how the laws are made ... ' He argued that
history also quickened a love of reading.[18] He agreed that too
much attention had been paid to battles and rulers, rather than the
people themselves.[19] The sort of history he asked for would
emphasise the recent rather than the ancient: not the swallowing
of dry bones of wholesale lists of the mere names of Saxon kings,
but rather 'getting the life and colour, so to speak, of the great
events of history'.[20] But the main focus of the syllabus should be
on the history of the English people.[21] His expectations of pupils
and pupil teachers in this field were considerable, and regarded as
too demanding by some of the Commissioners. He indicated he
had been employed as senior teacher of history in the Pupil
Teachers' Centres of Marylebone and Finsbury, and had asked
them questions like: 'Take the case of an educated nobleman living
in the time of Queen Anne; what books do you suppose you would

be likely to find in his library?' Similarly creative questions were asked of his own pupils, as on the occasion of a visit of the Principal of the Maria Grey College, when the children were told to write essays on the following subject: 'What man or woman that you ever heard or read about would you wish to be like and why?'[22]

History, he demanded, should be placed on the same footing as geography in the lower forms, and should be linked with it. Britain's involvement in various European wars could advantageously be used to introduce a good deal of the geography of other countries, for example.[23] Geography, he argued, should mainly be taught by *viva voce* and by maps. He would use *Geographical Readers* for home lessons chiefly.[24] He accepted that the study of English history could in practice be connected to the study of the whole world, but it could profitably be limited to a study of the colonies and countries related to us by commerce.[25]

Adams disagreed with the London School Board's view that the position of the history teacher was compromised by religious issues, though, on being challenged about the expertise of the general run of teachers, he accepted he should personally examine carefully the notes of teachers where religious questions were involved.[26] He felt the problem was that past history reading books had instilled a spirit of religious bitterness, making too much, for example, of religious persecution in the reign of Queen Mary and not enough of that in the reign of Queen Elizabeth, whereas he would emphasise the progress made from a time when the principles of religious liberty were not understood to the fortunate present, when 'everybody is allowed to worship God as they please'.[27]

His own school textbook, *Leading Events in English History*, was 'adapted to the requirements of the 1871 Code', and was published in 1872. The text was in two parts, the first running from Norman to Tudor times. The structure was divided into the main royal 'lines': Normans, Plantagenets, Lancastrians, Yorkists and Tudors, sub-divided according to 'Leading Events' such as the signing of Magna Carta. These sections were interspersed with biographies of such figures as Thomas à Becket and Mary Queen of Scots. The publishers, W. and R. Chambers, quoted HMI reports on Adams' history instruction, as 'quite remarkable for fullness and accuracy', a comment later attributed to Matthew Arnold.[28] Adams' intention was to get children to write down, in a coherent and intelligible form, the leading events in English history. To this end, the 'connecting links' between the events were prominently marked. Intended for the higher standards, the book was especially recommended as useful for home lessons. Each sub-section included a 'cause' at the beginning, and 'results' at the end, with the historical detail between. The writing style was heavy, making few allowances in the sophistication of its vocabulary. The book was written from a British point of view. The account of the Crusades, for example, was characteristic of that purveyed in textbooks over the centuries. The cause was the ill-treatment of Christian pilgrims by infidel Turks, guilty of 'insults, robberies and extortions' of pilgrims visiting the Holy Land.[29] *The Practical Teacher* also noted he had written two further texts for the publisher Stewart and Co., entitled *Biographical Sketches* and *Historical Notes and Queries.*[30]

There is also interesting evidence of Adams' teaching approach in history, obviously regarded by visitors to the school as far in advance of its time. He adopted a bantering, quiz-type, questioning style with his senior Fleet Road classes, intended both to impress the visitors with the detail of the knowledge of the pupils, but also to show his own mastery by 'flooring' the children with awkward, even trick questions. Charles Morley was astonished at the repartee-like nature of the interaction.

'A Bishop who was banished, quick.'
'Atterbury'
'A celebrated blind poet?'
'Milton'
'A naval Minister who kept a diary?'
'Pepys'
'Whose reign?'
'Charles the Second and James the Second'
'The founder of the Indian Empire?'
'Clive'

and so on.[31] The older pupils were taken on visits to Westminster Abbey and the Tower of London, and wrote up their experiences, the reward being a prize for the best work.[32] The upper classes were given carefully constructed and graduated sheets of notes, 'copied by the trypograph', so that the points of the lesson could be more easily followed as the teacher commented upon and illustrated the main points.[33]

As in almost all schools at the time, history was valued as a patriotic subject. Fleet Road was not unusual in celebrating the relief of Ladysmith in the Boer War with its children, summoning them to a flag-bedecked hall to sing the National Anthem and salute the victors.[34] Adams took the view that one of the school's purposes was 'to teach the children to grapple with difficulties and to become a self-reliant race, worthy descendants of those who had made England what she is'. The Queen was to be revered. Adams own contribution to the subject was recognised by his being elected, on the recommendation of Lord Aberdare, as a Fellow of the Royal Historical Society, 'in recognition of the value of his evidence before the Royal Commission on Education'.[35]

Adams was also keenly interested in English literature and drew attention to its connections with history. He was responsible for teaching both subjects in his Senior Department. He maintained he would always combine the two subjects.[36] He taught Shakespeare through this medium. If the Tudor period was the topic in history, they would also read the play of *Henry VIII*. Work on Shakespeare not only helped with history but also introduced children to the best literature possible. The pupils, he claimed, thoroughly mastered and analysed one play a year in the upper standards, with 'very good results'.[37]

Commercial Subjects

W.B. Adams believed in a degree of specialisation. He took the view that once they had achieved appropriate standards in the basic subjects, pupils in the final years in Standards VI, VII and Ex-VII should follow to an extent their own interests, and sharpen their general knowledge. For those not well-equipped to study mathematics, for example, he advocated tuition in shorthand and book-keeping, and French, because of their great commercial value.[38] French was taught, and while not euphoric over its success, Adams clearly supported its introduction.[39] He had a strong concept of providing a curriculum geared to the needs of London children. Commercial education was thus the third of Adams' curricular crusades, the others being the more practical orientation of the three Rs and history teaching, combined with literature. He appears to have been less interested in other subjects, not least sciences, which he regarded as more appropriate to northern and

Midland cities. Lyulph Stanley warmly applauded the commercial bent of the school, and spoke favourably of the ladder of opportunity which the London Chamber of Commerce certificates offered through being taken at evening continuation classes under one of the Fleet Road teachers.[40] Morley too was impressed by the school's commercial work, and gave an example of a shorthand lesson in operation, designed to fit pupils for careers in 'the Civil Service – the Telegraphs, the Post Offices'.[41]

Coeducation and the Curriculum for Girls

For its time, a forward-looking aspect of Adams' educational philosophy was his support for mixed schooling. At his time it was still a controversial form of organisation, seen as posing moral problems and tending to have a coarsening 'moral tendency' on the girls.[42] Toughly questioned by the Cross Commissioners on the issue, Adams stuck to his ground that the ideal state of the school should be that of the 'well-ordered family'. He argued that mixed schools had organisational advantages, and enabled boys to become more civilised without hardening the girls. The manners of the boys were improved, as were the academic expectations of the girls. The latter gained 'in courage and candour', while their presence improved the behaviour of the boys, 'who never like to be punished or disgraced before girls'.[43] The attendance of girls became more regular, as they were anxious to keep up with the attainments of boys, in a 'healthy spirit of rivalry'.[44] Adams agreed that the need to arrange for the girls to do cookery and needlework created logistical problems. But the boys could concurrently take different subjects, like algebra or French.[45]

These views generated stronger reactions than almost any other of his opinions from the Commissioners, concerned about the potentially injurious moral influence of mixed schooling, especially in districts where the scholars were 'drawn from the poorest ranks of society'.[46] While Adams did not entirely dismiss these objections, he emphasised he had never found not the slightest problems on these grounds.[47] Adams argued not only the widely held view that women teachers were better for younger children, but also, more controversially, that they were just as good as men in the upper standards. He also pointed out that women teachers curtailed the expenses on managers, being paid less than men, though he did not think this should be so.[48] On a later occasion he affirmed publicly that in future 'the younger children of our schools would be more and more entrusted to the care of females, and for this reason, among others, that their work taken as a whole, is superior to that of the sterner sex'.[49]

There is no doubt that the girls of Fleet Road stood out in the public view. This was in part a result of the initial influence of the redoubtable Louisa Walker in the infants' department, who through her games and action songs encouraged her girls to have career ambitions.[50] Both Morley and the *London* and *The Practical Teacher* correspondents were bowled over by the unexpected confidence of the girls, Morley, for example, by the 'depth and fire' of a recitation from *Henry V* of a girl of 13, 'with a most intellectual headpiece'[51] and *London* by one from *The Faerie Queene* 'said with all due inflections and proper feeling'. These reinforced the idea that girls could recite better than boys,[52] and also sing. Morley referred to the boys as musical barbarians: 'It is the girls of London, with the sweet soft voices ... enthusiastic lovers of good music ... to whom we must look then for reform.'[53]

His progressive instincts did not mean that Adams neglected the training of his girls for traditional domestic roles. He was a martinet where dropping litter was concerned, and saw domestic economy as promoting care, tidiness, order and thrift, as well as beneficial 'industrial' skills. It was a key subject for the girls of Fleet Road. It included far more than the technical details of cookery: the pros and cons of different ways of cooking meat, for example. The curriculum included health education, and among the topics followed were the diets presented as suitable for working men, for babies, and for sick people. Predictably, Adams used the prowess of the senior girls to prepare meals for visitors. Morley appreciated both the fare provided and the way it was served.[54]

Extra-curricular Activities

Music shared a place with history as one of Adams' great enthusiasms. Its association with school entertainments and prize-givings, as well as the notable London School Board choral music competitions, gave Fleet Road high public visibility, which Adams regularly exploited – and not only in the local press. Copy was sent back to South Wales, as in a report in *The Cambrian* of 1892 which headed a piece on Adams: 'HOW A SWANSEA BOY HAS SUCCEEDED AS A LONDON SCHOOLMASTER: THE WELSH LORD MAYOR'S VISIT TO A BOARD SCHOOL'. At this occasion great play was made on all sides about the family's Welsh connection. Adams himself, conveniently forgetting his discomforts as a student and as a teacher in the Principality, was now pleased to proclaim himself a Welshman. The Lord Mayor was in turn 'glad to know ... that the success of this particular school was due mainly to the efforts of a Welshman'.[55] The event was also featured in *The Schoolmaster*. A motto had been prepared in Welsh which meant: 'A hearty welcome to you, and a lifetime of peace.' 'Men of Harlech' was sung by the school choir.[56]

Similarly, in *The Cambrian* of 1896, there was an account of the annual Fleet Road prize distribution. W.B. Adams was described as 'one of the most able teachers in the United Kingdom' who had 'succeeded in stirring up a feeling of pride in the school ... something akin to the feeling that a public school boy has for the place in which he was educated'.[57] Again in 1900, when his son was well established as headmaster of Tenby County School, a local newspaper reported on the commemoration of the 21st anniversary of the school. Mrs Wynford Philips, wife of a Pembrokeshire MP, proposed the vote of thanks to Lyulph Stanley for awarding the prizes.

I am proud to think that this admirably conducted and great school is under the guidance of Mr. Adams, a Pembroke, and I may say, a loyal man. I am delighted to find that he has brought with him a love of music and art from that sweet land of song. For your sakes I should wish that my husband were here today.... I should like the member for Pembrokeshire to tell you how delighted the people of the county were to select, as head of their Intermediate School at Tenby, Mr. Adams' brilliant and gifted son.

A.J. Mundella proposed a vote of thanks to the staff and stated that it was easy to see that 'a master mind and a master hand were at hand in that exceptional institution'. Adams, responding, stressed that in his 21st year there he was still never so happy as among his staff and pupils. The little girl who presented the bouquet to Miss Stanley was the daughter of the only seventh Standard girl he had in 1879. He stated that the school's object was 'to keep pace with the times with regard to education, to teach the children to grapple with difficulties and to become a self-reliant race, worthy descendants of those who made England what she is'.[58] In his quest for recognition, Adams was aided and abetted by the London School Board and its luminaries, who were inclined to place the school on the itinerary of many visiting dignitaries, whether domestic or foreign. These included a much-publicised visit by Prince Damrong of Siam in 1891, and by an appointee of the Italian Minister of Public Instruction in 1897, both looking particularly at the musical training at Fleet Road, against which the latter judged the work in other countries of Europe as appearing 'pale by comparison'.[59]

One of Adams' most successful appointments was that of Jesse Harris as his master of music. Music was a highly organised activity, children from different standards being amalgamated for singing under different teachers with some qualification in music. Then twice a year Harris would go through the school to select the pupils with the best voices and musical ear and reading facilities for the special choir.[60] The school's successes in the London School Board Vocal Music Competitions represented the pinnacles of its musical achievement. These were no mean events, being held once each in the Royal Albert Hall and at Crystal Palace, and three times each at Exeter Hall and the Queen's Hall. They were attended by well-known music critics, including George Bernard Shaw.The Fleet Road choir won on three occasions before the competitive element in the occasion ended in 1898.[61] The second outcome was that the school's favourable publicity locally was enhanced by the famed choir's appearances at annual concerts and entertainments.[62]

In addition to its concerts and prize-givings, the school engaged in competitive sports, again publicising its successes in cricket, football and athletics. Adams ensured that Fleet Road was further kept in the public eye by invitations to teachers' associations to hold meetings there, including even one from the Metropolitan Board Teachers' Association, with which he had such a tense relationship, at whose quarterly meeting in February 1882 Mrs Burgwin, the redoubtable headmistress of Orange Street Board School in Southwark, spoke on 'Over-pressure in Girls' and Infants' Schools'.[63] More frequently, Fleet Road hosted the Marylebone Teachers' Association meetings. In 1887, for example, Adams organised a particularly prestigious Saturday afternoon conference on the 'Higher Training of Teachers', at which members of

Oxford colleges, the London School Board, the inspectorate, and the vice-Principal of Borough Road College attended. It was closely concerned with a topic near and dear to Adams: 'The Status of the Profession'. During the discussions, he argued for raising the standards of training of elementary teachers by widening the intellectual range of the course. which would require its extension to three years. It was noted that the 120 attending the meeting partook of tea afterwards, supervised by Mrs Adams, after which a concert, interspersed with recitations and followed by dancing, concluded the evening.[64]

CONTROVERSY AND CRITICISM

Professional modesty was not one of William Bateman Adams' character traits, and just as his father had had to face the criticism of over-publicising himself and his family, so his son provoked similar comment. Much of this came from peers heavily involved in teacher trade unionism, towards which W.B. Adams was ambivalent. In his evidence to the Cross Commission, for example, on being asked whether he belonged to the National Union of Elementary Teachers, he stated that he believed his name was on its list, but he was not a working member.[65] In fact he was a founder member of one of its branches, the Marylebone Teachers' Association.

The Marylebone Association, at its opening meeting in December 1872, resolved to be affiliated to the NUET. Adams was elected as its Treasurer. It was agreed there should be a committee of mistresses to look after the interests of female teachers, and Mary Adams served on this committee.[66] Adams was perhaps keener on the Association's social events than its political activities. Among other things, they gave him the opportunity to hold meetings at his schools. The pattern was to put the business part of the meeting first, then follow it with social activities, at which Adams sometimes performed. Annual summer outings were organised to nearby beauty spots, where walks, cricket, quoits, and croquet were all popular, followed by a meal and indoor entertainment in the evening. In 1877 Adams was elected President of the Marylebone Teachers' Association, and later continued as a regular member of the organising committee. There is every evidence that he was a loyal supporter at the local level, therefore, but at the same time was regularly highly critical of the Union at the national.

Adams was not a regular attender at the national conferences, but was present as a Marylebone representative at Bristol in 1873, London in 1874 and 1877 and, predictably, at Swansea in 1897. This last homecoming may have served to reinforce his satisfaction at having moved to London nearly 30 years previously, for the blackness of the industrial environment impressed itself on the delegates. *The Board Teacher* observed graphically, on the rainy weekend of the Conference: 'Only sombre Dante could, on that awful Saturday, have enjoyed the view, just east of the Conference town.... Well-nigh every member it made dismal and doleful.... Hardened old sinners took to "nap", maturing ones to whist, the rollicking boys to rousing choruses, and all the sweet souls to bed.'[67] Perhaps surprisingly, there was no evidence in either the local or national press that Adams actively participated in the conference, nor that he used the occasion locally to publicise his exploits in London.

The lack of common ground between Adams and his fellow conference-goers was already evident at the London meeting at the Birkbeck Institution in Chancery Lane in 1874. In the one recorded documentation of his making a contribution, he spoke strongly against a proposal to recruit HMI from the ranks of elementary school teachers. He was 'not dissatisfed with the present staff of HM Inspectors', and complained about this subject again cropping up when there were so many others of more pressing importance. He thought the conference was agitating 'merely upon a question of sentiment'. It nevertheless supported the original proposal.[68] Regular tensions were also evident between the Marylebone Association and of the NUET's journal *The Schoolmaster*. In 1883, for example, its editor commented critically on the low attendances at the branch, pointing out that in this populous area with over 260 certificated teachers, an important issue was decided by a mere 11 votes to three. Indeed, over the years the Marylebone branch became a byword at NUT Conferences for its low membership and meagre contributions. In turn Adams objected strongly to the Union's attempt to appoint supervisors of local associations, which he denounced as 'useless and an exercise of undue interference'. Though ostensibly advisers, they would end up giving instructions.[69]

A further brush with peers arose from what some of them regarded as Adams' over-deferential attitudes towards influential members of the Inspectorate. A number of these had of course, materially assisted the advance of his career. On the occasion of HMI Alderson's elevation to become a Charity Commissioner in December 1885, for example, Adams presided over an assembly at Fleet Road of 500 teachers to present him with an address. In his response, Alderson stated that Adams 'seemed to him to represent the body of Marylebone teachers in a very eminent degree'.[70] A letter from an anonymous teacher the following February took a contrary stance.

> There is a considerable number of us, headteachers in this district, who fail to recognise their late Inspector in the Fleet Road eulogy. We refused to join the presentation party because we suspected (and the event has completely confirmed our suspicions) that the address would be couched in terms to which we could not conscientiously assent.
>
> That the gentleman in question is a good examiner of children no one doubts, but that he had any visible sympathy with teachers is a very recent discovery.[71]

Adams' great respect for the older generation of the inspectorate was again apparent on the death of Matthew Arnold. At the quarterly meeting of British Teachers' Association, held at Borough Road in May 1888, he moved the resolution of 'unfeigned sorrow' at his passing. As HMI for British Schools, the BFSS had 'never had a more consistent or warmer friend. Sympathetic to teachers, he upheld the finest traditions of the Inspectorate, with a 'delightfully free and easy way of examining'. He trusted people: 'his teachers honoured him for it, and, as a natural consequence, the whole tone and character of the profession was placed on a higher level.'[72]

On Adams' re-election to the post of President of the Marylebone Teachers' Association in 1890, he further lambasted the Union for its attacks on the Inspectorate, not least on Joshua Fitch, claiming that it was not merely unrepresentative in its membership and views, but also had no 'right to attack public men in this way without producing a shred of reliable evidence'. He insisted that his experience of Inspectors like Bowstead, Arnold and Alderson had been very favourable and that he always looked forward to their annual visits with feelings of pleasure.

Included in this attack was sarcastic comment about William J. Pope, a former President of the Union and of the Metropolitan

Board Teachers' Association. Pope had made criticisms of unsuitable arithmetic questions being offered by inspectors to children, one of which he claimed could not be answered by graduates of Oxford and Cambridge.[73] Following a further confrontational exchange of letters, Pope repeated his observation that Adams was over-respectful of inspectors, and launched into a savage attack on Adams and what he stood for, alleging that Adams had for years 'resolutely opposed the work of the Union, and done his best to back up those who would perpetuate the bondage of teachers'. He noted that he and the Union had been responsible for upsetting the 'grinding tyranny' of such as the London School Board and Whitehall: 'we are on the eve of seeing our fellow teachers treated as men and women, the efforts of Mr. Adams to the contrary notwithstanding'. He drew attention also to Adams' equivocal response to the Cross Commission on union membership. He concluded: 'If the Marylebone Inspectors favour Mr. Adams, as they appear to do, no wonder he becomes their apologist, and favours officials with his laudatory speeches.'[74]

In what he described as his 'final rejoinder', Adams reiterated that he had subscribed to the Union since the time of its formation. He regarded Pope's implication that he had served to 'perpetuate the bondage of teachers' as scandalous. At no time had he ever felt in bondage. He maintained that it was useful to have as Inspectors 'gentlemen of culture, with broad and liberal educational views untrammelled by professional prejudices' – in other words, he did not favour the appointment of a teacher inspectorate. If he was opposed to the work of the Union, it was only because he dissented from Pope's line of reasoning. He finally accused Pope of orchestrating a campaign to exclude him from the Union, and said he would appreciate this outcome if Pope's ideas were to be guide its counsels.[75]

In the last letter of the correspondence, Pope accused Adams of running away, and demanded that he retract his falsehoods. He claimed Adams had no place in the Union, and instanced that only 43 of its members belonged in 1889 to the Marylebone Branch, out of a total of 800–900 in board and voluntary schools in that district, referring to it as 'the weakest spot on the Union', and blaming it on Adams' influence. He urged Adams to apologise for what he had done and deployed Carlyle's phrase: 'his regeneration must be preceded by his deep repentance'. He submitted that while every member was entitled to his opinions, one who 'for years has specially tilted against the London members of the Executive, and traversed the entire programme of the Union, should not be in it'.[76]

Even so, Adams continued to play a prominent role in the Marylebone Teachers' Association. In 1895 he chaired a complimentary dinner held in a Holborn Restaurant by the Association to celebrate Edmond Barnes's fourth election as member of the London School Board at which, intriguingly, two of Adams' arch-opponents, T. Gautrey and W.J. Pope, were present. Characteristically, one of the vocalists at the associated 'excellent' musical entertainment was J.W.B. Adams.[77] Characteristically, again, while Adams was an erstwhile member of the Marylebone Teachers' Association, and also of the London School Board Head Teachers' Association, he rarely enrolled as a member of the Metropolitan Board Teachers' Association. An exception was in the years 1901–02. An uncharitable view would be that this was to help him gain his Fellowship of the Educational Institute of Scotland, and then to publicise his achievement, for in the MBTA lists for 1902 he is listed as W.J.B. [*sic*] Adams, FEIS.

Adams was again to meet with strong Union opposition following the London School Board's approval of the plan for the reorganisation of Fleet Road after his wife's retirement in 1898. In his evidence to the Cross Commission Adams had already signalled his view that there would be an advantage in joining senior and junior departments of large mixed schools under one headteacher, and on his wife's early retirement from the headship of the Fleet Road Junior Mixed Department, the London School Board's School Management Committee proposed that W.B. Adams, at no additional salary, be made headteacher of the combined school, supported by a senior assistant mistress in the Junior Mixed Department. An amendment was tabled, among whose supporters were T.J. Macnamara and T. Gautrey, to refer the matter back and have the post filled in the usual way. The amendment was lost. In its comment on the interchange, *The Board Teacher and London School Board Review* (to give it its full title) reported that Gautrey had commented critically that the action would reduce Adams to the status of a mere 'shopwalker' looking after 22 assistants and a pair of pupil teachers.[78]

On 5 May, the journal *London* had noted that Gautrey 'evidently does not admire Fleet Road School because the head master does not join the teacher's Trade Union, of which he is secretary'. It criticised Macnamara for language and tone lacking in 'dignity and polish' and condemned him for opposing administrative reforms, and for speaking as a teacher representative rather than as one for his constituency. The whole London School Board system would not break down because one 'superfluous teacher' was removed from Fleet Road School.[79] Macnamara, editor of *The Schoolmaster*, defended himself in that journal the following week:

There is a Board school in Hampstead which I think *London* told us ... was the 'the finest elementary school in Europe'. The headmaster of this school is a very estimable person, whose skill as a schoolmaster is only excelled by his anxiety to impress upon School Board members, the Press, and the public generally what a most splendid school his is. Recently the head-mistress of what is known as the 'Junior Mixed' department of this school resigned. Whereupon the idea is at once floated – Heaven forbid that I should suggest by whom – that it would be a good plan to let this wonderful schoolmaster take charge of his own and her departments. Yea, and he is found quite ready to do so without any addition to his salary.

So, in good time, this proposal is submitted to the Board. Whereupon Mr Gautrey ventures to oppose. As an educationist he doubts the ability of even this rare genius properly to supervise the daily routine of two departments accommodating some 1,176 children; as a trade unionist he objects to the wiping out of one of the few chances of promotion for our thousands of thoroughly efficient assistant mistresses.

A correspondent in turn complained that Macnamara should earlier have been leading a campaign against what he belatedly identified as a 'sinecure post' at Fleet Road, and also against Adams' evident underemployment previously, as apparently now he had time at no extra salary to take over the junior department.[80]

Similarly scornful abuse had previously been heaped upon Adams in *The Board Teacher* by a columnist, presumably Gautrey, noting the various self-congratulatory plaudits included in the school's magazine, with its motto *Semper Floreat Fleetonia*. These included the assertion of Sir George Kekewich, Secretary of the Education Department, that Fleet Road was 'the best elementary school in the kingdom':

We congratulate the Board upon having 'the very aristocracy of masters and pupils' in at any rate one of its establishments; we congratulate Eton upon being considered worthy of comparison with Fleet Road; and we congratulate Mr. W.B. Adams, F.R.Hist.S., upon having the largest staff of any school in England. In the list of staff we notice a choir-master, but no trumpeter. Perhaps Mr. W.B. Adams, F.R. Hist. S., does not need a trumpeter.[81]

This was not the only attack in *The Board Teacher*. In a thinly veiled piece, again responding to the public eulogising of Fleet Road School, the columnist wrote of a 'Mr. A. Shynynge Lyte ... the respected master of Swallow-street Board School' who had obtained an excellent merit grant for the tenth time in succession. Her Majesty's Government had despatched 'General New Sance' to inspect the drawings of the budding Royal Academicians at the school. 'Our readers will have noted that the Imperial Authorities have granted Mr. Lyte a diploma as teacher of drawing.' Reference was also made to the visit of 'H.R.H Burrabaloo, King of the Cannibal Islands', 'who expressed himself greatly interested in the well-fed appearance of the pupils' He was told that the trophy on the wall of the school hall was one which 'the nigger troupe of the school had carried off three times, in competition against all other schools in the Metropolis'.

The columnist concluded:

Gentlemen, there is every reason for believing that you have excellent schools. Their excellence may, in a measure, be due to the highly respectable character of the districts whence you draw your pupils, but no one wishes to deny also that it is, in a measure, due to your skill and assiduity. You must, however, be very ignorant or very vain if you really think there are not many other masters up and down the land as skilful, as assiduous, and as successful as you. The puffs of friendly newspapers may raise you in the esteem of those who cannot undergo the fatigue of judging for themselves, but loveliness needs not the foreign aid of orna-ment, and sensible people are apt to believe that merit which needs the aid of puffery cannot be very great. You evidently have considerable influence with certain journalists; if you do not exert it to check the exuberance of their panegyrics, the uncharitable will say that you inspire them. It would be considered unprofessional for a successful doctor to advertise his cures, or for a successful barrister to advertise his forensic triumphs; and why should medicine or the law have a higher professional standard than teaching?[82]

EXAMINATIONS AND REPORTS

Like other schools, Fleet Road had to build its reputation on the scrutiny not only of government, but also of local, in this case, London School Board, inspectors. The Board's Inspector quickly prophesied success for the school. 'This large school is in excellent hands and promises to become, very shortly, one of the best conducted schools in my district.... The discipline and tone are remarkably good, and the instruction is, in the circumstances, highly creditable....'[83] The Government Report of 1884 was specially praiseworthy, noting with approval that nearly 35 per cent of the scholars were in Standards V, VI and VII, while 70 scholars had gone up two standards in the year.

The Singing, which is of high quality, gives evidence of very careful training on the part of the teachers who undertake this portion of the instruction. The cricket and football clubs are both popular and flourishing, and I am glad that the teachers take an active part in the various sports and amusements of the scholars. The discipline is effectively maintained. I think in the matter of discipline, if the habitual tone of voice of some of the male teachers were more subdued, its influence on the boys would be decidedly beneficial. This school ranks as Excellent.[84]

While there was an occasional caveat, HMI Reports were consistently effusive. That of 1892 commented that it was 'rare to find a school which is so well taught throughout'.[85] There was no let-up in their praise in the Reports in Adams' final years so far as the quality of the work was concerned. That of 1901, for example, included the comment: 'This large Mixed School reflects the greatest credit upon Mr. Adams and his staff. The organisation is admirable, the curriculum is wide and well chosen.'[86]

There had, however, been crucial technical criticism in 1897 from HMI J.G. Fitzmaurice, accusing the school both of not working sanctioned timetables and of not keeping full records of children's attainments in subjects like geography, history, mental arithmetic and recitation. The examinations had been held by the teachers of the classes concerned and not by the headmaster. 'A more uniform system of marking and entering results should be arranged for the whole school.' There was unusual criticism of the work of Standards III and IV, alleging that Adams was not properly supervising the work of the classes, allowing some of it to be 'more highly marked than it should be'. This was followed by an ameliorative letter from Fitzmaurice's superior, Chief Inspector T.W. Sharpe, indicating to Adams that what Fitzmaurice needed to know was whether sufficient time was being allotted to the subjects of instruction for which grant was available. This was more than ever necessary 'since examination has become a thing of the past'. The note was sent to Adams via Fitzmaurice, who tersely commented: 'The suggestion made by Mr. Sharpe had better be followed.'[87]

By this stage memoranda were circulating round the Education Department that gave no cause for comfort either to Fleet Road or the London School Board. There is no doubt that Fleet Road was taken as a test case in the growing attack on advanced elementary provision. The type of work of the older pupils of the school was manifestly in secondary rather than elementary mode. It was predictable that the Department should question whether grants were being properly used. The Fleet Road timetables caused some official consternation, particularly the so-called 'extraordinary classes' attached to the main timetable. 'But do we pay grants for them?' was the question put on the relevant memorandum. Fitzmaurice reassured the Department that these classes were indeed part of the main school, but three of the teachers took no part in the elementary work at Fleet Road. Adams for a long time had recognised that he was sailing close to the wind. He was also known to have stated unofficially that he had classes working outside and beyond the Education Code. Adams' long-held view that 'there was room in this great capital of ours for every variety of instruction'[88] was not shared by official opinion.

Scholarships

The most important single factor reinforcing Fleet Road's reputation was its success in scholarship-winning, the scholarship ladder movement being regularly referred to by Lyulph Stanley and other luminaries of the London School Board as a most important element in the scheme of popular education.[89] By the 1890s two sets of scholarships were available. The London School Board itself did not have the power to offer scholarships, but from the early 1870s it persuaded individuals and private companies to do so. To gain a scholarship, children had to have passed Standard V, and to have sat a testing examination. The later London County Council Technical Instruction Board scholarships were at three levels: junior, intermediate and senior. Basically, the junior scholarships allowed deserving children to stay on to the upper standards of schools like Fleet Road, which was officially recognised for this purpose. The intermediate took them on to secondary education, and the senior scholarships to higher education. The numbers jumping each hurdle dwindled alarmingly as the number of scholarships decreased greatly at each level. In general, children of blue-collar workers gained many of the junior scholarships. The social balance skewed upwards for the intermediate scholarships, won more by the children of white-collar workers.

One of the great virtues of scholarships, so far as gaining publicity was concerned, was that they were countable, both in numerically and pecuniary terms, and provided a basis for compiling league tables of London schools. In the 1887 London School Board examinations, Fleet Road exceptionally provided the first two boys and the first two girls. The monetary value of scholarships became another criterion of achievement. Fleet Road had won nearly £2,500 worth by 1890 and nearly £25,000 worth of School Board scholarships by the time of Adams' death. In 1896 the *Daily Telegraph* noted that Fleet Road must have 'either exceptionally clever masters and mistresses, or phenomenally brilliant scholars' in winning no fewer than 19 scholarships in the year, and two years later recorded that for the second year in succession the school had won the largest number of Junior London County Council Scholarships.[90] In the following year, in an article entitled 'The Educational Ladder: the London Scholarship Record: the Most Successful Schools', the *Daily News* analysed the results over three years and, on the basis of both sets of scholarships, offered a league table to show that Fleet Road was the 'Champion School', first in the Technical Instruction Board scholarships, second in the London School Board scholarships, and first overall.[91]

ADAMS' ATTITUDES TO TEACHERS AND TRAINING COLLEGES

Perhaps because of his negative early experiences, Adams was critical of teacher training institutions with the exceptions of the British and Foreign School Society's Normal Schools he favoured, Borough Road for men and Stockwell for women. He regarded teaching as one of the lost arts, or at least a neglected one. 'I have to do with a very large staff of assistants, and really, when they come to me from training colleges, they seem to know everything except the art of teaching.'[92] None the less, Adams was happy to receive many visitors from Training Colleges, and to receive students on teaching practice, as from Maria Grey Training College, and King's College, London.

Adams' relations with his staff were, on the face of it, if not warm, then certainly supportive. He selected staff very carefully, giving preference to those from Borough Road and Stockwell, with which he kept in close correspondence. In a letter dated 2 July 1879 to the Secretary of the British Society, he appealed for a 'thoroughly efficient man' from Borough Road to replace a senior assistant about to leave, and noted that 'all the Stockwell students ... are doing well'. As early as 1879 Adams expressed his conviction that an appointment of a good prospective teacher to Fleet Road would be a sure road to promotion, as he stated in a letter to the BFSS dated 5 July 1879. This indeed came to pass. John Sadd soon left to take over Haverstock Hill Board School, and in fact returned to succeed Adams at Fleet Road in 1903. Harry Dare was a local boy who had attended voluntary schools. Appointed to Fleet Road in 1880, he was to take charge of the celebrated scholarship class. Fourteen years later he secured a headship at Barrow Hill Road Board School. At least three of the female teachers became headmistresses of girls' departments in Board Schools, and two were appointed as 'mistresses of method' at Nottingham University Day Training College. In the period between 1893 and 1903 all his staff held First or Second Class certificates. At an entertainment in 1884 it was announced that three of the assistants had had their certificates raised to the First Class.[93] The number of probationers in the Senior Mixed Department was kept to a minimum. By the latter part of the 1890s graduate teachers were being attracted. By 1900 there was a strong core of experienced staff. In the three departments of the school eleven were aged over 40, eleven 30–40, 16 25–29, and only six were under 25. There was a higher proportion of younger staff in the junior and infants' departments.[94]

Like his brother John Frederick, W.B. Adams was keenly aware of the need to improve the intellectual quality and specialist skills of teachers in the light of the success of schools like his own in going beyond the narrow confines of the elementary codes. Thus, as President of the London School Board Head Teachers' Association School Board, he visited Oxford with his colleagues at the request of the authorities of Lincoln College. There he made a strong plea for promoting more advanced teaching in elementary schools, and bringing training colleges into closer touch with universities.[95]

MARY ADAMS AT FLEET ROAD: THE JUNIOR MIXED DEPARTMENT

From the start of her appointment late in 1883 as headmistress of Fleet Road's Junior Mixed Department Mary Adams received equally good reports as the Senior. In general, however, sandwiched as she was between arch-publicists in the persons of her husband in the senior mixed department and Louisa Walker in the infants, she was much less of a public figure, usually recognised for arranging the small-scale musical costume sketches and the exhibitions of drill that played a subsidiary part in the school entertainments. After these Mary Adams characteristically was thanked for providing the children with buns and fruit, and entertaining distinguished visitors to tea in prettily decorated classrooms. The Junior Mixed Department earned an 'Excellent' grant in its first year under Mary Adams. The Report of 1885 was even better: 'The general condition of this School is highly satisfactory, and the excellency of its tone is, I think, greatly due to the personal influence of Mrs. Adams.... Musical drill has been introduced with very happy results; it is in itself useful, and tends to lighten the monotony of the elementary work of a Junior School.'[96]

There were, however, flaws in the 1887 Report: 'But for certain blemishes in two of the classes of the First Standard, the general condition of the school would be as highly satisfactory as it was last year. The discipline of these classes is not as exact as it should be, their Reading is not much above fair, and the formation of letters and figures argues a want of care in revision. These defects call for Mrs. Adams' immediate attention.'[97] By 1888 it was reported that these faults had been 'amply cured. The condition of the school as to discipline and attainments, both in Elementary and in Class subjects, is highly satisfactory'.[98]

One of the problems caused by the popularity of the school was overcrowding, causing great pressure on the school hall and toilet accommodation. As a result of consistently good inspectors' reports, Mary Adams' salary progressively increased. Soon after her appointment, based on a new scale of calculation, she was receiving £225 per annum, which increased annually with £4 increments over the next ten years to £260 in 1894. But the pressure of coping with the large numbers of children in the Junior Mixed Department took its toll. During the summer of 1895 Mary Adams lost 60 days through 'nervous debility'. In the autumn of 1896 she was away for 12 days with colds and indigestion, and in the autumn of 1897 16 days with headaches and insomnia. She retired early, in her mid-fifties, in 1898.

Much was made of her retirement occasion, almost certainly orchestrated by her husband. Sir George Kekewich presided. One of the Hampstead papers entitled its account of the occasion 'The Apotheosis of the School Mistress: a Unique Presentation', and suggested that no mistress in an elementary school had ever earned such as testimonial of respect.[99] The list of subscribers to her testimonial, 300 in all, was formidable. It included members of the nobility, Sir Joshua Fitch, Sir John Gorst, Joseph Chamberlain, Dr James Martineau, at least eight members of the Inspectorate, at least eight Principals or senior members of Training Colleges, and influential members of the London School and the local community. Lord George Hamilton MP, a former Vice-President of the Committee of Council and a past Chairman of the London School Board, wrote: 'I consider Mrs. Adams to be an admirable illustration of what an instructress of the young should be.'

The Chairman of the meeting, Edmund Barnes, paid tribute both to Mary Adams and her husband in making Fleet Road 'unsurpassed by any school in the Kingdom'. He testified 'to the admirable manner in which Mrs. Adams had done her work, "sandwiched" as her school was between the great and noble Senior Mixed School and the equally notable Infants' School'. He was glad in a way that she had retired, 'for of all men in the world who needed a peaceful home those connected with education should have it. . .'. Characteristically, Mary Adams responded very briefly by giving thanks for the honour and the gifts presented to her, but asked that her husband should respond on her behalf, because she felt undeserving of the praise which had been showered on her, and he would not allow her to say that. His response, equally characteristically, offered some though hardly a shower of praise to his wife. His speech focused on the school. He claimed that it was 'in the natural order of things when she joined him at Fleet Road ... one end and aim only should exist for the advancement of the school as a whole without any division of authority.... The recollection of that day would always be regarded as a radiant spot in the memory of Mrs. Adams and himself'. A vote of thanks to Kekewich and his wife was responded to by Sir George who pointed out that the world of education knew 'what great assistance Mrs. Adams had rendered to her husband in creating a great school...'. He reflected, not recognising perhaps the fact that they had two servants, that 'lady teachers had harder work than men, for they had to look after children at home as well as at schools, and besides disciplining their scholars had to discipline their husbands (laughter)'.[100]

Mention of Mary Adams' being sandwiched between her husband's Senior Mixed Department and Louisa Walker's Infants' excites speculation about the relationships between these three fine headteachers. There is little documentary evidence of much contact. The Walkers were not recorded as mourners at Adams' funeral, though the Infants' department sent a tribute. On the other hand Adams promoted the idea of sponsoring a portrait of Louisa Walker's husband in recognition of their joint efforts in support of the Marylebone Teachers' Association.[101] It is certain, however, that Louisa Walker resented the fact that Mary Adams and her successor in the Junior Mixed Department earned more than she, in accordance with a London School Board ruling on the salaries of infant headteachers. 'Injustice always rankles in one's breast, and I do most frankly say that every month a bitter pang has gone through me when I have seen my colleague's name on the pay sheet receiving £14 more than myself for a school half the size.'[102]

Between the time of her retirement and her husband's death Mary Adams undertook some supply work at the school. She seems otherwise to have retired completely from the public gaze, having to face the stresses of her husband's death in 1903 and later her son's divorce and subsequent service in the armed forces during the First World War. She died on 18 February 1918 at her residence in Willow Road, aged 73, from heart failure. Her husband's personal estate on his death in 1903 had amounted to £1,304. She left £1,743 14s 6d.

THE ACHIEVEMENT OF
WILLIAM BATEMAN ADAMS

William Bateman Adams died in harness. On 5 March 5 1903 Adams' senior assistant noted in the log book: 'Mr. Adams seized with apoplexy at noon.' The school was closed that afternoon and the following day as the doctors recommended he be kept in school. He returned home on 8 March. Although he was tended by Mrs Adams and two nurses, and his condition seemed to improve, he had a second attack leading to heart failure on 14 March. His funeral took place on 17 March, a considerable crowd waiting at the gates of his Willow Road residence, and at Hampstead Cemetery. Here his favourite piece, 'The Pilgrim's Chorus' from Wagner's *Tannhauser,* was conducted at the graveside 'in a storm of rain'. The funeral was attended by his brother Richard, his son, John William Bateman Adams, two brothers-in-law, and 13 headteachers or staff from London board schools. Mary Adams, presumably too shocked to attend, sent a letter which conveyed her heartfelt thanks to those who had supported her 'in the great affliction that has befallen me'. It was agreed that a memorial tablet to Adams should be established in the school hall, which was unveiled the following October. Again Mary Adams was not present but wrote to say that she was with the occasion in spirit.[103]

Though it was asserted in the *Hampstead Record* that Adams 'did not actively concern himself locally with other branches of public life',[104] this was not entirely true. As we have seen, he was one of the founder members of the Marylebone Teachers' Association. He was also a member of the London School Board Head Teachers' Association.[105] He was a loyal and influential member of the British Teachers' Association. This held quarterly meetings, and Adams seems also responsible for introducing smoking concerts, held in the first place in the Mitre Tavern in Chancery Lane.[106] The meeting was followed by a smoking concert which included popular and 'irresistibly comic' songs. Adams proposed the vote of thanks to the performers and said the success of the occasions meant they would be starting a new season in October.[107] At another such concert in December 1891 his brother J.F. Adams, equally well known as Clerk to the Tottenham School Board, was in attendance, as was D. D. Salmon, Principal of Swansea Training College.[108] Adams became a member of the Committee of the

British and Foreign School Society in 1892. At one of their annual re-unions, at the New College, Isleworth, he noted that the British Teachers' Association was the oldest association of its kind, and had had much to do with the forming of other associations, including the NUT.[109]

Apart from his Fellowship of the Royal Historical Society for his services to history in schools, he was also elected to a Fellowship of the Educational Institute of Scotland, its equivalent of the NUT, at the annual meeting at the Royal High School, Edinburgh, in 1900. The Fellows were normally Scottish teachers, but in this year four English teachers too, including Adams, were elected.[110] 'Foreigners' proposed had to satisfy the Institute that they were members of an equivalent organisation in another country. At the next prize-giving at Fleet Road the teachers presented Adams 'as a mark of esteem' with the robes of his Fellowship which he was gratified to wear at the occasion.[111]

Adams was also a founder member of the Pembroke County Club, designed to 'enrol within it every Pembrokeshire man that resides in the great metropolis', a chairman of its Committee and the first president of its annual dinner. By 1895 it was reported that it had 'taken so firm a hold that it will unquestionably become one of the recognised social functions of London. It was hoped it could be developed into a regular form of Club, at which visiting Pembroke men could stay'.[112] The *Tenby Observer* sent its correspondent to the annual New Year's smoking concert at the Mitre Hotel, High Holborn, in 1897, at which members of the Carl Rosa Opera Company and Woolwich Artillery Band performed. Adams' son, newly appointed headteacher of Tenby Intermediate School, was present. W.B. Adams was described as 'the ideal chairman', conducting the occasion with 'his usual grace and felicity, and in warm spoken tones'. 'For Pembrokeshire, sentiment held sway', with Pembrokeshire men urged to stick together, and time spent amid the county dialect 'a complete restorative to tiredness in this London wilderness'.[113]

One of Adams' last attendances was at the annual dinner in March 1902, again in Holborn, at which patriotic fervour was at its height. Loyal toasts were offered to 'The Imperial Forces of the Empire', 'The Pembrokeshire County Club and Pembroke our County' and The Houses of Parliament.'[114] Due tribute was paid to Adams at the Club's annual dinner in 1903, soon after his death which, as General Laurie, MP, indicated, 'cast a semi-gloom over the occasion'. 'The Chairman of the Committee in his tribute stated that Adams' whole heart and soul had been in the club, and he had sacrificed all other interests to attend committees and reunions. 'They felt they were doing the right thing whenever Mr. Adams advised it.'[115]

Adams' own epitaph might have been his effusion to the correspondent of *The Practical Teacher* in 1894: 'My school is my hobby. With delight I have watched its development.... When I opened the Fleet Road School ... I found it a wilderness: it is now to me a large and beautiful garden, with my boys and girls for fruits and flowers.'[116] While Adams' most pungent opponent, the columnist of *The Board Teacher*, was resistant to such hyperbole, he at the same time recognised the achievement in a barbed though warm tribute on Adams' death, in a comparison with a School Board Inspector, of a more self-effacing disposition, who had died at about the same time. Under a heading 'Two Notable Deaths' he wrote:

The Board has lost by death during the last month one of the oldest of its inspectors and one of the most successful of its teachers, and we sincerely deplore both. That Mr. Landon performed the many delicate duties of his office with judgment and tact is proved, if proof were necessary, by the fact that during his long office his name has never been mentioned in these 'Notes'. The name of Mr. Adams has been mentioned, but only because it was so often mentioned in the newspapers that regularly recorded the triumphs of his school. That those triumphs were many and great we would be the first to admit. Fleet Road was a credit to the Board and to himself....[117]

FLEET ROAD: THE FINAL ANALYSIS

How good was Fleet Road? In his habitual eulogies about the school, Lyulph Stanley was at the same time not uncritical. He was aware that it did not achieve the standards of the higher grade schools and science schools of northern cities, but he blamed the London School Board, not Adams and his staff, for that.[118] He was entirely in tune with Adams' objectives, appreciating the school's particular offerings in educating boys and girls together, in equipping themselves to specialise in history and in fitting scholars for the Civil Service, rather than merely maintaining an average in all subjects.[119]

Though school managers and newspaper columnists claimed that Fleet Road was the best elementary school in England and Europe, on any dispassionate appraisal it is doubtful whether it was even London's best. In the first place, the Senior Mixed Department was not strictly elementary, as Adams agreed. In addition, while Fleet Road was very far above the average, and in quantitative terms was the leader in winning scholarships, other schools gained more of the higher level scholarships. Others also gained similar proportions of scholarships in less favourable social areas. Fleet Road's particular curriculum emphasis meant that it could not be chosen as one of the four prestigious science schools in London. The Board felt that an industrial training was more appropriate in Greenwich, Plumstead, St. Pancras and Lime-house. Not being a science school lowered status in some eyes, such as those of the Education Department and, from 1900, the Board of Education, suspicious of the commercial thrust of schools like Fleet Road. HMI J.G. Fitzmaurice, who knew the school well, was publicly supportive but privately caustic, as in a Departmental memorandum: 'Fleet Road is an ambitious school and has been most successful in obtaining scholarships, but I have always felt that bright children (I may be wrong) were unduly pressed in order to run for scholarships ... It is a school that advertises itself (?unduly)' (the latter crossed out).[120]

Fleet Road was therefore at the heart of discussions between the London School Board and the Board of Education as to what constituted a Higher Grade School. As early as 1886, in a letter dated 15 February to the BFSS, Adams was claiming that his was 'a Higher Grade School, in all but name', pointing out that he had over 500 scholars in Standards V, VI and VII, and 'also a class working outside, and beyond, the Education Code'. The unsatisfactory *ad hoc* system continued. In 1895, for example, the Editor of *The Board Teacher* lamented London's 'puny but costly system of Seventh Standard schools' and argued that primary education 'must more and more aim at secondary education'.[121] It was widely agreed that London had nothing to compare with the recognised and celebrated Higher Grade Schools of the northern towns and cities, such as Bradford and Sheffield.

By the end of the decade, London School Board was designating Higher Grade departments,[122] 79 in all, of which Fleet Road was one. But they were not recognised Higher Grade Schools.

Indeed in 1900 London School Board decided to define them as Higher Elementary Schools under Board of Education (which had by then taken over from the Education Department) Minutes, rather than under the Directory of the Science and Art Department.[123] The School Board was at this time still asking the Board of Education for recognition. But it was extremely reluctant to allow the change, not wishing to pay the higher grants for Higher Elementary education.[124] At Fleet Road's annual Christmas concert that year Lyulph Stanley passionately argued the superiority of the School Board's judgement over that of the Board of Education. It regarded Fleet Road as a Higher Grade School, with 800 scholars in the fifth standard and above over 200 in the ex-seventh standard: '... if the Government refused to recognise it as such, then so much the worse for the Government'.[125] Of course it was to prove so much the worse for the School Board. In 1900 the querying of elements of London School Board's expenditure by the district auditor on the grounds that it was not being devoted to elementary purposes was confirmed legally in the so-called 'Cockerton Judgment', which led to the demise of the school boards.

It may be assumed that Adams revelled in the accolades heaped upon the school at its prize-givings and entertainments. He may have needed them to compensate for the scorn he excited among some of his peers and indeed among certain portions of the local population. Notwithstanding the hyperbole, by any standards Fleet Road was an outstanding school and Adams an exceptional headmaster. One of his most positive qualities was his high expectation of children. He was totally unsympathetic to any call to minimise the curriculum and restrict what in modern parlance would be termed the entitlement to a broad and balanced curriculum that combined liberal and vocational elements, and the practical and the cultural. He resisted, on the one hand, the idea that the three Rs were ends in themselves and, on the other, the notion of over-pressure, very much in vogue in the 1880s. He pointed out that Fleet Road parents, far from believing in it, had kept their children at school until they had all passed the standards, in many cases at great personal sacrifice.[126]

Like his father before him at Goat Street, he cast Fleet Road in his own image. 'Fleet Road School was Mr. Adams, and Mr. Adams was Fleet Road.'[127] Perhaps the most balanced and differentiated tribute the Adams received appeared in the *School Board Chronicle* on the occasion of Mary Adams' retirement.

Fleet Road ... has for years past stood as an object-lesson in the practical possibilities of School Board management.... The children of that school have had the happiness to fall into the hands of a headmaster and mistress, in the persons of Mr. and Mrs. W.B. Adams, who perceived opportunities of service and success in their position under the Board, which others might have overlooked. They were not satisfied with working in a groove, nor with the mere fulfilment of the specific duties of their position. They sought and found occasion for such liberal enlargements of the conception of their office, as have made Fleet Road School the distinctive corporate entity which every school some day will become ... amongst the elementary schools of London. Fleet Road has led the way towards that healthy individualism, those human relationships between teachers and scholars which are the invaluable characteristics of the life of the English public schools. They had the good fortune, at a fairly early stage, to enlist the personal interest of several influential members of the Board in their plans and endeavours. But that interest was gained and retained because their work was good and their ideas were practical as well as lofty. What Fleet Road is, every Board School, according to its own sphere and circumstance, may be.[128]

The many references in the press to Fleet Road's aim to instil the spirit of the public school system should not obscure the fact that in essence nothing could have been further from Adams' mind than implanting its value system, based on privilege and exclusion. He was a meritocrat, desiring to provide pathways to social and economic advance. But he was equally an opportunist and a realist, caught in a transition period between two different systems of career advance, the earlier one of patronage and the later of formal credentials. He did not eschew personal connection in seeking promotion for himself and his family, as will also be instanced in the case of his equally famous brother, John Frederick Adams, the subject of the next two chapters.

REFERENCES AND NOTES

1. W.E.Marsden, *Educating the Respectable: A Study of Fleet Road Board School, Hampstead, 1879–1903* (London: The Woburn Press, 1991).
2. *Hampstead and Highgate Express*, 21 March 1896.
3. *Hampstead Record*, 15 Dec. 1900.
4. *Hampstead and Highgate Express*, 3 Oct. 1885.
5. CC, *2nd Report* (1887), p.45.
6. *The Cambrian*, 27 March 1896.
7. *Hampstead and Highgate Express*, 19 Dec. 1894.

8. *School Board Chronicle*, 3 Dec. 1898, p. 627.
9. *Tenby Observer*, 20 Feb. 1902.
10. CC, *2nd Report* (1887), p.51.
11. *Swansea and Glamorgan Herald*, 9 April 1879.
12. Ibid., 5 July 1879.
13. CC, *2nd Report* (1887), pp. 45–6.
14. Ibid., p. 63.
15. Ibid., p. 46.
16. Ibid., p. 59.
17. *Hampstead and Highgate Express*, 24 July 1897.
18. CC, *2nd Report* (1887), p. 46.
19. Ibid., p.56.
20. Ibid, p. 46.
21. Ibid., p.57.
22. Fleet Road Senior Mixed School Log Book, 3 March 1898.
23. CC, *2nd Report* (1887), p. 47.
24. Ibid., p. 52.
25. Ibid., p. 62.
26. Ibid., p. 63.
27. Ibid., p. 62.
28. *Educational Record*, Vol. 13 (1891), p. 326.
29. W.B. Adams, *Leading Events in English History*, (London: W. and R. Chambers, 1872), p.9.
30. *The Practical Teacher*, Vol. 15 (1894), p.4.
31. C. Morley, *Studies in Board Schools* (London: Smith, Elder and Co., 1897), pp. 92–3.
32. Ibid., pp. 103–4.
33. *The Practical Teacher*, Vol. 15 (1894), pp. 3–4.
34. Fleet Road Senior Mixed School Log Book, 1 March 1900.
35. *Hampstead Record*, 27 Oct. 1900.
36. CC, *2nd Report* (1887), p. 62.
37. Ibid., 52.
38. Ibid., pp. 47–8.
39. I bid., pp. 52–3.
40. *Hampstead and Highgate Express*, 3 March 1900.
41. Morley, op.cit. (1897), p.101.
42. *School Guardian*, 7 May 1887.
43. *The Practical Teacher*, Vol.15 (1894), p.4.
44. CC, *2nd Report* (1887), p. 49.
45. Ibid., p. 64.
46. Ibid., p. 66.
47. Ibid., p. 57.
48. Ibid., p. 49.
49. *The Schoolmaster*, 12 March 1887, p. 405.
50. See Marsden, op. cit. (1991), pp. 149–51.
51. Morley, op.cit. (1897), pp. 91–2.
52. *London*, Vol. 7 (1898), p. 154.
53. Morley, op.cit. (1897), p. 119.
54. Ibid., pp. 95–9.
55. *The Cambrian*, 30 Sept. 1892.
56. *The Schoolmaster*, 1 Oct. 1892, p. 557.

57. *The Cambrian*, 27 March 1896.
58. *Tenby and County News*, 7 March 1900.
59. Fleet Road Senior Mixed School Log Book, 5 Aug. 1897. See also Marsden, op.cit. (1991), pp. 232–3.
60. *Magazine of Music*, Vol. 10 (1893), p. 129.
61. See Marsden, op.cit. (1991), pp. 218–31.
62. Ibid., pp. 233–8.
63. *The Schoolmistress*, 16 Feb. 1882, p. 194.
64. *The Schoolmaster*, 9 April 1887, pp. 555–7.
65. CC, *2nd Report* (1887), p. 45.
66. *The Schoolmaster*, 21 Dec. 1872, p. 249.
67. *The Board Teacher*, 1 May 1897, p. 110.
68. *The Schoolmaster*, 11 April 1874, pp. 225–6.
69. Ibid., 2 June 1883, p. 701, and 8 March 1884, p. 337.
70. Ibid., 12 Dec. 1885, p. 905.
71. Ibid., 13 Feb. 1886, p. 261.
72. Ibid., 12 May 1888, p. 686.
73. Ibid., 22 Feb. 1890, p. 293.
74. Ibid., 15 March 1890, pp. 390–1.
75. Ibid., 22 March 1890, pp. 425–6.
76. Ibid., 29 March 1890, pp. 470–1.
77. *The Board Teacher*, 1 Feb. 1895, p. 43.
78. London School Board School Management Committee *Minutes*, 25 March 1898. See also *The Board Teacher*, 1 May 1898.
79. *London*, Vol.7, 5 May 1898, p. 146.
80. Ibid., Vol. 7, 12 May 1898, p. 312. The 'Incident at the Board', Macnamara's response and that also of the representative of the Bricklayers' Union were also recorded in *The Board Teacher*, 1 June 1898, pp. 146–7. The protesting letter appeared in the following month's edition, 1 July 1898, p.162.
81. *The Schoolmaster*, 17 April 1897, p.719.
82. *The Board Teacher*, 1 Feb. 1897, p.33, and 1 April 1898, pp.82–3.
83. London School Board *Minutes*, May 1880.
84. Ibid., Dec. 1884.
85. Ibid., Dec. 1892.
86. Ibid., Feb. 1901.
87. Ibid., March 1897.
88. *Hampstead and Highgate Express*, 4 May 1895.
89. See Marsden, op.cit. (1991), Ch. 10, for a fuller account than can be given here.
90. *Daily Telegraph*, 24 July 1896 and 24 Feb. 1898.
91. *The Daily News*, 11 Aug. 1897.
92. CC, *2nd Report* (1887), p.49.
93. *Hampstead and Highgate Express*, 29 Nov. 1884.
94. See Marsden, op.cit. (1991), pp. 168–78 for further material on Adams' relations with staff at the school, and pp. 178–83 for his very favourable relations with the school managers.
95. *Educational Record*, Vol. 15 (1900), p. 297.
96. London School Board *Minutes*, Dec. 1885.
97. Ibid., Nov. 1887.
98. Ibid., Nov. 1888.

99. *Hampstead Record*, 26 Nov. 1898.
100. *Hampstead and Highgate Express*, 11 Nov. 1898.
101. *The Schoolmaster*, 17 April 1897.
102. *The Head Teacher*, 16 June 1902, p. 215.
103. *Hampstead and Highgate Express*, 21 and 28 March, and 17 Oct. 1903.
104. *Hampstead Record*, 13 June 1903.
105. *The Schoolmaster*, 2 Dec. 1893, p. 970.
106. Ibid., 7 March 1891, p. 446.
107. Ibid., 2 May 1891, p. 796.
108. Ibid., 5 Dec. 1891, p. 950.
109. Ibid., 26 Oct. 1895, p. 650.
110. *Educational News*, 29 Sept. 1900, p. 658.
111. *Hampstead Record*, 27 Oct. 1900.
112. *Tenby and County News*, 3 April 1895.
113. *Tenby Observer*, 21 Jan. 1897.
114. Ibid., 27 March 1902.
115. *Tenby and County News*, 25 March 1903.
116. *The Practical Teacher*, Vol. 15 (1894), p.7.
117. *The Board Teacher*, 1 April 1903, p. 78.
118. *Hampstead and Highgate Express*, 21 March 1896.
119. *Hampstead Record*, 4 May 1895.
120. PRO ED 14/41.
121. *The Board Teacher*, 1 June 1895, pp. 133–4.
122. Ibid., 1 Jan. 1899, p. 20.
123. Ibid., 1 June 1900, p. 123.
124. PRO ED 14/102.
125. *Hampstead Record*, 15 Dec. 1900.
126. *Hampstead and Highgate Express*, 29 Nov. 1884.
127. Ibid., 13 June 1903.
128. *School Board Chronicle*, 3 Dec. 1898, p. 627.

5

John Frederick Adams as Teacher

Like his elder brother William Bateman, John Frederick Adams was trained as a pupil teacher at Goat Street School. In 1859 he was presented with a drawing prize for success in the government School of Art examinations at Swansea's Royal Institution, as was his fellow pupil teacher, William Fulford, to be involved in the following year in the court case with John Adams.[1] John Frederick went on to win a First Class Queen's Scholarship to Bangor Training College, and was first on the list of 50 would-be entrants. In recognition of his achievement, he was presented by the school managers with a volume of Milton's works.[2] He entered Bangor Training College one year after his brother and left it with a certificate in the First Division.

J.F. Adams' first appointment was at 'Swansea Normal College', a private school in the buildings of the first Swansea Training College, which had closed down in 1851. Under its headmaster Evan Davies, the school had achieved a good local reputation by sending its scholars to universities. Here John Frederick was for a short time as part of a teaching team offering 'a sound and liberal English course', as well as classics, mathematics, modern languages, and a range of technical and scientific subjects. During his time there he maintained the family tradition of mutual professional support, in this case by conducting a public examination for his father at Goat Street in December 1863.[3]

THE LLANDOVERY EXPERIENCE

In January 1864, not yet 21, John Frederick Adams was appointed as headmaster of Llandovery British School. Its front elevation is shown in Figure 5.1. The school opened in 1820 and moved to a

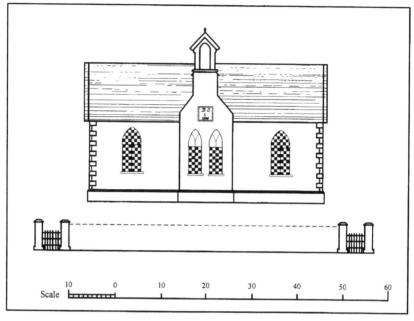

Figure 5.1.   Llandovery British School, front elevation, 1848

new building in Stone Street in 1848, next door to one of Llandovery's small breweries (Figure 5.2). It was a normal type of British School, in this case for boys and girls, with a large schoolroom including spaces for drafts, desks, and two galleries, which could be separated by curtains. A teacher's house was provided.

John Frederick Adams maintained close contact with Swansea. He returned home regularly, as evidenced by late arrivals back at school, recorded in his log book, on some Monday mornings. The rail journey from Swansea to Llandovery at this time took over two and a half hours. His father reciprocated his son's support by visiting Llandovery to examine his classes. J.F. Adams recorded in his log book the usual problems of an elementary headmaster of this period, including low attendance on fair days and at the time of the hay harvest. On their return from the harvest he noted that some of the children had 'left a good lot of their learning in the hay field'.[4] He complained about the restrictions of the Revised Code and a serious want of reading books, slates and other apparatus. Parents were criticised for allowing poor attendance, and he was in turn confronted by them when pupil teachers struck

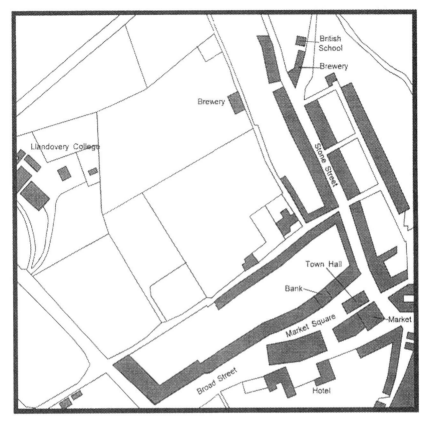

Figure 5.2. Map: Llandovery British School

children, or when he gave too much in the way of home lessons. He registered his own reservations about the value of corporal punishment, although he used it as a penalty for, for example, indolence, reckless conduct, defiance of pupil teachers, dirtying reading cards and breaking slates. More positively, involvement in cricket matches was highlighted.

During his probationary year at the school, Adams was assisted by four pupil teachers and an uncertificated sewing mistress. Apart from a major reservation about claims being made for pupil teachers who met neither the requirements of the Code of 1860 nor those of the Revised Code, HMI Bowstead's Report of 1864 was good, commenting that the school had increased in numbers and was in 'a prosperous and efficient state. It has passed a fair examination under the Revised Code'. But more slates and desk accommodation were needed. Two hundred and twenty-six pupils were present at the examination, 14 passing at Standard VI level, 12 at Standard V, 30 at IV, 34 at III, 36 at II and 28 at I. There were 59 children under six years of age.[5]

Adams was generally satisfied with his pupil teachers, regretting that one of them, the best he had come across, had decided not to go forward for a Queen's Scholarship, while another left for a situation as a bank clerk in London. Two others did compete for Queen's Scholarships. These he had also found 'trustworthy and persevering young men, being always most gentlemanly in their conduct, and industrious in their work...'.[6] On the other hand, an unsatisfactory pupil teacher, found guilty on more than one occasion of striking children, was dismissed.[7] At the beginning of 1865 new desks and books and apparatus arrived from the British and Foreign School Society to Adams' evident satisfaction. About this time four of his girls were withdrawn to 'finish their education' at Llandovery College.[8] In March the BFSS Inspector visited and described the school as 'flourishing.... Its large attendance, admirable discipline and the advanced state of all the classes reflect most creditably upon Mr. Adams'.[9] The following Government Report was equally satisfactory and Adams duly completed his probationary period successfully. Government grant increased as a result: 'The Managers are much gratified and have complimented me on the success of the school under my care. The pupil teachers and myself have all been duly paid our several gratuities.'[10]

By 1866 he had achieved a Certificate of the Third Class in the First Division, following another good HMI Report. It noted that Llandovery was a large school which had been conducted by Adams with 'ability and success', satisfactory in the elementary subjects and useful in other branches of instruction in the upper classes. On the negative side, and a harbinger of things to come, two of his pupil teachers had been found to copy from each other in their examination and were failed, leading to a significant reduction in grant of £20. Adams resigned from Llandovery British School in September 1866.

During his short time in Llandovery, John Adams engaged in small-town social activities in his leisure time. He performed recitations and in plays in local entertainments in the town hall, called the 'Penny Readings'. The local newspaper reporter indicated that these were supported by a large number of the working classes, which 'spoke well for their intelligence and taste for literature'. In December 1864, Adams selected for his contribution 'a most laughable piece from Valentine Vox'.[11] Writing about another of the 'Penny Readings, at which Adams read a piece entitled 'The Göttingen Barber', the reporter described the occasion as extraordinary. 'We may safely challenge a town of equal size to produce such an interesting and good amateur programme.'[12]

From an early date, Adams involved himself in local educational politics and disputations. In March 1866 a large meeting of British School teachers appointed him as Honorary Secretary of an initiative to open a subscription to recognise the 'long and valued services' in the area of HMI Joseph Bowstead.[13]. His views on the Revised Code were revealed in a combative correspondence in *The Welshman*. Starting it under a pseudonym, 'C.M.', Adams argued that the Revised Code penalised small rural schools, and illustrated how they were bound by their very nature to lose income, however industrious the master. This he regarded as unfair to a class of schools most in need of public aid.[14]

His contentions were countered by another anonymous correspondent, 'C.T.', who maintained that the Revised Code was designed not to pay schools, but to pay for results. Under the old system, children undertook a variety of subjects, gained a smattering of knowledge, but did not actually learn anything.[15] In his next letter Adams signed himself openly as master of Llandovery British Schools, and dismissed this argument as substituting 'dogmatical assertion for logical argument'. He accepted that too much had been attempted under the old system, but considered that a switch had been made to the other extreme, and one which meant that 'the cultivation of the mind is comparatively neglected.' He described the advantages of teaching a broader curriculum, including geography and history, as 'numerous and self-evident' and said he was pleased that 'instruction in them is almost imperatively demanded by the more intelligent parents, who look upon their children as rational beings, and think that the province of education includes the development of powers as well as the formation of habits and fitness for the discharge of social, relative and national duties'.[16]

An offended 'C.T.' retorted that Adams had misrepresented his argument, which was not related to differences between town and country schools 'but between the principle of paying for instruments of education, and of paying for education itself'. Large grants had been paid under the old system and yet children had come out of it 'lamentably deficient in the barest elements of knowledge'. In ordinary business 'value for money' was demanded and this should be true of education. Thus so important a principle should not be abandoned for the convenience of country schools.[17]

Adams returned to his attack on the mechanical nature of instruction and examination in the 'basics'. Arithmetic, he claimed, had lost its previous ' severe, mental discipline', and condemned the opinion of many in authority that the working classes should not receive too much education and thus 'obtrude into the ranks of their superiors'. He quoted well-known Inspectors' reports to reinforce this argument that the Revised Code had brought with it 'enormous evils'.[18]

'C.T.' in turn maintained that, having read HMI reports himself, two-thirds of Inspectors had declared in favour of the new system and accused Adams of selective and dishonest quoting from their reports. He was scornful of Adams' 'wretched twaddle' about the higher branches of education. In answer to the question 'What is education?' he insisted that it was the three Rs that were 'the foundation of learning ... There is no sham in such training'. Boys who could read and write well had 'the key which opens the golden gate.' Adams' argument about keeping the working classes down was denounced as 'a foul calumny ... too despicable for refutation', on those who paid for their education.[19] In his final response, Adams spurned C.T.'s defence of a Code which, he now added, limited the entitlement of the poor: 'Let me ask C.T. would it not be a miserable consolation for him to have been told in his youth that he was too poor to learn (Higher) Mental Arithmetic, English Grammar, or Geography, even of his native county, or any such profitable branches?'[20]

THE LLANELLY EXPERIENCE

Adams' next appointment was at Llanelly British School, one of the largest in Wales. The *Llanelly Guardian*, in welcoming Adams, quoted the latest HMI Report for Llandovery and hoped that 'the same success will follow him' in Llanelly.[21] In 1866, at almost the same time as his older brother, John Frederick Adams had chosen to move from a small market town environment to that of a rapidly growing manufacturing centre. Llanelly, like Merthyr Tydfil, was experiencing a cholera outbreak: 164 deaths were recorded in the town between the middle of July and the end of August.[22] Its population had risen from nearly 8,500 in 1851 to an estimated 13,000 in 1866. Llanelly was already noted for its heavy metal and coal mining industries. His new school was a large boys' department in the centre of the town (Figure 5.3).

While John Frederick Adams stayed longer at Llanelly than William and Mary Adams in Merthyr, his experience was even more frustrating and, indeed, wounding. From the start he appears not to have settled in, complaining in his log book entries about finding the upper standards deficient, classification of children difficult, attendance moderate, behaviour unsatisfactory, accommodation wanting and qualified teaching power, apart from himself, absent. A new classroom was being built, but the draughts associated with the building had given him a severe cold followed by the concern that 'rheumatism has almost deprived me of the use of my arms'. For a whole week he was off work, returning feeling still not well.[23] A new classroom and gallery improved teaching conditions. (Figure 5.4). The school was divided into two rooms, one with galleries and one with desks. As usual, a space was left for teaching drafts of children, again divided by a curtain. The girls' school was separate.

Adams was constantly vexed by the behaviour of the children and the attitudes of the pupil teachers. A cleaner complained that older boys were 'interfering' with her daughter. Having punished boys for lateness, he decided to stop using corporal punishment, but was forced to resume it: 'some ill-disposed boys have taken advantage of it to play the truant – made an example of them.'[24] Early in 1867 he found the children difficult to control, as the schools, boys' and girls', were agog with the rumour that the previous headmaster and headmistress of the schools had eloped with each other.[25] He noted that the children preferred geography and history to other subjects, but argued that 'these subjects are not so important as grammar, either regarded as a means of mental discipline or as to their practical value'.[26] He found the biblical knowledge of the youngest children 'irreparably associated with

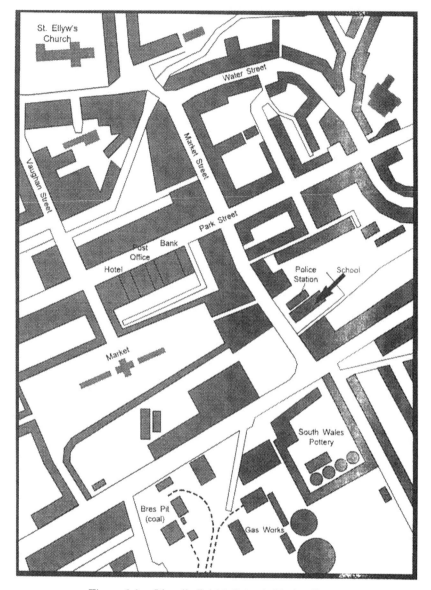

Figure 5.3.   Llanelly British School, Market Street

the Welsh language.'[27] He regarded the lack of understanding of
English among some of the Standard I and II children as 'a
sad impediment to their improvement',[28] and the attempts of
Standard I to learn to read as, for this reason, 'remarkably dull'.[29]

Adams' first examination, by HMI D.R. Fearon, was, neverthe-

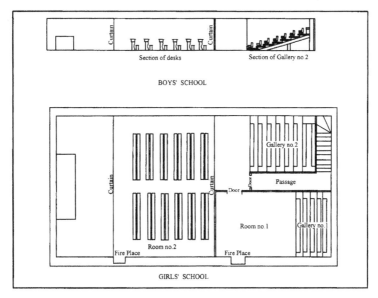

Figure 5.4.   Plan: Llanelly British School, Boys' Department

less, satisfactory. 'The discipline in this school is fair, and the scholars have passed a fair examination.... The new master who has only been in charge six months appears to be working the school with much vigour and good method. For the tone and attainments of the scholars he is not as yet responsible.'[30]

Adams found Llanelly parents a continuing trial. Apart from grumbling that they kept their children at home for their own convenience, they were slow to pay the school pence. In March 1867 he sent out about 60 bills for arrears and claimed that three-quarters of the parents calling to pay the pence disputed the amount.[31] But the 1866–67 session ended more optimistically, his younger brother arriving to fill in for a sick pupil teacher: 'Find work much easier with assistance of Mr. R. Adams.'[32]

The following term opened well, with a 'red letter day' in the history of the school. The children were invited by the inhabitants of Llanelly to attend 'a monster tea party'.

The weather was everything that could be desired and at two o'clock the boys and girls assembled in the playgrounds. There were 632 present. We proceeded to a field ... where they were supplied with ... cake *ad libitum*. Previously to this we paraded the town singing school songs in procession. Crowds of people were watching the long line of happy faces and everybody bestowed the highest praise upon the Managers of these schools for the orderly manner in which the children conducted themselves.[33]

The *Llanelly Guardian* agreed that the 'clean and respectable appearance and conduct' reflected favourably upon their teachers.[34]

The British and Foreign School Society Inspector, David Williams, called and said he had never seen better writing.[35] Adams resolved once more to give up using the cane. He attributed deficiencies in arithmetic to too much reliance on books: 'Will take up the blackboard again'.[36] He expressed pleasure at receiving new sets of class books and wall maps, and at his children performing well in the drawing examinations. He taught some music. He found the Welsh language problem affected his history as well as scripture and reading teaching. He recorded giving the boys an hour's lecture on 'Poor boys who have become great men', and that his managers had told him it had been the most successful year in the history of the school.[37] He maintained contacts with his roots, including arranging 'a very interesting juvenile cricket match' against his father's school. Llanelly won by 49 runs, some of its boys 'showing remarkably good play'.[38]

During his time at Llanelly Adams also attended meetings of the South Wales Teachers' Association. At one of these, held at his father's school in Swansea, he gave a paper on 'Teaching Arithmetic in Standards I and II according to the requirements of the Revised Code', a Code whose principles he rejected entirely, as it offered 'a premium to teachers to neglect the proper training of the children of the working classes'. The reporter recorded that Adams was a teacher 'of some experience' who presented his paper in 'a practical and scientific matter'. All present congratulated him 'upon his successful paper'.[39] David Williams, BFSS Inspector, was in the chair, and a 'sumptuous repast followed'.[40]

Adams' resolve to discontinue corporal punishment was strongly tested after two months, when he found a boy truanting with four others, when taking them to 'the match'.[41] Serious troubles with pupil teachers were brewing. On one occasion when Adams was absent a criticism lesson had degenerated into a 'burlesque'. He spoke to the pupil teacher about his 'ungenerous conduct'.[42] In the February examination disaster struck, when Fearon dismissed his best pupil teacher from the examination for speaking: 'incomparably the most eligible candidate in every respect'.[43] Adams clearly decided something had to be done about his pupil teacher force, and these became a major preoccupation thenceforth. One named William Ace was criticised for speaking to other pupil teachers while Adams was engaged in a classroom elsewhere,[44] and soon after this for taking 'his usual weekly half-holiday'.[45] The pupil teachers were lambasted for not stopping children from jumping over desks and breaking things.[46]

Adams' attempts to maintain his non-corporal punishment policy came to an end when a Standard V boy who had 'already corrupted another boy by his bad habits', arrived late, almost immediately walked out again, and was impertinent: 'Flogged him', Adams recorded.[47] But it was the pupil teachers who continued to exercise Adams' patience, chatting around the fire, for example, when they should have been ushering the boys in after lunch. Not for the first occasion when Adams had told them he would be slightly late, William Ace once more left school at lunch-time before the boys. Adams told him not to return and indicated he would be reported to the managers. At the end of his tether, Adams recorded that he would not be responsible for the further progress of his pupil teachers 'if this unjustifiable and trifling conduct is persisted in'.[48]

The HMI Report of March 1868 was ominous.

This school is in good order, but the results of the examination shew that the instruction in the elementary subjects requires considerable improvement. The pupil teachers do not seem to receive sufficient instruction, especially in arithmetic and English grammar.

My Lords will not be able if they receive an equally unfavourable report next year to authorise only such reduction in the grant under Article 44 as the number of failures effects of itself. They will have to impose a special reduction also (of one or more tenths) of the total grant conformably to Article 52 (a).

Note also Ace and Evans have to improve very greatly during the ensuing year if their apprenticeships are to be recognised under Article 91.[49]

After a quiet summer, Adams returned to the fray the following October, proceeding further to lose control of his pupil teachers. Ace had again absented himself without leave, and Gough was described as 'exceedingly idle, very disobedient, and to which recently added impertinence. Feel this might positively be put to an end without delay'.[50] Evans was also unsatisfactory, and disorder at lunch time was blamed on him and Ace letting the boys do what they liked.[51] There was a brief respite in which Adams reported that the pupil teachers had improved in their work, and had achieved satisfactory results in their examination.[52] But soon after this Gough was accused of not completing his home lessons, having been to a 'low opera' in the town. The following day a boy informed him that while he was out the pupil teachers had been fencing with their pointers and canes. He found the school in confusion as a result.[53] At the end of October he ordered two of the pupil teachers home for disobedience.[54] In early November many windows were broken as a result of most of the pupil teachers engaging the boys to play with them.[55] By the end of term, Adams had more or less disowned William Ace, saying he had never before had such trouble in getting a pupil teacher to study, nor one whose conduct was so disobedient. 'I wish to state I shall not be responsible for his passing.'[56]

In January 1869 the BFSS Inspector visited and expressed what was to prove to be an over-confident judgement that the school was well prepared for the forthcoming examination.[57] In the event the 1869 Report was again a bad one.

This school seems to be in fair order, but the results of the examinations are only partly satisfactory. The middle part of the school, comprising the 2nd and 3rd Standards, passed a very fair examination. The upper portion of the school, the 4th, 5th and 6th standards, passed a very indifferent examination in everything, and does not appear to have been well instructed during the past year. The first class was examined in English grammar for the extra grant, but the knowledge of grammar possessed by the great majority of the boys was very meagre and unsatisfactory.

The Report commented, however, that the pupil teachers had been 'well taught'. Far more serious was the accusation that the registration records, both for the evening class operation run by Adams, and for the boys' school, were untrustworthy.

With regard to the boys' school, HM Inspector has given a number of detailed instances which seriously discredit the returns, and My Lords have hesitated long whether they ought to withhold the Grant altogether under Article 5(d). They have decided, however, to be satisfied with reducing the Grant on the present occasion ... by four-tenths. If anything of the kind occurs again, the Grant will inevitably be withheld.[58]

The log book entries became ever more attenuated, two months of activity being covered on one page, symptomatic of Adams' demoralisation. A May entry was, however, very different, and was headed with the red inscription: 'This cannot be altered but by a subsequent entry.' In this remarkable statement, Adams effectively dismissed himself.

The Secretary of the school handed me a copy of the Inspector's Report which in my opinion is malicious, untrue and unjust. ... The failures in the day school I attribute to a great degree to the nervous manner of the inspector and his indistinct utterance and the frequently bad English which he spoke which often caused the elder pupils to laugh.

It is to be regretted that he could only discover three errors in the Registers of 300 boys after 'hawking' the town and looking over them for such a prolonged period. It so happened that neither of the cases were of the slightest benefit to me.

I declined in principle to attend a committee meeting summoned at the instigation of the Inspector (Williams), having previously explained the cases to him, where he again abused his position by prophesying that my certificate would be cancelled and grant withheld – and also before the case was submitted to his superior telling the managers that they must change the Master and Mistress. (The Report on the girls' department was in fact worse than that on the boys). Having been engaged in this profession since I was 13 years of age, I never before saw but gentlemen raised to such a position and never before saw such malice precede common fairness and justice.[59]

J.F. Adams, like other members of his family, based his inspectoral role model on such men as Arnold and Bowstead, and not on those they perceived as jumped-up ex-teacher sub-inspectors appointed following the Revised Code to deal with all the mundane detail of the examination. Adams had local supporters in David Williams, the BFSS Inspector, and the late David Rees, the most influential of the managers. The historian of the school suggests that had Rees still been alive and well, Adams might have remained.[60] A new, albeit temporary, headmaster was already in post by 18 May 1869. His first log book entry was : 'Found everything in a very neglected state.'

There is some evidence that the new chief HMI, D.R. Fearon, was demanding greater stringency than had been the case with his more benign predecessors. Thus in his general Report for 1867 he noted that Bangor Normal College had produced most of the certificated teachers in his district, which included Carmarthenshire, in which Llanelly was located. Among a number of criticisms, he indicated that he was not satisfied with the training of pupil teachers, and particularly with the way in which registers and log books were kept. He also found the discipline deficient in many British Schools, and instanced bad habits such as lounging with elbows on desks and feet on benches, spitting on the floor, standing in class with hands in pockets, entering school without removing caps, and scribbling on outside walls. Fearon also provided a tabulated assessment of the 50 or so certificated teachers for whom he had been responsible. Two of these were noted as having trained as pupil teachers at Goat Street and were at Bangor in the time of Adams. Clearly one of them must have been John Frederick, though it is not certain which. In the worse case, the discipline and work in the higher subjects were categorised as bad; in the better case as fair.[62] Whichever it was, J.F. Adams' teaching prowess at this stage was not regarded highly by Fearon.

Another reasonable conjecture would be that Adams now and later gained more satisfaction from extra-mural activities than from the teaching role. On a number of occasions both at Llandovery and Llanelly he recorded in his log books being late back at school. In October 1866, he was appointed as the Honorary Secretary of the Llanelly Mechanics' Institution, one of the most famous in Wales, a 'flourishing institution', as the *Llanelly Guardian* later described it.[63] He continued from where he left off in Llandovery by taking part in the 'Athenaeum Readings' at the Institution. In a recitation entitled 'Dr. Pangloss and his Pupil', Adams played the pupil, and the 'fast young swell character' he portrayed 'caused much laughter which continued throughout the piece.' Unfortunately the occasion was disturbed by 'young fellows' at the front who kept up 'a continual buzz of conversation and giggling'. The newspaper reporter demanded that in future they should be 'publicly exposed and summarily ejected'.[64] As Secretary, Adams informed the press that had he known about the disturbance he would have asked the Chairman to ask the youths to leave, judging from their conduct that the entertainments of the pot-house would be 'far more congenial to their tastes than anything that would be in connection with the Llanelly Mechanics' Institute'.[65]

In the third of the Athenaeum Readings, Adams performed the part of Antonio the merchant in the enactment of a scene from Shakespeare's *The Merchant of Venice*.[66] During 1869, he was appointed to conduct drawing classes at the Llanelly School of Art, and for a short time was recorded as its Headteacher. In May 1869 Adams announced his resignation both from this position and as Honorary Secretary to the Llanelly Mechanics' Institution, coinciding with his demise at the British School. He had clearly been an assiduous and responsible Secretary, producing extremely informative annual reports, which went well beyond extolling the achievements of the institution. They provided considerable detail on the social background of the membership, for example.[67] The broad cultural sweep and moral uplift of an adult education institution was evidently more to Adams' liking than the stresses induced by the recalcitrant behaviour of the boys and pupil teachers in his day school.

TEACHING IN LONDON

Finchley British School

No documentation has been found on what happened to John Frederick Adams between the time of his dismissal from Llanelly British School and his arrival at Finchley in 1870. What is apparent was that the family support system soon came to his rescue. Knowing that his brother William Bateman was leaving, the Finchley managers in a letter dated 28 April 1870 requested the BFSS to find someone to succeed him. This was followed up by another communication on 25 May thanking the Society's Secretary for his response, but indicating that 'we are provided with an excellent teacher in the brother of our late master'.

John Frederick Adams also settled into the residence vacated by his brother, in Stanhope Road, across the main thoroughfare from the Finchley school (see Figure 3.8). Here, aged 27 in 1871, he is recorded as residing with a young housekeeper/servant, her husband (a plumber), and a schoolgirl from the same home town as the housekeeper. In Finchley he benefited from children who came from more respectable homes than those of Llanelly, and from being visited by one of the old breed of school inspectors, namely Matthew Arnold, who declared himself well pleased with the state of the buildings, and the evidence that 'these schools aim at something more than instruction in the three Rs'.[68]

Concerts were regularly held in aid of the school funds. The reporter of the *North Middlesex Chronicle* declared that the attendance at one in November 1871 was 'quite brilliant, most of the leading families in Finchley being represented, and the company comprised a very large and fashionable audience'.[69] The following concert was designed to find funds for an extension of buildings and numbers which would need the engagement of a mistress 'to assist the present very efficient master'.[70] Not everything was satisfactory to Adams, however, for on 23 November 1873 he wrote to the BFSS to complain of the 'continual interference of some new members of the Committee in matters of detail and principle' which had made up his mind to leave when an opportunity presented itself. He therefore asked the Society to place his name on their books, and to be considered for a headship of a boys' school in London or its neighbourhood. He claimed he had the highest certificate he could get by examination, and had 18 years of experience. He was fully certificated as a teacher of science and art, and could if necessary teach Latin and French, having already done so in 'high middle class schools'. The salary he wished for was 'the highest I could get'.

During his stay at Finchley he demonstrated a continuing interest in educational issues through involvement in union affairs and letters to the press. By 1872 he was well established in the London Association of British Teachers, at whose quarterly sessions at Borough Road College he was always ready to put forward an opinion. Hence at a meeting in February 1872 he raised objections to the NUETs proposed pension scheme, speculating on its possible negative effects, arguing that it would cause a large (and presumably, in his view, undesirable) influx into the ranks. Later that year, Adams helped to sustain 'a most entertaining and lively discussion' on 'What shall we do with our dunces?'[71] Before long, he had been elected by the Association to represent it at the Annual NUET Conference at Bristol.

In 1872 he also wrote to the fledgeling union paper, *The Schoolmaster*, to welcome its presence, but also to criticise some of its emphasis. He argued against the over-prominent and 'imaginary grievance' the journal put forward about the social position of teachers, arguing that status was a personal matter and accrued from 'what we are as citizens, without much reference to our profession'. He also objected to the preoccupation over the difficulties of elementary teachers gaining entrance to the inspectorate, which he did not consider as fundamental to the welfare of the profession. He wished on the other hand that more attention be devoted to issues connected with the Codes and other official regulations he regarded as negative, and also for space 'to discuss subjects connected with the art of teaching'.[72]

In 1873 he complained, also in a letter to *The Schoolmaster*, about what he considered as the unrealistic questions that had been set in the early examinations for scholarships associated with the London School Board by the headmaster of the City of London School, the famous Dr Abbott. Adams affirmed that experienced elementary teachers would not have been surprised that entrants found it excessively difficult to define terms like 'constitutional government', 'democracy', 'executive' and 'despotism'. He had tested some ex-City of London schoolboys on these questions and found they could cope tolerably with only two of them. The editor of the journal supported his view.[73]

Whitfield Tabernacle School

Despite the problems at Finchley, it was not until 1876 that he was able to make a move, to the Whitfield Tabernacle School in Finsbury, just off the City Road (Figure 5.5), an independent and undenominational school run on British lines. According to Booth's team the area around the school was 'largely composed of factories, workshops and showrooms, notably in the furniture trade, in which many of the inhabitants of the large number of tenement dwellings here find employment'.[74] Of the 11,000 or so people living in this particular block to the east of the City Road, Booth recorded 26.6 per cent as in poverty and 73.4 per cent in comfort, with the vast majority on the margins between the two, that is in streets coloured purple and pink.

Whitfield (often written as Whitefield) Tabernacle was founded in 1753 in the Moorfields area by the evangelist and Calvinistic Methodist, George Whitefield, a contemporary and an opponent of Wesley. The *North Middlesex Chronicle* recorded Adams' appointment was unanimous, and that he would be succeeded in Finchley by a tutor at Borough Road College and an undergraduate of London University.[75] Again there is little record of his success or otherwise at this school, at which he stayed until his appointment as Clerk to the Tottenham School Board in 1880. At about the time of his Whitfield Tabernacle School appointment, John Frederick Adams had applied for the post of Inspector for the Swansea School Board, and was on the final short list of two, but was defeated by the headmaster of Swansea National School.[76]

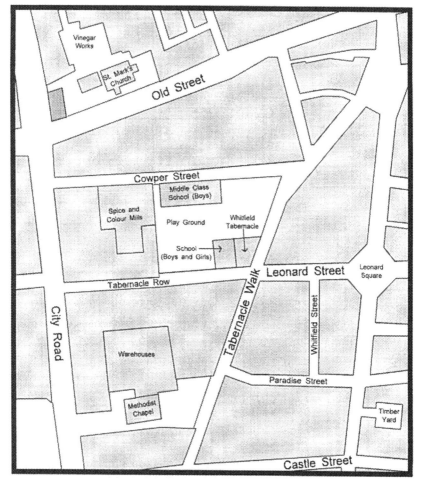

Figure 5.5.   Map: Whitfield Tabernacle School, London's East End

J.F.ADAMS AND THE NATIONAL UNION OF
ELEMENTARY TEACHERS

By the time he was appointed to Whitfield Tabernacle School Adams was a well-established public speaker. He had already been invited to contribute to the meetings of the Finsbury and City Teachers' Association, which followed similar activities to those of the Marylebone and British Teachers' Associations. Here he reviewed the proceedings of the recent 1877 NUET Conference in London and, among other things, condemned the policy of the

Union in seeking direct representation in Parliament.[77] He also attempted to use the local Association to influence the Inspectorate, arguing that the new English History requirements were too vague, and the period covered, 1485–1877, was too long, and likely to promote cramming 'in a subject which he found to be a most valuable aid to education in giving boys a love for reading and research'. He proposed a letter be sent to the district HMI requesting him to give a fuller idea of the nature and extent of the knowledge he would require. His peers considered this to be injudicious. Adams withdrew his proposal but reserved the right to reintroduce it.[78] The meetings of the Finsbury Association were often held at Whitfield Tabernacle Schools. As at Marylebone, social events were arranged, such as a railway outing in special carriages from Liverpool Street to Hertfordshire, an area near the River Lea with historical points of interest. At the hotel luncheon Adams proposed the toast to the ladies. The afternoon was spent boating on the Lea or rambling in the grounds of the hotel. After tea, there were glees, solos and dancing.[79]

The Schoolmaster was keen in its praise of the work of the Finsbury Association, commenting that it had 'plenty of energy. Its teachers are well known to be among the most active within the metropolitan area. They keep a sharp look out in the days of election, and they are seldom found napping when the season comes for activity'. The Association had just organised a major bazaar in Islington at the same time as a local cattle show, which brought a lot of people into the area. The Lord Mayor opened it and J.F. Adams acted as master of ceremonies. The President and other members of the NUET were present, and were introduced by Adams to the Lord Mayor, to whom they explained their objectives. Credit was given to Adams and a colleague for 'the completeness of the arrangements for the opening ceremony and for the comfort of the visitors in every particular'.[80] The Finsbury Association was also regularly praised for its high numbers and active money-raising, occasioning 'repeated cheers' at Union conferences. It was a stick with which to assail the miserable efforts of its neighbour Marylebone. In one year, it was recorded as having 824 members, and raising £324 4s 6d for the Union, as against Marylebone, with its 122 members, raising a mere £6 10s 6d.[81]

In March 1880 Adams resigned as General Secretary of the Finsbury Association on the grounds that he did not have time to do the duties properly. In receiving his resignation with regret, his colleagues congratulated him on his recent appointment as Clerk to the Tottenham School Board.[82] One of his last duties was to sit on a delegation of the Association to interview parliamentary candidates for the Finsbury constituency, bringing to their consideration various educational topics.[83] Finally, he reported back from the Brighton Conference, which he described as 'tame', with the questions discussed, in his opinion, not such as to interest educationists or the public generally. A colleague agreed that teachers were too fond of relating their own experiences.[84]

At the time of his resignation, Adams was residing at 77 Walford Road (Figure 5.6) in Stoke Newington, together with three other boarders, two schoolmasters, a student undergraduate of London University, and a 21–year old housekeeper. In Booth's classification, it was a district in the solid pink of respectability.

For a time, Adams functioned also as Honorary Secretary of the Metropolitan Teachers' Association.[85] He remained active in the British Teachers' Association, and in 1878 responded to a paper on 'The Evils of Centralisation'. He stated that it was a privilege to belong to an organisation at which so excellent a paper was read, and had noted for himself that his own work had become 'more and more of a routine character ... there was little time left for what ought to be the true aim of a teacher'.[86] The following year he objected to the process of centralisation being applied to the training of pupil teachers at specialised centres, proposing that they were better catered for by being overseen by principals who could see them at their regular work.[87]

At the Plymouth Conference in 1878 J.F. Adams was elected to the Executive of the NUET, coming twenty-third out of 24 among those elected.[88] At the Nottingham Conference the following year he was re-elected, in thirteenth position. At this meeting he was sufficiently established in the Union to be invited to attend the Annual Dinner and propose a toast, in this case to 'The Clergy and Ministers of all Denominations' whom he presented as major pioneers of education, claiming that most teachers present had entered the profession under the auspices of a local clergyman or minister. He also, oddly, paid tribute to the work of voluntaryists on school boards. Additionally, he acted as Master of Ceremonies at the Teachers' Ball, attended by 280. During the year he had

Figure 5.6.   J. F. Adams' lodgings, Walford Road, Stoke Newington

attended 44 meetings, including 20 of the full executive, and others of its committees, including the Provident Society and Orphanage Council.[89]

In 1880 Adams' NUET attendance dropped to 25 meetings, including 16 of the Executive. He was re-elected again at the Brighton Conference, coming sixteenth out of 24 candidates. Arrangements were made at that conference for a reunion of old Borough Road students. Though not one himself, having attended Bangor Training College, he was made Vice-Chairman for the occasion, at which 50 met in the banqueting room of Brighton Pavilion.[90] In the following year he attended only 12 executive meetings and three other special committee meetings, presumably in part because he had now left teaching. In any event, he either did not put himself forward, or was voted out, as an executive member for the following year.[91] By then, of course, he had been appointed as Clerk to the Tottenham School Board. He had during his early years in the metropolis developed a taste for national conferences, both for professional and social reasons. As we shall find in the next chapter, they helped to set the seal on a national reputation.

REFERENCES AND NOTES

1. *The Cambrian*, 25 Nov. 1859.
2. *Swansea Mercury*, 8 Feb. 1862.
3. *Educational Record*, Vol. 6 (1864), p. 59.
4. Llandovery British School Log Book, 4 Sept. 1865.
5. Ibid., 20 June 1864.
6. Ibid., 13 Dec. 1864.
7. Ibid., 6 Feb. 1865.
8. Ibid., 20 Jan. 1865.
9. Ibid., 1 March 1865.
10. Ibid., 28 Aug. 1865..
11. *The Welshman*, 16 Dec. 1864.
12. Ibid., 9 March 1866.
13. Ibid., 25 March 1866.
14. Ibid., 6 Oct. 1865.
15. Ibid., 13 Oct. 1865.
16. Ibid., 27 Oct. 1865.
17. Ibid., 17 Nov. 1865.
18. Ibid., 1 Dec. 1865.
19. Ibid., 15 Dec. 1865.
20. Ibid., 22 Dec. 1865.
21. *Llanelly Guardian*, 20 Sept. 1866.
22. Ibid., 30 Aug. 1866.
23. Llanelly British Boys' School Log Book, 21 Sept., 12 and 22 Oct. 1866.
24. Ibid., 28 Nov. 1866.
25. Ibid., 7 Jan. 1867.
26. Ibid., 3 Dec. 1866.
27. Ibid., 11 Dec. 1866.
28. Ibid., 6 June 1867.
29. Ibid., 24 Oct. 1867.
30. Ibid., Report included with Feb. 1867 entries.
31. Ibid., 18 March 1867.
32. Ibid., 2 July 1867.
33. Ibid., 30 Aug. 1867.
34. *Llanelly Guardian*, 5 Sept. 1867.
35. Llanelly British Boys' School Log Book, 25 Sept. 1867.
36. Ibid., 22 Oct. 1867.
37. Ibid., 31 Dec. 1867.
38. *Swansea and Glamorgan Herald*, 5 Oct. 1867.
39. Ibid., 22 May 1867.
40. *The Cambrian*, 24 May 1867.
41. Llanelly British Boys' School Log Book, 13 Dec. 1867.
42. Ibid., 2 Dec. 1867.
43. Ibid., 21 Feb. 1868.
44. Ibid., 26 Feb. 1868.
45. Ibid., 6 March 1868.
46. Ibid., 28 Feb. 1868.
47. Ibid., 12 March 1868.
48. Ibid., 18 March 1868.
49. Ibid., Report appearing in the March 1868 entries.
50. Ibid., 1 Oct. 1868.

51. Ibid., 6 Oct. 1868.
52. Ibid., 8 Oct. 1868.
53. Ibid., 15 Oct. 1868.
54. Ibid., 30 Oct. 1868.
55. Ibid., 4 Nov. 1868.
56. Ibid., 21 Dec. 1868.
57. Ibid., 26 Jan. 1869.
58. Ibid., Report included with Feb. 1869 entries.
59. Ibid., included with May entries.
60. E. Jones, *Their Hard-Earned Pennies* (Llanelli Borough Council, 1990), p.30.
61. Llanelly British Boys' School Log Book, 18 May 1869.
62. *RCCE*, 1867–8, pp. 313–19.
63. *Llanelly Guardian*, 20 Dec. 1866.
64. *The Welshman*, 15 Feb. 1867.
65. *Llanelly Guardian*, 14 Feb. 1867.
66. Ibid., 18 April 1867.
67. Llanelly Mechanics' Institution, *Annual Report*, 28 April 1868.
68. *North Middlesex Chronicle*, 20 April 1872.
69. Ibid., 4 Nov. 1871.
70. Ibid., 2 Dec. 1871.
71. *The Schoolmaster*, 24 Feb. 1872, p. 82, and 12 Oct. 1872, p. 146.
72. Ibid., 16 March 1872, p. 118.
73. Ibid., 19 July 1873, p.29.
74. C. Booth (ed.), *Labour and Life of the People in London*, 1st Series, Vol.2 (London: Williams and Norgate, 1891), Appendix, p. 17.
75. *North Middlesex Chronicle*, 4 Dec. 1875.
76. *Swansea and Glamorgan Herald*, 5 Jan. 1876. No initials were given for the candidate was referred to as Mr Adams in the newspaper report. It was almost certainly J.F. Adams, as W.B. Adams was making clear to the BFSS at this time that he wanted only a London appointment, while Richard Adams was clearly not yet experienced enough to have been considered for the post.
77. *The Schoolmaster*, 12 May 1877, p. 463.
78. Ibid., 2 Sept. 1877, p. 306.
79. Ibid., 28 Sept. 1877, p. 317.
80. Ibid., 13 Dec. 1879, p. 646.
81. For example, see *The Board Teacher*, 2 April 1894 and 1 April 1899.
82. *The Schoolmaster*, 6 March 1880, p. 312.
83. Ibid., 27 March 1880, p.371.
84. Ibid., 1 May 1880, p. 523.
85. Ibid., 13 April 1878, p. 402.
86. Ibid., 30 Nov. 1878, p. 578.
87. Ibid., 1 March 1879, p. 238.
88. Ibid., 27 April 1878, p. 456.
89. Ibid., 19 April 1879, pp. 442, 451 and 470.
90. Ibid., 3 April 1880, pp. 430 and 451.
91. Ibid., 27 April 1881, p. 481.

6

John Frederick Adams as School Board Clerk

THE TOTTENHAM SCHOOL BOARD
1879–88

From the early 1870s, the Education Department registered increasing concern over the inadequate supply of school accommodation in Tottenham. The introduction of workmen's cheap return fares on the Enfield to Liverpool Street was a watershed for Tottenham, transforming it from 'a pretty residential suburb ... into a huge working class area – a London over the border.'[1] In 1881 Tottenham's population was 46,441; by 1891 it was 97,166. During the 1870s, the voluntary agencies engaged in a frenzy of school expansion but had little chance of stemming the tide of demand in the face of Tottenham's inexorable population growth. They managed to stave off a School Board for nearly a decade.

In covering the election of the first Tottenham School Board in 1879, the editor of the *Tottenham and Edmonton Weekly Herald* divided the 26 candidates into three groups: those who for years had laboured zealously for the cause of education; those who had laboured equally zealously to bring upon the parish the burden of a School Board; and those whose education had been 'so sadly neglected that they are but indifferently qualified for the office they seek'.[2] Those elected consisted of five churchmen and four Nonconformists. Most had claimed economy as their watchword. At the first meeting, prophetically held 'amidst thunder, lightning and rain', the local newspaper reckoned that the 'ebulliency ... unhappily displayed' by the Rev. McSorley, an unashamed voluntaryist, was demonstrated in his 'questionable taste' in making 'a personal fling at one of his colleagues'. A warning was issued against sectarian battles already being fought at the Board's first meeting.[3] Elected Vice-Chairman, McSorley proposed also that each meeting be opened by a prayer, a move that was defeated.[4]

One of the Board's earliest tasks was to appoint a Clerk. There were 260 applications, of which 16 were selected by a committee for further consideration. The salary was to be £180 per annum. John Frederick Adams (Figure 6.1) was one of three interviewed and received as many votes from the committee as the two other candidates put together. The terms were that he should devote his whole time to the service of the Board and not take on other duties. He accepted these conditions.[5] At the time of his appointment, Adams was still resident in Stoke Newington, but soon moved to 2 Page Green Villas (Figure 6.2), where he was living at the time of his marriage in October 1881 to Kate Beck, daughter of a Great Western Railway official, born in Warwick, a teacher, and twelve years his junior. They later moved to a more prestigious residence, Leamington Lodge (Figure 6.3) which, like Page Green Villas, was conveniently located by the Tottenham High

Figure 6.1.   J.F. Adams, Tottenham School Board Clerk

Figure 6.2.   J.F. Adams' residence, Page Green Villas, Tottenham

Road. In 1891, their household included a teacher lodger and a servant. Kate Adams became well known for her philanthropic work in Tottenham, raising funds through organising activities by board school children for the local hospital, for example.[6]

Adams soon became adept in the deployment of delaying tactics in the face of regular queries from the Education Department over the accommodation question. The new Tottenham School Board was informed by the Education Department that there was a deficiency of 2,000 places, but the Board's own census suggested one of over 3,000. Adams gave his Board notice that in view of the discovery that the shortfall was much greater than the Department

Figure 6.3.   J.F. Adams' residence, Leamington Lodge, Tottenham

had previously indicated, there would be a need to provide temporary accommodation, to include a Temperance Hall, a Congregational school room and a Mission Room. In addition there were plans for schools to be transferred to the Board. The first newly built board schools were opened in September 1881.

Adams had necessarily to be proficient in treading the tightrope between, on the one hand, the demands of parents for accommodation and, on the other, the accusations of extravagance by ratepayers and the voluntary agencies. His skills were quickly recognised by the Board and in February 1881 it was moved that his salary should be raised to £230, with an increase to £250 the following year, and £25 thereafter to £300. The proposer stated that it was

impossible to find a better clerk than Mr. Adams in the kingdom. He had shown himself beyond praise. The amount of correspondence that he had conducted, and the statistics he had prepared, were wonderful perform-ances ... working late and early, he had placed the affairs of the Board in a most satisfactory condition ... He had done many things which ordinary clerks could not do, and had saved the ratepayers a large amount of money.[7]

Adams replied to the effect that he had found it a pleasure to work 'under a body of gentlemen', and that he hoped that the education of children would in all cases be entrusted to one 'actuated by such high principles as this Board...'.[8]

The first Triennial Report was outstandingly well put together, and there is no little hint that it included some of Adams' own views on school provision. It was pointed out that in planning schools it was decided that as Tottenham was a metropolitan district it should not make provision inferior to that found in London. It had therefore visited London board schools, and worked on the same principle that it was cheaper *pro rata* to build large than small schools. It had also adopted the accommodation principle of the classroom or Prussian system, that is, a central hall with classrooms off it. One problem the Board had had to face was that in a fast-growing community, sites were scarce and fabulous prices were asked. The Report noted that the children in the Board Schools were for the most part in a 'very backward con-dition. The cry of over-educating, which has been echoed for some time, is simply absurd'. In publishing a summary of the Report, the *School Board Chronicle*'s view was that the first Board had been conducted, notwithstanding the presence of members whose prime motivation was to protect the voluntary schools, in a relatively liberal spirit.[9]

Tottenham's second School Board was increased in size to twelve members, reflecting the rapid growth in the district's population. Eight members of the old Board were re-elected. The balance of power altered a little, with five churchmen and seven dissenters making up the new Board. It continued to plan for new schools, but in 1883 it came under increasing criticism from the local press. The *North Middlesex Chronicle* saw it as, on the one hand, pressing too hard on poor parents for fees which they just could not afford to pay, yet on the other being guilty of extravagance, the School Board rate having gone up to 4d in the £. The editor warned the Board that it was 'fast losing the strong position' it once occupied in the estimation of the parishioners.[10] He returned to the attack over small but significant queries raised in the annual audit of the Board's accounts. He observed that the Clerk 'acted, if we may so call it, for the defence of the Board ... with considerable zeal and ability, being well up in the various points presented, which in several cases might have otherwise been legitimate disallowances and surcharges'.[11]

This attack heralded problems to come at the official audits of the School Board's accounts, at which ratepayers were in attendance to challenge items of the Board's expenditure. One of the early queries was over the Board issuing its own hymn book. This led to a surcharge, against which the Board appealed to the Education Department. Singularly, one of the Board's own members, who had voted against the provision of the hymn book, attended the auditor's meeting as a ratepayer.[12] In the next half-yearly audit there was a protest at fees being paid for the conduct of a scripture examination, on the grounds that this too was not provided for in the Act. Adams argued forcefully that while there was a prohibition on any sectarian teaching in Board Schools, the Bible was not a sectarian book and that was what was being examined. He concluded: 'If it is legal to teach a subject it is legal to examine a subject; the former has to be paid for, why not the latter?'[13] On this occasion Adams was proved right.

The third Tottenham School Board contained many familiar faces, eight members of the previous Board retaining their places. The *School Board Chronicle* noted the unusual feature of the poll being headed by a woman, Mrs Collett, wife of a local dairyman. She had been proposed by the parish doctor, a strong opponent of popular education. Similarly, the second in the poll, a Roman Catholic priest, was known for his antagonism to the School Board system. The cumulative vote system was condemned for producing an election result 'widely regarded as a complete failure to express the real feeling of the ratepayers'.[14]

The thrice-elected Chairman no doubt sensed trouble when Mrs Collett claimed that as she had headed the poll she should be able to chose which committees she sat on. She objected to being put on the Bye-laws Committee without her agreement and on

this one alone, while other members were on two such committees. She wanted a place on the School Management Committee.
She innocently claimed 'not to understand motions, and those sort
of things'. Having implied that the Chairman and Clerk had
colluded on her committee membership in 'an irregular manner',
the former complained that his honour had been impugned.[15] Mrs
Collett's conduct was again castigated when she circulated a 'private' report to her son-in-law, who wrote to the press about
it. This the Rev. McSorley, who reckoned he had been misrepresented in the letter, argued was 'a very grave breach of
privilege'. The Chairman believed 'that no man in the room would
be guilty of such an Act'. At the same meeting Mrs Collett made
four proposals, not one of which acquired a seconder. She complained that 'she was not wanted there, but should stop her time
out'.[16] In the event, she died in June 1888.

Such incidents were the harbingers of other bitter exchanges in
which Adams was embroiled, and which excited increasing im-
patience from the *North Middlesex Chronicle*. Its editor maintained
that the Board was descending to a third-rate position as a public
body, referring to the 'frivolous discussion' and 'littleness' of its
proceedings. By this stage Mr Botterell (whose occupation was as
Clerk to the Nene Valley Commissioners) was questioning a number of actions of the Clerk, for example in calling a meeting without giving adequate notice. This Adams had done on the practical
ground of the need to appoint a temporary teacher, and after consultation with the Chairman. Adams denied more than a very
technical breach of procedure. If meetings could not be called at
short notice no appointments of teachers could be made.[17] The
issue was seen as significant enough for the *School Board Chronicle*
to highlight as 'an alleged illegal board meeting'.[18]

In November 1886, following a tabulated return of the salaries
of clerks on other school boards, it was agreed Adams' salary be
raised from £300 to £350, with a promised increase of £25 for the
next two years, a resolution carried by 10 to 1. The objection was
made by the Rev. McSorley, purely on the grounds of the heavy
burden of local taxation on the ratepayers, he claimed. He spoke
in 'the highest terms of Mr. Adams' ability and devotion to
duty'.[19] Meanwhile the accommodation problem worsened. The
Board reported that at the beginning of 1887, following the
closure of various temporary schools, there was certified accom-

modation for 7,048 pupils. But there were 9,248 on the books and 7,258 in average attendance. Adams was authorised to send a letter to the Education Department seeking 'all possible in- dulgence ... as the parish is a very poor one', asking for permis- sion to keep open some of the temporary buildings. The Department was of the view that the temporary accommodation was 'too bad to be any longer accepted', but perforce had to make concessions.[20]

In the meantime Adams had taken on the responsibilities of examiner in the Board's schools, including the examining of pupil teachers. This brought him another tribute in the Triennial Report of 1888, which concluded that as a result of his help in conducting 'examinations of schools under the Board, and of candidates for pupil teachers, it has been possible to dispense with an Inspector of the Board's schools'.[21]

The half-year audit in March 1888 was sufficiently notable for it to be the subject of an article in the *School Board Chronicle*. The auditor disallowed sums of over £7 expended on the setting up of school savings banks, and nearly £5 for the purchase of Bibles as scripture prizes. Both of these Adams argued were legitimate expenses, but he lost this battle. Selected ratepayers, often self- evident supporters of the voluntary system, continued to attend the audits to question minute details of expenditure. Predictably, they regarded spending on harmoniums and even copy books as going beyond the provisions of the Codes. The scripture prizes issue excited a complaint from the North Middlesex Branch of the Secular Society objecting to sums 'recklessly expended' on 'fanci- ful whims and religious instruction'. The purchase of Bibles was described as 'the thin end of an unmistakably injurious wedge ... the Board was extravagant, and the clerical element upon it mate- rially made use of its operations for propagandist purposes'.[22]

In retrospect 1888 was a pivotal year for Adams and for the Board. During it he became a Barrister-at Law, with Chambers at 5, King's Bench Walk, Temple. He was also appointed as Return- ing Officer for the election of members to the new Local Govern- ment Board for Wood Green, which the *North Middlesex Chronicle* suggested would give 'eminent and widespread satisfaction'. He possessed 'plenty of first-rate ability and a good supply of common sense, an entire absence of obsequiousness, but an ample amount of respect, and a remarkable talent for despatching work'.[23]

THE FOURTH TOTTENHAM SCHOOL BOARD,
1888–1891

The fourth Tottenham School Board contained only six members of the previous Board. In the build up to the 1888 election, the editor of the *North Middlesex Chronicle* pleaded that no more parsons should be elected: 'They may be good men, but admittedly they are the worst men of business in the whole community.'[24] The new Board was to achieve national notoriety, culminating in its dissolution in 1891. Two of its members, T. Piper and J.E. Watson, both of whom had stood as unsectarian candidates, were of a particularly combative disposition. They immediately challenged what they regarded as Adams' over-privileged position, the former querying whether Adams was now giving his whole time to the Board, having acted as Clerk to the Wood Green Local Board. It was explained that the previous Chairman had granted him permission to take on the responsibility as a temporary measure. Watson made clear that he was against such practices, and considered Adams should be bound by the original terms of his agreement. Adams asked what was meant by the term 'whole time', claiming he devoted always nine and ten and sometimes 15 and 16 hours a day to the Board's work.[25] At the next meeting Watson and Piper formally objected to Adams' temporary assumption of the Clerkship at Wood Green and the previous Chairman's approval of this. Rev. Father Bayley complained that if such a motion were minuted 'it would be a disgrace to the Board for ever.' All the other members who spoke did so in support of Adams, and the motion failed.[26]

The *North Middlesex Chronicle* became increasingly scathing in its indictments, referring in October 1889 to a section of the Board as 'being wholly incompetent to discharge the duties of the posts to which they have been elected. They are charged with ignoring the interests of education to vindicate their self-importance. The sound of their own voices, it is said, is to them the sweetest melody, while it savours strongly of discord to others'.[27] By the end of the year, the unremitting intrusion of personal animus into the debates led to the Chairman suggesting that they should seek the permission of the Education Department to dissolve the Board. By the next meeting he had had second thoughts, having sought Adams' advice. The Clerk was unable to see how the

Board had been in default of its duties, which he claimed were being properly performed: 'therefore any proposition such as you suggest making would be practically void and of no effect'. The Chairman therefore withdrew the motion for dissolution, but indicated that in future he had 'determined to put down all personal remarks with a high hand'.[28]

In February 1890, Adams was accused of a 'grave irregularity' in not having paid a sum of money to a former headmistress of one of the Board's schools, but a smaller amount to her predecessor, 'in error'. The implication was that he had pocketed the rest. An explanation was forthcoming but the Finance Committee regretted what had happened and resolved 'to adopt prompt and stringent measures' to prevent a recurrence.[29] During 1890 the *North Middlesex Chronicle* maintained its tirade against the Board, rating it as 'one of the worst School Boards in the kingdom.... The rank and file of the Board consist of nothing more than a set of educational hucksters'. The attack was also directed at what the newspaper perceived as the Board's progressive policies. There had, for example, long been debate in the area about priority being given to establishing higher grade schools, regarded as an 'expensive fad'. The editor protested against the 'shameful extravagance of teaching science to poor little girls ... a School Board of a poor district who insists on science being taught to starving children are fit subjects for a lunatic asylum'.[30] A public meeting was held on the higher grade school issue and a memorial from ratepayers, protesting against the extravagance of the Board, was sent to the Education Department. One of the leading figures in the protest was J.E. Watson, a member of the Board.[31]

By November 1890 *The Schoolmaster*'s attention had been attracted to the Board's problems, the editor referring to his 'unhappy lot' in directing the attention of readers to the 'inner animosities of the Tottenham School Board.... They allow their angry passions to rise too freely'. On the other hand, it praised the Board for its defence of its teachers from outside attacks, over the corporal punishment issue in this case. *The Schoolmaster* made considerable play of the fact that the barrister defending a Tottenham teacher summoned for assault was none other than J.F. Adams, and pointed to the advantage of having a Clerk who had been both a practising teacher and a lawyer himself. Adams' skills resulted in the case being swiftly dismissed.[32]

The 1891 Débâcle

Affairs at Board meetings went from bad to worse. At one, Adams and the Chairman were rebuked for privately conferring while members were asking for a ruling: 'if it was to be persevered in there need be no regular Chairman at all, because the Clerk might hold his own position and that of Chairman as well.' McSorley proposed that in the light of the 'gladiatorial conflict' at meetings and 'owing to the combativeness of dogs', a 'muzzling order' was needed. He proposed that no speech to the Board should be allowed to exceed ten minutes in duration. He noted that under this Board over 200 points of order had been raised.[33]

At its December meeting the Rev. Fotheringham, a Presbyterian minister, proposed that the Board should petition for its own dissolution to allow the ratepayers to elect a new body. He complained that no question that came up 'could be discussed on its merits, but according to the views and peculiarities of the members who were likely to take part in the discussion'.[34] The Chairman seconded the motion, agreeing that the Board was 'a standing disgrace to the parish'. Other members insisted that they would not pass votes of censure on themselves maintained that the current Board had done a good job. The motion was lost.[35] The editor of the *North Middlesex Chronicle* thought this meeting 'even eclipsed its former notorious proceedings', including three hours of wrangling, leaving the proper business untouched. He referred to the dissolution motion as 'a consummation assuredly devoutly to be wished'.[36] He was not too long in achieving this wish, for the Board was about to fall foul of its auditor again.

The affair of the Tottenham tellurium was celebrated enough to merit a column in *Punch*.

'If you please,' said the Auditor of the Tottenham School Board accounts, 'would you explain to me what that curious thing is that you have got in your hand?'

'With pleasure,' replied the White Knight, who had recently been elected a Member of the Board. 'It's a Tellurium.'[37]

Reporters from the national press, it was later recounted, were attracted to meetings of the Board to record for the nation the 'titter all round' in its discussions over the surcharge for the tellurium.[38] To one local newspaper editor, the tellurium was a luxury 'unknown even to the London School Board'.[39] The promoter of the purchase of the tellurium, Thomas Piper, was to the ratepayer group a lethal combination of an 'unsectarian' and an 'educational expert', as well as being Chairman of the Board's Finance Committee. He was a lecturer at St Katharine's Training College, Tottenham, and an unashamed proponent of expenditure on broadening the elementary curriculum. The tellurium he described as a teaching aid: a model worked by wheels and levers, showing the relative motions of the sun, the moon and the planets, and was used in meeting the requirements of the physiography syllabus, one of the specific subjects of the Code. As Piper argued, by the help of 'this beautiful little instrument' children acquired a more meaningful view of how the heavenly bodies were disposed in space, enhancing their chances of success in public examinations. This meant the Board received larger grants from the Science and Art Department. Piper concluded, tendentiously: 'We may therefore define a tellurian as an instrument for reducing the rates'.[40]

In a letter headed 'Educational Experts (?) and the Result', Piper was personally attacked by a colleague on the Board, J.E. Watson, for favouring some schools in Tottenham rather than others. It was the master of the Noel Park Boys' School, opened in 1889, who had been responsible for ordering the tellurium. If Piper had sanctioned it for this school why not for others? The answer was that its head was a friend of Piper: one of his 'anointed'. The writer explained that he now rarely attended Board meetings because of Piper's abuse against himself and 'exhibitions of ranting'.[41]

Another acerbic set of exchanges was recorded in the on-going dialogue between the District Auditor and the Clerk. Adams was clearly aware that some of the purchases, if not that of the tellurium, were entering into grey areas for school board expenditure, such as the financing of evening schools. But as the local newspaper commented, he was a lawyer with the capacity to make black seem white, and two and two add up to six. On this occasion expenditure on a large number of items of scientific equipment, in addition to the tellurium, was challenged. There was also what the Auditor took to be illicit spending on materials for kindergarten work. During the discussion, Adams was asked what physiography was. He described it as a newly invented science about ten years old (in fact it was one promoted by T.H. Huxley) which included 'a little chemistry, a little electricity, physical science, and geography'.

The auditor questioned whether physiography was required to meet the demands of the 1870 Education Act. Adams correctly indicated that it was a specific subject option included in the current Educational Code. Schools did not have to offer it, but the Board had given the subject its support. The auditor reflected that if the Science and Art Department wanted such advanced science to be taught, it need not be in Tottenham's elementary schools. For this and other expenditure deemed to be illegal, the Board was surcharged. The cost of the tellurium was £4 14s 6d.[42] Eighteen months later, the Local Government Board arbitrated in favour of the Board. It pointed out that the articles in question, 'if not clearly necessary for the instruction of the children were, as regards most of them, at least useful for that purpose, and the items might be regarded as judicious expenditure on the part of the Board'.[43]

An illustration of the extraordinary confrontations Adams faced at the public audits can be culled from that of the summer of 1891. Knives sharpened by the tellurium affair, the regular ratepayer opponents of the Board led the attack with the auditor apparently seeing his role to arbitrate. The *School Board Chronicle* quoted some of the exchanges *in extenso*.

Auditor: Now, there are some other items: a doll, a doll's house and furniture for a doll's house; flags and a mariner's compass – all for an infant school. These seem extraordinary items. What can infants want with a mariner's compass? ...
Adams: Infant education has undergone great changes. The Kindergarten system has completely altered it. The old system of teaching A B C as in dame schools has been superseded and the intellects of children are now being trained and developed.
Ratepayer 1: That's all nonsense. Teach them as before. It will be more useful to them ...
Ratepayer 2: Let them have some mud pies to play with; they'd be happy then ...
Auditor: Now, Mr. Adams, what are these four dozen flags ... and musical dumb-bells?
Adams: The flags are part of the appliances for flag drill and physical exercises called musical drill.
Ratepayer 1: What nonsense! They can sing without flags.
Ratepayer 2: Is it the Union Jack?
Adams: This is getting frivolous. I have told you about the new kind of instruction which is taking place in infant schools under the Government Code.

Ratepayer 1: It's beside the question altogether. Look at our expenditure. This is not the proper teaching for infants, and Mr. Adams ought to know it.... I don't blame him for making the best of his case, but he ought to know better.

Auditor: There are some pictures – Henry VIII, Charles I, and General Wolfe, by the Art for Schools Association. What have they to do with elementary education?

Adams: What would English history be without Henry VIII and Charles I? Nothing but a scene of spasmodic fighting. These were pictures towards historical teaching. You surcharged geographical pictures last year, and the Local Government Board upset your decision, and certainly they will do so if you disallow these, for they are historical ...

Ratepayer 1: It is all part of a piece of extravagant policy. No doubt there are a lot more items, mixed up in big accounts, which have not come under notice.

The auditor gave his assurance that every item would be gone through carefully, and indeed disallowed all the items except the pictures, at the same time indicating he did not agree with them as expenditure coming under the Elementary Education Acts.[44]

The *School Board Chronicle* used the Tottenham case as clinching evidence in a campaign against the School Board voting system: it was the 'miserable and mischievous' cumulative vote that was at fault, and what was needed was a restoration of the rule of party. The cumulative voting system meant that individual electors could 'plump' all their votes (twelve in the case of a twelve-member Board) for one candidate. Tactical voting could place a minority group in power. The *Chronicle* argued that there were several good men on the Tottenham Board, but because of the voting system they did not work together. 'They are mere items, each man with notions and objects of his own and wholly without party feeling ... there are only two methods of getting work done, by Despotism or by Government by Party.'[45]

Meanwhile, the *North Middlesex Chronicle* editor had concentrated his attack on Adams who, in taking up the Board's case he claimed 'with all his historical padding and incisive sentences', merely proved the old axiom, which is 'No case, then abuse the other side'.

We have had occasion, from time to time, to compliment Mr. Adams generally on the able way in which he performs his public duties. He is a man of resource and tact, and has probably more brains than half the united quantity which belongs to the members of his Board, but we are afraid that, since he has become a member of the legal profession, he has

most of the faults of the lawyers. Knowing, as he must do, that the Board
are distinctly in default for not performing their duties, and seeing, as he
also must, meeting after meeting, the mere pantomimes by the members,
he has, consequently, forgotten the truth in stating his case, and
descended to the position of an irrepressible, cavilling local attorney, and
given out stale history as a substitute for facts, figures and strong argu-
ments. We hope the Education Department will rebuke him for his
effrontery, and that they will do speedy justice and dissolve the Board
forthwith ... It would probably be a blessing for the Clerk, for we feel
sure that his abilities would find a better market, even if it took them to
the Old Bailey.[46]

The Education Department had been made aware both through
local representation and in the press that the Board's priorities
were not sufficiently concentrated on the accommodation problem, and it would seem had found a reason to show that the Board
was indeed in default. In April the Department required it to find
sites for two new schools. Adams had given warning the previous
March that there was a serious deficiency of places and a requisition might be issued. At this point Tottenham's Board alleged that
it was an 'irresponsible local assembly' that had brought the issue
to the attention of the Education Department[47]. The letter from
Adams to the Department was presumably that referred to by the
local editor as 'effrontery'. At the Board's meeting early in May,
Adams estimated there was an educational deficiency of 4,454, the
1891 census showing Tottenham's population to be well over
95,000. The letter just received from the Department was in effect
a final order. The Board went on the defensive, claiming that what
the Department was asking for was an impossibility.[48]

The final order was followed up quickly. The Education
Department again wrote to Adams. He replied, pointing out that
the Board in 1891 supplied 10,500 Board School places, and the
voluntary agencies only 2,759. He maintained that the Education
Acts operated inequitably on working-class suburbs like Tottenham, which helped to produce the wealth of London, but left poor
districts like his with crippled resources in the face of abnormal
demands. He quoted nearby Hornsey, with greater rateable
value, having to supply but one-third of the board school places of
Tottenham. Adams argued that the Department had been at fault
in not allowing them to go ahead with an earlier school project,
and that was the cause of any default. He complained also of the
Department listening to the views of irresponsible local vested

interests.[49] Some members of the Board dissociated themselves from Adams' letter, the Chairman maintaining that he had jeopardised his position by acting on the instigation of an internal clique, and including matters in his letter that the Board had previously rejected. Members of the Board were angered also because Adams had recently implemented a Committee decision about purchasing a site without it going to the full Board. He defended his action on the grounds that it was his first duty to protect the Board and prevent it from going by default, with a possibility of the district being disenfranchised. On this explanation, the Chairman exonerated Adams from blame.[50]

Following a special meeting of the Board, Adams wrote to the Department on the same defensive lines as previously. He concluded by anticipating Tottenham's disgrace to come, saying that as reward for their service they did not look 'for that public gratitude which seldom if ever comes to members of public bodies, but they do consider that to be ousted from office before the expiry of time for which they were duly and honourably elected is an act which is apparently arbitrary rather than just or equitable'.[51] The Education Department now dispatched HMI T.W. Sharpe to administer the *coup de grâce*. An acrimonious meeting between the Board and Sharpe followed.[52] He was unsympathetic to the claim that the Board had been vigorously negotiating to find sites since the April requisition. He noted that while letters had been passed since then, no action had been taken, despite the Board's protestations to the contrary. There remained a deficit of 2,500 places. He contended that the Board had proved ineffective because of the strident hostility endemic in its proceedings, not helped by weak chairmanship. It had done too little. He recommended that the Board should be regarded as 'in default', dissolved under Section 66 of the 1870 Act, and a new election ordered.[53]

The Education Department's decision evoked a storm of local protest, particularly through its ploy to advise the nomination of a Board rather than the holding of an election. Tottenham interpreted this as disenfranchisement. In the event, seven nominated 'gentlemen' refused to serve on this less than formal basis. The *School Board Chronicle*, reporting the protest meeting, also quoted the *Methodist Times* as complaining that the Department's approach to 12 gentlemen had largely been confined to churchmen. Dissenting denominations had been excluded. Strong objection was raised against children being handed over 'to a clique in favour of sectarian and denominational education'.[54] A deputation of Tottenham and Wood Green ratepayers was sent to Whitehall to point out that a poll was imminent, requesting the Department to hold its hand. The Department retracted its decision, and agreed that a new election should be held on 14 November 1891.[55] Officials made it clear to the organiser of the deputation, however, that it expected its influence would be used to elect a 'satisfactory working Board' which would give priority to the provision of accommodation.[56]

THE POST-1891 TOTTENHAM SCHOOL BOARDS

Seven of the members of the now defunct Board were re-elected. W. Low, the weak former Chairman, was not. Neither was R.J. Robinson, an accountant and valuer, the most vocal ratepayer opponent of Adams at the audits, who had also been unsuccessful on previous occasions. But his vote increased greatly, from 358 to 2,386, a warning sign to opponents that his attacks on the Board's expenditure had registered. The *School Board Chronicle* judged that the new Board consisted mainly of liberals, but lamented that the cumulative vote system had again operated, and no local association had been formed with seven candidates and a 'defined and united school policy ... and a joint platform.' It hoped a majority of members elected would do this.[57]

Another local newspaper analysed the election returns in the light of the confrontation between the forces of progress and reaction on the previous Board. The seven progressives gained in all over 32,000 votes. The four 'undoubted reactionaries' polled 17,969. The other elected member was labelled a 'doubtful', veering towards the reactionary. The result was seen as a blow to the two most pronounced reactionaries, Low and Robinson, and the lesson it taught Tottenham was unmistakably that the new Board was for progress. It was noted that were now three clergymen, as against five on the old Board.[58] The new Chairman, Colonel Durrant, was by the following March being congratulated by the *North Middlesex Chronicle* for getting through the Board's business 'with success, gentlemanly ease, and good temper'.[59] The meetings were still not equable, but the confrontations were mostly over side issues. On the essential question of accommodation the Board made good progress. In the light of the 1891 census figures, and bearing in mind that the population would rise as they were building new schools, Adams estimated that there was a gross deficiency of 5,578 places.[60] By January 1893 the Chairman was reporting that progress on two new Board Schools and the start on a third was well in hand. In addition, another was being enlarged. In July 1894 Adams indicated that for the first time the Tottenham School Board had received favourable comment in the recent Department Blue Paper: 'In Tottenham the supply is never quite equal to the demand, but the Board are doing their best to meet the prodigious increase in population.'[61] The Board indeed received unprecedented special grants from the Education Department of over £2,000 because the work being undertaken was out of proportion to the rateable value of the district.

Confrontations continued at the public audits, with Adams and Robinson again the protagonists. In January 1894, Robinson raised a huge number of detailed queries over what he regarded as dubious expenditure. Adams forced Robinson to withdraw insinuations about teachers having made garments out of materials supplied by the Board for public entertainments. So far from this being true, teachers had paid large sums from their own pockets to raise funds for the benefit of poor children. On this occasion, the auditor was critical of Robinson for making statements 'which have a very nasty flavour'. Adams concluded his defence of the expenditure in upbeat and oratorical mode:

As to all the other items, he had answered them so often that he was tired of doing so. Mr. Robinson had as usual trotted out the names of some scientific apparatus which the Board had every right to buy and happily would go on buying.... It was not within the power of the Auditor to disallow any of the items. The Code said the Board 'may', the Board construed that to mean should, and they would.

The auditor made no disallowances or surcharges on this occasion.[62] In September 1895 there was another altercation. By now the auditor was cautious. Adams was well established as a powerful opponent, with a keen mind and a legal training. He had already generally had his cases supported at a higher level: 'You see, Mr. Robinson, my power is limited. I have considerable sympathy with several of your objections, and I have previously made disallowances, and my decisions have been reversed in respect to items similar to those you name.' Adams confidently asserted that there was no doubt about his position. The auditor could not disallow items it was within the powers of the Board to purchase, nor challenge the price, unless there was a *prima facie* case of paying unreasonably highly for them. He was contemptuous of Robinson's queries about the purchase of portable lavatories, and of linoleum for teachers' rooms. 'Who ever heard of such extravagances?' On the latter, Adams retorted: 'Who can possibly object to articles for comfort, convenience and cleanliness in teachers' rooms? These rooms were also sometimes used for Committee meetings. How could anyone object to decent furniture?'[63]

By 1896 Adams' salary had reached £450, and it was proposed it should be increased in two instalments of £50. One member queried this in the absence of information on what other clerks were receiving, and also enquired about the amount of Adams' salary as a barrister. Adams gave the assurance that he was frequently refusing briefs because of his School Board commitments, and that his practice was small. It was clarified that proportionally Adams' salary was not high, and the increase was unanimously approved.[64] By this time Tottenham's Board rate was 1s 7¼d, one of the highest in England and Wales. In the following year Tottenham was cited as one of the six most necessitous boards in the country, and stood to receive £4,574 from a new Bill for the aid of necessitous school boards.[65]

The high School Board rates were presumably a reason why the Wood Green ratepayers wished for a separate Board. In February 1896 Adams led a deputation taking Tottenham's case to Middlesex County Council, arguing that while Wood Green would not gain financially, Tottenham would lose. He claimed there was no large disaffection in Wood Green, though its supporters claimed its three members on the Tottenham Board could easily be outvoted. He was congratulated by the Chairman for the able way in which he had put the case. Part of this was, as Adams argued, that large boards were more efficient, and moving to smaller ones would be a retrograde step.[66] His success in this dispute can be construed as having helped him achieve a salary rise, the Board believing it was his skills which turned the decision of Middlesex County Council in Tottenham's favour on this occasion.

By the time of the 1897 election the Board had made good progress in providing schools, but was judged in the local press to be incorrigibly extravagant. 'Vote for Economy' thundered the *North Middlesex Weekly Standard*, quoting one former Board member as saying 'I don't care a tinker's curse for ratepayers.' A columnist referred to the progressives as 'The Party of Waste'. The 'Moderate' group agreed on a combined election advertisement, contending that their best efforts would be directed to checking similar extravagance in the future.[67] By contrast the *Tottenham and Stamford Hill Times and Stoke Newington Chronicle* supported the Progressive Party, and was congratulated by one of its correspondents for unmasking the 'sinister designs' of the voluntaryist 'sacerdotal six'. It was satisfied that their 'economic dodge' had not succeeded. Analysing the figures, it claimed that the maximum strength of the sacerdotalists was 26,000 and the minimum of the 'progressive unsectarians' was over 47,000. It condemned the former for not drawing attention to the truly splendid work of the previous Board, in improving average attendance, in achieving successes in Queen's Scholarship examinations, in lowering the average cost per child, and raising proportionally higher earnings of government grant than the London Board.[68]

During 1898 Adams' salary was increased from £500 to £550 per annum. His reputation in 1898 was at its peak. He was frequently invited to speak at local meetings, at one giving a paper to 'a bumper house ... full of men' on 'Hooliganism', using his usual amalgam of good humour and the support of statistics. Referring to his own terrier as a hooligan for destroying his folio of notes, Adams' theme was that the cost of educating people was much less than that of convicting them and sending them to prison. Ninety-seven per cent of prisoners were very imperfectly educated. Only 2 per cent could read and write well and only 1 per cent had received superior education. All people had two sets of faculties, the higher and the lower, and the best strategy was to appeal to the higher gifts of nature. All 'infliction of the lash' he denounced as brutalising and served to 'knock the devil in instead of knocking him out'. Amid laughter and applause he ridiculed the policy of confining local parks and open spaces to nice-looking nursemaids and babies, and of regarding boys and girls as natural enemies. He pressed for the teaching of athletics, 'as no true athlete could ever become a rough'.[69]

Early in 1900 Tottenham School Board moved into new offices in the grounds of one of the board schools. They were opened by Sir George Kekewich, Secretary of the Education Department who, as a local newspaper implied, seemed to stand in some awe of Adams: 'The frequent references by Sir George to Mr. Adams ... show that the latter is well-known, if not dreaded, at the Education Department.... I rather think he has cornered Sir George more than once.... May our School Board Clerk's bow long abide in strength.'[70]

Adams and Tottenham felt in need of support in the course of promoting a campaign of the Association of School Boards against the new Education Code. This Adams claimed was the most radical change since the Revised Code of 1862, and was based on a deceptively simple principle of a block grant to schools which would mean that while poor schools would gain, successful schools like those of Tottenham would lose, as would all boards who had pursued an 'advanced policy'. He claimed it was a means of giving dole to the inefficient schools of the villages and, by implication, to voluntary schools, whereas the large and efficient board schools of towns and cities would suffer crippling blows.[71]

The continuing growth of Tottenham allowed for an increase to 15 seats on the Board at the 1900 election. The *North Middlesex Weekly Standard* maintained its strongly anti-progressive stance, alleging that the 'discredited majority on the School Board' had put up 'dummies' to enable the 'extravagants to slip again into power'. It condemned the exorbitant School Board rate, by then over two shillings in the pound, accusing it of living on 'cant and humbug' and housing itself 'in costly buildings'. Of its 'political and educational creed, its jobbery and caucus-like work, Tottenham ratepayers are fairly sick'. The Board had been 'extravagant beyond all comparison with its predecessors'.[72] On this occasion the paper was triumphant, for the 'economists' won handsomely over the 'extravagants'.[73]

It is much to be doubted whether Adams was as comfortable with the new philosophy as that which had guided the progressive fifth, sixth and seventh Tottenham boards. But he was not to be with it for long. In May 1901 what was to be his final illness was reported, serious enough to cause him to miss his first meetings in all his time at Tottenham.[74] In the previous year, the Cockerton judgment had been announced, prompting a move by the Board to discontinue all payments of money that might be contravening it. Adams was not there to clarify doubts, or to suggest how far the Board could go.[75] He had, however, already foreseen the problems. 'It seems to me to be abundantly clear that the whole tendency of educational legislation and practice at present is to confine the School Boards to elementary branches of instruction only.' He was concerned that the vitality of higher grade and science provision in Tottenham was being sapped.[76]

THE SCHOOL BOARD CLERKS' CONFERENCES

In 1898 John Frederick Adams' respected services to the School Board Clerks' conferences were recognised when he was elected the Association's President. In his presidential address he noted: 'This is an age of associations and conferences for all sections of the community, and we cannot but be struck with the infinite number of public meetings held, and the number of speeches which are constantly being made in the various assemblies connected therewith.'[77]

The School Board Clerks' Association was formed as a result of a preliminary meeting held at Sheffield in January 1875. The initiative came from the clerks of large northern and midland boards, including Liverpool, Sheffield, Leeds, Newcastle, Hull, Birmingham, Manchester, Nottingham, Leicester and Bolton. Before this they had informally consulted to help each other in dealing the great difficulties they grappled with in the 'largest class of towns'. The qualification for membership was acting as clerk for a district of 50,000 or more inhabitants.[78] The *School Board Chronicle* featured the proceedings of the succeeding conferences in some detail, regarding them as one of the most progressive educational agencies in operation: 'There is gathered within the focus in this Conference, year by year, and presented in a compact and assimilable form, the essence of all the most practical experience of educational administration in its breadth and in its detail, in its internal economy and in its relations with external interests, gathered over a great and widely representative area....'[79]

The annual meetings were held all over Britain. The conference experience often began with a long railway journey. For the Glasgow conference in Adams' presidential year, for example, members and visitors from the south of England travelled 'by a pre-arranged route – on the Midland service – which, passing through the beautiful Peak country, will bring them to the rendezvous at the Windsor Hotel, Glasgow'.[80] Programmes of events were arranged, including visits to schools, industrial undertakings, and attractive scenic locations, including Loch Lomond and Clyde shipyards for the Glasgow conference. There was the pleasure of the social intercourse available at and after the evening dinners at the hotel. Wives were allowed to attend, and Mrs Adams was present at at least three of the conferences.

Adams was one of the most celebrated members of the Association, attending his first conference at Nottingham in 1885. He had already established his reputation as an outspoken commentator on the educational questions of the day and, like his elder brother, was not afraid of offending the sensibilities of his peers. Even though regarded generally as supportive of teachers, in 1882, he upset a columnist in the recently established journal *The Schoolmistress*, by suggesting that the standard work of elementary schools could as well be done in half a year as a whole one. Its columnist remarked tartly: 'It may be asked whether other teachers of twenty years' experience do not hold a somewhat different opinion.'[81]

Adams was a regular contributor to the conference debates, and at many gave one of the keynote papers, his first on 'Some Practical Deficiencies of our Educational System' at Brighton in 1886. In this he demanded a more liberal and complete elementary system, to be elaborated by 'a body of distinguished literary men from our universities and public schools', rather than relying on 'the perpetual annual patching of the existing Code ... a sorry thing at its birth, and age and alteration has not much improved it'. Like his brother W.B. Adams, he was a fervent proponent of graded schools, asking for a ranking of free schools of a first grade, offering simple and rudimentary instruction, then a second grade of average elementary schools, teaching more or less the present range of subjects, and finally a third grade of schools starting at the fourth Standard, from which students from the other schools would be drafted at no increased fee. These would offer a more liberal and technical education. In retaining a sense of balance and realism, however, he referred also to the over-pretentious instruction he discerned in the lower grade of schools, and agreed that teaching chemistry to girls was 'going a little in advance of public opinion'.[82]

Another of Adams' recurrent themes was the narrowness and

fickleness of the government Codes which determined the nature of the elementary curriculum. He pointed to the huge expense caused by the changes in them from one year to another. His speeches shed real insight on the impact on the ground of these changes, although there was clearly an element of playing to the gallery in his style of address. At Sheffield in 1896 he attacked the legislation making 'Varied Occupations' compulsory. In the conference arena his stance was predictably different from that he had taken at meetings with Tottenham School Board's auditor.

Great ignorance, of course, prevailed amongst school boards, managers and teachers at that time as to what type of occupations were really of educational value. An immediate – I was going to say mania – arose for acquiring knowledge in these arts. Classes were formed at considerable expense ..., and stock – some of it of the most expensive kind – was freely purchased ... We all know, if I may borrow a Stock Exchange term, that there's a slump in Kindergarten materials at present – (laughter) – and they are not likely to rise again to where they stood.[83]

Adams was a spokesman for meritocratic values, drawing on attitudes embedded during his family upbringing and later professional experience, and reflected in the practices of many of the great urban school boards. Such was evident in his contribution to the discussions of the social difficulty as related to free education at the Huddersfield Conference in 1891.

Parents who were respectable and pretty well off, and whose children therefore came from good homes, would not like their children to associate with the poorest class, many of whom were far from clean.... The Board with which he was connected had two schools (higher grade) where 9d per week was charged; they were both crowded, and the parents were glad to pay the money. ... He did not wish to be misunderstood – he would not limit the child's education by the amount of fees it paid – but he was satisfied that to free all schools would be a step fraught with some difficulty.[84]

Like his older brother, John Frederick Adams had a keen sense of history. Without ever revealing his own traumatic experiences with pupil teachers, he regularly harked back to the origins of the pupil teacher system, the iniquities of the Revised Code, and the like. At the Wolverhampton Conference in 1893 he gave a wideranging paper on 'School Staffing'. He made reference to three epochs of schooling in the nineteenth century: the first of masters and monitors; the second of masters and pupil teachers, with assistant teachers rarely found except in the most favoured schools; and the third, where head and assistant teachers were becoming the order of the day and pupil teachers were gradually being eliminated. Rural areas he regarded as stuck in the second epoch, while the major school boards were well into the third. He looked forward to a fourth epoch in which there would be many more graduate teachers. He thought it sound sense to have the younger classes, even in boys' schools, taught by women teachers, replicating the view of his brother, W.B. Adams. But for the higher classes he argued passionately for more qualified and specialised teachers, generalists not being able to cope with the full range of subjects demanded. He was pleased to note that his own Board were now appointing graduates: 'future plums of the profession will go to men who have thus not been content to march in the ordinary rank and file and to roam early in life upon a tableland that can go no higher'. But teachers must be decently paid, otherwise the laws of supply and demand would dictate, and there would be a crisis.[85]

Progressive though his views were, he manifestly could not escape from the time-warp of current practices, including the norms of class sizes in that period. His 'perfect arrangement' for school staffing was one 50–sized and three 60–sized classrooms, each under certificated assistants, a 70–sized classroom under a certificated teacher and a young pupil teacher, and an 80–sized room under an assistant and a good pupil teacher. Fifty scholars in the upper standards, not more than 60 in Standard III, and 70 in Standards I and II he thought a 'fair distribution'.[86] Adams approved the post-monitorial arrangement of a central school hall with classrooms off. At a later conference at Manchester in 1897, by which time he was Vice-President, he deplored as a 'retrograde movement' the use of these central halls for teaching. 'They were not intended for this purpose', and formed 'the lungs of a large school, and thus added to the health of the children'. To see a class there occasionally was one thing, 'but to see the hall habitually used as a classroom was most objectionable and quite opposed to progress in school buildings and their plans'.[87] The editor of *The Schoolmaster*, T. J. Macnamara, made generally favourable comment on Adams' contributions to this Wolverhampton conference, particularly the plea to reduce the 'multifarious foreign duties' expected of a headteacher, reinforcing Adams' words: 'it is worse than wasting eminent pedagogic ability to keep a Head Teacher chained to his desk as a mere copying clerk'. Macnamara was more forward looking than Adams on class sizes, however, complaining: 'But why, oh why should he count on the staff for sixty scholars?'[88]

Adams' trenchant criticism of ideas he did not support could arouse heated responses, but he usually expressed his appreciation of the value of a well-made speech even if he was in conflict with its content. At the Hull Conference of 1894 he was taken seriously to task by the editor of the *School Board Chronicle* for his support of the idea of exemption by age and attendance (rather than age and examination). Adams claimed that if parents caused their children to attend a certified efficient school over the requisite number of years, they had fulfilled their responsibilities. The theory of the individual examination was now dead, and teachers should be trusted to classify their scholars. Most other delegates were not happy, nor was the editor.

The Conference of 1894, if it had no other claims to remembrance, would be memorable for having produced one School Board Clerk who has a word to say in favour of exemption by age and attendance. The distinction of this unique position among his official brethren belongs to Mr. J.F. Adams; yet in spite of the fire of his emphasis of the hapless project of the N.U.T ... not even Mr Adams' conspicuous gifts could make a really presentable case out of that forlorn and retrograde project.[89]

On the other hand, the journal *The Head Teacher* paid tribute to Adams' general contributions, observing that he was 'as usual on the side of common sense and of the teachers'. He had argued that more trust should be put in teachers, who could be relied on to take care of themselves. The columnist concluded: 'But then Mr. Adams speaks with the knowledge that comes of contact. Would that every School Board had as sensible a clerk as he.'[90]

As it had been for William and Mary Adams, so 1898 was an *annus mirabilis* for John Frederick. In that year he was elected as President of the School Board Clerk's Conference. In his presidential address he referred to the uniqueness of the conference in preserving 'a calmness and amenity of temper' that was uncharacteristic of the current acrimony in education. None the less, it was also an attacking speech, suggesting that the advantages of the dual system were rapidly disappearing and, while praising the previous efforts of the voluntary sector, pointing out that their schools were 'running a most unequal race with the School Boards'. Similarly, like the *School Board Chronicle*, he showed hostility to the cumulative system of voting for School Board, claiming that the plumping principle allowed the election of 'angular men' with pet ideas or hobbies or 'cranks who have only a very remote or indirect connection with education at all', and some 'thoroughly opposed to Board Schools altogether'. He was similarly antipathetic to small school boards, some of which acted with efficiency and vigour, but others did their best to frustrate the intentions of the Education Acts, with the power of one or two reactionaries doing great mischief. He also attacked the half-time system: 'that wretched system ... which mocks our much-vaunted civilisation, and still permits 110, 654 children of tender years to undertake part-time labour in some parts of the country'.

In his concluding peroration, demanding the continuing advancement of education, he ended with a quote from Aristotle: 'Education's greatest and highest aim is to make virtuous and good citizens, to secure happiness arising from the blamelessness of life, to lead to the perfection of man's social and moral nature, and to encourage those great and noble deeds which dignify and adorn a country.'[91] His performance at the Glasgow conference, the largest gathering there had been, was warmly received by the *School Board Chronicle*, which remarked that Adams

sustained most admirably the traditions of his office.... His speeches in acknowledgement of the courtesies extended to the members at one point or another of the proceedings were distinctive in character and eminently happy in expression.... Whether it be in public speech, in writing, or in familiar conversation, the able Clerk of the Tottenham School Board has the faculty of always engaging interest. He has his point of view, and does not hesitate to take it. And when his point of view involves some actual or seeming conflict with another, he does not at all mind hearing the point argued.[92]

The Schoolmaster, on the hand, was much cooler, complaining that: 'In the course of his address Mr. Adams dished up many of the "Facts and Figures" given on these columns on 21st May ... (And considering the labour involved in the compilation referred to, we think it would have been a graceful act on Mr. Adams' part to have made public acknowledgement of the source of his inspiration).'[93]

His presidential address in 1898 was indeed his swan song, for though he attended with his wife the Brighton and Bristol conferences of 1899 and 1900, his contributions were small. He was unable to attend the Edinburgh conference of 1901, writing to say that 'the unfortunate state of my health will make my attendance impossible, unless, indeed, there is a marvellous improvement, which at present hardly seems possible'. His wife indeed confirmed on 13 May that he had been forced to cancel all engagements.[94]

THE ASSOCIATION OF SCHOOL BOARDS' CONFERENCES

Having cut his teeth at NUET conferences, and having made his name at those of the School Board Clerks, Adams now became associated with a third conference body, the Association of School Boards. Their annual meetings, which began in 1894,[95] were different in nature from those of their Clerks. They were not confined to the larger school boards, and not only the clerks were represented. Thus Adams was normally accompanied by two of the members of the Tottenham School Board. The *School Board Chronicle* regularly urged that the interests of small as well as large boards be considered, remarking rather condescendingly in 1898 that 'the modest dignity, common sense and practical reasonableness of several representatives of the rural School Boards ... were not the less favourably impressive for an occasional touch of dialect or homely idiom'.[96]

Very many more attended these London meetings than the conferences of the School Board Clerks' Association. The first was held in 1894 at London's Westminster Palace Hotel. The Association was formed in a context of increasing official antagonism against the school boards, and was designed to move towards 'a basis of common action' and provide 'a medium of mutual helpfulness'.[97] Adams was soon in action. At the first annual meeting he proposed that, in the light of the 'famine of teachers', the government should provide enough residential training college accommodation for those eligible for admission. At present less than half those with scholarships were actually admitted. What the government had done was to provide for day training colleges, which had not taken off, and he was glad of it. He spoke in favour of the two-year residential training college course, where students

were taught by 'trained and cultivated persons'.[98] At the 1895
meeting, Adams was again in the forefront of discussion, in this
case proposing something close to his interests as Clerk to the
Tottenham School Board, in demanding that boards should be
given stronger powers of compulsory purchase, the normal hiking
up of the price where sites were scarce being of a pronounced disadvantage to the boards. What he was demanding was that they
should have at least the same powers as other public bodies, such
as parish councils.[99]

Adams made contributions to all these conferences, often
reflecting on issues that had interested the School Board Clerks'
Association also. In 1899 he moved a resolution, overwhelmingly
supported, that it was unjust to rate Board Schools, and in so
variable a way as between areas, while voluntary schools were
exempted.[100] His final interjection was in 1900, when he complained its committees were not necessarily representative of the
Association as a whole. He claimed that the Executive Committee
was taking too much into its own hands in respect of an internal
proposal, for conference purposes, to associate boards in districts,
with each cluster rather than each board sending representatives,
presumably to reduce pressure on space. Representation, Adams
contended, was the very life of the Association. 'Once the Executive did not represent the country, fairly and fully, then the Association, instead of talking about some Boards not going in, would
very soon hear of some Boards going out.' ('Hear, hear,' and
laughter) He admired the ability of the platform very much, but
possibly there was as much ability in the room as well (laughter)
for although he liked to be governed, he did not like too much of
the grandmother in it (laughter)'.[101]

THE ACHIEVEMENT OF J.F. ADAMS

John Frederick Adams died from stomach cancer on 18 August
1901, his prolonged and painful illness having rapidly worsened
during the summer. At his funeral, attended by W.B. and J.W.B.
Adams, but not Richard Adams, the Rev. Fotheringham, an old
acquaintance on the School Board, said that he preferred to draw
a veil over Adams' religious views, which were 'something between
himself and God, but he died in God's service.... Neither would
he lift the veil to disclose the happiness of his family life'. The

most heartfelt tribute was from one of the later members of the School Board, S. Dash, for a short time its Chairman: 'full of energy, alert in duty, untiring in work, he is with us still – we hear him speak in indignation in the presence of wrong; we see his flashing glance as, with restless sarcasm, he withers a false doctrine, or denounces a glaring inconsistency.... The cool, placid face, which lit up with recognition as he passed us on the side-walk, could become a lashing picture of power when confronted with any attempt to destroy or impair the thoroughness of educational work.'[102]

The local newspapers were as one in their praise referring, among other things, to Adams as one of the Tottenham ratepayers' 'most shining lights', having saved them many times from having to put their hands in their pockets 'to avoid litigation'. He was described as a man who 'possessed in a larger degree than is vouchsafed in many of us the power of analysing the character and traits of his fellow men – of him it may be said that he never halted between two opinions ...', and as an active force in the field of politics, a man who espoused the Liberal cause, though in his later life as one 'of the older school', not following 'the tenets of modern radicalism'.[103]

At both metropolitan and national levels, further tributes poured in. The *School Board Gazette*, for example, received with 'extreme regret' the news of Adams' passing. It recorded that during his 22 years at Tottenham he had 'vigorously discharged the duties of his position, bringing into play an apt intelligence, a ripe experience (for he was once an experienced schoolmaster), and a love for his work, which have earned for him in Tottenham and elsewhere the esteem of a wide circle of friends'.[104] Both the obituarist and the editor of the *School Board Chronicle* also paid homage to one who was through his own educational history and legal training 'the ideal School Board Clerk'.

Mr. Adams has for many years been a figure of distinction, and a strong, characteristic personality, in the public life and work of education. At first a teacher, his great faculty for administration found a congenial sphere, and his expert knowledge a wider scope and opportunity, when he became a School Board Clerk in a new and fast-growing district of Greater London. To his qualifications for the official service ... he joined the special learning and the combined quickness and certainty of intellectual movement, developed by his later studies and practice as a barrister-at-law. Of temperament combative – though at heart always kindly and well-meaning – and keen in the dialectical fray, he was a force to be reckoned with, and one, moreover, apt to be found on the winning side of the cause in which he was required to engage.[105]

The *Chronicle* reproduced in addition a fulsome series of tributes from members of the Tottenham School Board. Two quoted the remark made centuries previously about Christopher Wren: 'If they wanted his monument, look around', in this case of course to the many 'great public schools' that had been erected in Tottenham and Wood Green under Adams' clerkship.[106]

The tribute at the School Board Clerks' Association was somewhat more muted, perhaps because the subsequent conference took place so long after his death. The President referred to him as one 'always ready to defend his views ... At the same time he was a chivalrous opponent in debate and a staunch friend'. The meeting was enjoined to mourn the loss of 'an able and beloved colleague in the work of education'.[107] The President had reported much earlier on a response from Kate Adams which confirmed that her husband's presidency of the Association had been 'a source of pride and gratification to him.... If anything could soften the sense of terrible loss I have sustained, it would be the kind and sympathetic expressions of genuine feeling, from those with whom my late husband was officially connected in the great work of education'.[108]

Intensely embroiled, like his elder brother, in all the advances pioneered by the progressive urban school boards such as those by which they were employed, one in London and one in Tottenham, John Frederick Adams was angered beyond measure by what he sensed would be the ultimately successful efforts of reactionary forces to subvert the achievement. He died, however, before the final blow was struck.

REFERENCES AND NOTES

1. See P.J. Prior, 'The Higher Grade Schools in Tottenham and Wood Green, 1884–1918', (unpublished University of London MA thesis, 1981), p.5; also *North Middlesex Standard and Tottenham and Wood Green Echo*, 23 Aug. 1901.
2. *Tottenham and Edmonton Weekly Herald*, 29 Nov. 1879.
3. *North Middlesex Chronicle*, 3 Jan. 1880.
4. *School Board Chronicle*, 10 Jan. 1880, pp. 38–9.
5. TSB *Minutes*, 29 Jan. and 5 Feb. 1880.
6. *North Middlesex Weekly Standard*, 9 Feb. 1900.
7. *North Middlesex Chronicle*, 12 Feb. 1881.

8. Ibid., 2 Dec. 1882.
9. *School Board Chronicle*, 20 Jan. 1883, p. 68.
10. *North Middlesex Chronicle*, 19 May 1883.
11. Ibid., 21 July 1883.
12. *School Board Chronicle*, 10 May 1884, p. 469.
13. Ibid., 15 Nov. 1884, p. 479.
14. Ibid., 7 Nov. 1885, p. 457.
15. Ibid., 13 Feb. 1886, pp. 176–7.
16. *North Middlesex Chronicle*, 6 March 1886.
17. Ibid., 25 Sept. 1886.
18. *School Board Chronicle*, 2 Oct. 1886, p. 341.
19. Ibid., 27 Nov. 1886, p. 579.
20. TSB *Minutes*, 29 Jan. 1887.
21. TSB *Triennial Report*, Dec. 1888.
22. *School Board Chronicle*, 5 May 1888, p. 449.
23. *North Middlesex Chronicle*, 1 Sept. 1888.
24. Ibid., 13 Oct. 1888.
25. *School Board Chronicle*, 23 Feb. 1889, p. 201.
26. Ibid., 2 March 1889, p. 234.
27. *North Middlesex Chronicle*, 26 Oct. 1889.
28. *School Board Chronicle*, 4 Jan. 1890, p. 9.
29. TSB *Minutes*, 11 Feb. 1890.
30. *North Middlesex Chronicle*, 3 May and 7 June 1890.
31. Ibid., 14 June 1890.
32. *The Schoolmaster*, 8 Nov. 1890, p. 694.
33. *North Middlesex Chronicle*, 11 Oct. 1890.
34. *Tottenham and Stamford Hill Weekly Times and Stoke Newington Chronicle*, 11 Sept. 1891.
35. *North Middlesex Chronicle*, 10 Dec. 1890.
36. Ibid., 13 Dec. 1890.
37. 'Auditors in Wonderland', *Punch*, 10 Jan. 1891, p. 15. A fuller account of the affair can be found in W.E. Marsden, ' "Educational Experts (?) – and the Result": the Tottenham Tellurium', *History of Education Society Bulletin*, No.51 (1993), pp. 48–51.
38. *Tottenham and Stamford Hill Times and Stoke Newington Chronicle*, 11 Sept. 1891.
39. *Tottenham and Edmonton Weekly Herald*, 2 Jan. 1891.
40. Ibid., 6 Jan. 1891.
41. Ibid., 30 Jan. 1891.
42. *Tottenham and Stamford Hill Times and Stoke Newington Chronicle*, 15 May 1891.
43. *School Board Chronicle*, 29 Oct. 1892, p. 467.
44. Ibid., 6 June 1891, p. 619.
45. Ibid., 23 May 1891, p. 540.
46. *North Middlesex Chronicle*, 7 March 1891.
47. TSB *Minutes*, 2 March 1891.
48. *North Middlesex Chronicle*, 9 May 1891.
49. PRO ED 16/213.
50. *School Board Chronicle*, 29 Aug. 1891, pp. 203–4.
51. Ibid., 29 Sept. 1891, p. 325.
52. Ibid., 3 Oct. 1891, p. 360.
53. PRO ED 16/213.

54. *School Board Chronicle*, 18 Oct. 1891, p. 391.
55. Ibid., 24 Oct. 1891, p. 459, and 31 Oct. 1891, p. 496.
56. Ibid., 7 Nov. 1891, p. 557.
57. Ibid., 21 Nov. 1891, pp. 621–2.
58. *Tottenham and Stamford Hill Times and Stoke Newington Telegraph*, 20 Nov. 1891.
59. *North Middlesex Chronicle*, 5 March 1892.
60. *School Board Chronicle*, 23 Jan. 1892, p.88.
61. TSB *Minutes*, 21 July 1894.
62. *School Board Chronicle*, 13 Jan. 1894, p.40.
63. Ibid., 28 Sept. 1895, pp. 314–15.
64. Ibid., 17 Oct. 1896, p. 378.
65. TSB *Minutes*, 12 April 1897.
66. Greater London Record Office, MCC/SB/6/9.
67. *North Middlesex Weekly Standard*, 5 Nov. 1897.
68. *Tottenham and Stamford Hill Times and Stoke Newington Chronicle*, 12 Nov. 1897.
69. *North Middlesex Weekly Standard*, 2 Dec. 1898.
70. Ibid., 16 Feb. 1900.
71. Ibid., 23 March 1900.
72. Ibid., 26 Oct. 1900.
73. Ibid., 2 Nov. 1900.
74. *School Board Chronicle*, 18 May 1901, p. 533.
75. Ibid., 15 June 1901, p. 681.
76. TSB *Minutes*, July 1900.
77. *School Board Chronicle*. 11 June 1898, p. 626.
78. Ibid., 26 May 1883, pp. 542–3.
79. Ibid., 15 June 1895, p. 663.
80. Ibid., 28 May 1898, p. 571.
81. *The Schoolmistress*, 6 April 1882, p. 308.
82. *School Board Chronicle*, 2 Oct. 1886, p. 347 and p. 363.
83. Ibid., 6 June 1896, p. 657.
84. Ibid., 30 May 1891, p. 582.
85. Ibid., 19 June 1897, p. 720.
86. Ibid., 3 June 1893, pp. 629–31.
87. Ibid., 3 June 1893, pp. 629–30.
88. *The Schoolmaster*, 27 May 1893, p. 927, and 950–1.
89. *School Board Chronicle*, 26 May 1894, p. 582 and pp. 597–8.
90. *The Head Teacher*, 9 June 1894, p.2.
91. *School Board Chronicle.*, 11 June 1898, pp. 626–9.
92. Ibid., p. 625 and p. 659.
93. *The Schoolmaster*, 4 June 1898, p. 678.
94. *School Board Chronicle*, 8 June 1901, p. 657.
95. *School Board Gazette*, 3 March 1899, pp. 232–6.
96. *School Board Chronicle*, 21 May 1898, p. 539.
97. Ibid., 11 May 1895, p. 521.
98. Ibid., 7 April 1894, p. 380.
99. Ibid., 11 May 1895, pp. 525–6.
100. *School Board Gazette*, 6 June 1899, pp. 458–60.
101. *School Board Chronicle*, 26 May 1900, pp. 568–70.
102. *Tottenham and Stamford Hill Times and Stoke Newington Chronicle*, 23 Aug. 1901.

103. *North Middlesex Standard and Tottenham and Wood Green Echo*, 23 Aug. 1901.
104. *School Board Gazette*, 3 Sept. 1901, p. 241.
105. *School Board Chronicle*, 24 Aug. 1901, pp. 199–200 and p. 204.
106. Ibid., p. 238.
107. Ibid., 7 June 1902, p. 607.
108. Ibid., 31 May 1902, p. 556.

7

Richard Adams in Swansea

EARLY YEARS

Richard Adams was the fourth and youngest son of John and Eliza Adams, and the third to make teaching his career. He was born in the master's house of the British School at Pembroke Dock on 17 April 1849. His first schooling was at Pembroke Dock, but his father moved to Goat Street when he was six, where he was a scholar and later a pupil teacher. Early in 1868 it was announced that he had been successful in winning a Queen's Scholarship, of 'substantial value', allowing two years' residence and free tuition at a training college.[1] Unlike his brothers, Richard was able to attend Borough Road, in what was to prove the only metropolitan experience of his professional career. He was allowed to do this because the 'impediment' which had previously forced young Welsh unsectarian students to attend Bangor had in 1867 been removed, a circumstance 'highly appreciated' by South Wales teachers, assistants and managers.[2]

At Borough Road he passed his examinations adequately, though his record was far from distinguished. In his first-year assessment he was one of the bottom two students, placed in the Third Division, and was one of 17 still in this division at the end of his second year. As we have seen, during his time at Borough Road he was allowed to go out on 'supply' to Finchley to take over from William Bateman, during the time of his illness. Apparently he had taken the initiative himself, as revealed in his letter written in from Finchley back to Borough Road, dated 19 September 1869, saying he had been asked

to keep school for my brother, as he is quite unable to attend to his duties in consequence of a severe attack of quinsy. I take the liberty of writing to you, as I am much concerned about one point in connection with it, viz. that you may think I am taking a liberty in not having first obtained your permission. The fact is, I was unacquainted with the matter when I left college on Saturday noon, and was therefore unable to do so.... If, Sir, you consider I have acted wrongly, it has arisen from matters over which I had no control.

The Finchley managers had also asked for him to act as a stand-in. The arrangement was allowed.

At Borough Road, Richard Adams received a prize for proficiency in drawing and developed a taste for sport. Early in 1870 he was appointed as assistant at his father's school in Swansea.[3] He was to remain in the town for the remaining 40 years of his teaching career. There is little of note to mark his time as an assistant at Goat Street that could be separated from the experiences associated with his father (Chapter 2). It would appear that he was active in union matters for a time, being a member of the Glamorgan and Llanelly District Union of Teachers.[4] As already noted, by the 1870s the Goat Street building was something of an anachronism, and its managers proposed in 1874 it be taken over by the Swansea School Board, which was agreed in 1875. He and his father were re-appointed to their positions under the revised arrangements.

The family interest in cricket was maintained, and there was an account of a cricket match between Goat Street and the National and Parochial Schools in which Richard Adams played. He was 'one of the good bowlers, taking four wickets'.[5] By the end of his time at Goat Street, Richard Adams had achieved a Second Class, Third Division certificate. The general opinion of the local press was that he helped his father to sustain the reputation of what was by then dubbed 'Adams' school'. On the closure of Goat Street the *Swansea Journal* recorded that while the schools had long been condemned, they remained high in efficiency as a result of the efforts of the Adams.[6] The *Swansea and Glamorgan Herald* welcomed the fact that they would be in charge of the new school, both 'thoroughly up to the work. The senior member of the family is ripe with experience – the junior, principal of nineteenth-century "go."'[7]

THE RUTLAND STREET YEARS

As described in Chapter 2, the children of Goat Street were marched through the centre of Swansea to their new school in

Rutland Street in April 1881. Richard Adams had been promoted to become the headmaster of the senior boys' school, while his father took on the junior boys until his death in 1883. During nearly 30 years at Rutland Street under the Swansea School Board, and then the County Borough Council, three matters loomed large. The first was the issue of School Board extravagance; the second confrontations over teacher salaries; and the third progressive curriculum change.

The Opening Years of Rutland Street Schools: School Board Extravagance

As early as 1875, the Swansea School Board was seeking a site for new schools in the central area of the town. The preferred location was on the corner of Frog Street, a notorious slum district where, it was said, the houses 'adjoining the churchyard, were in very bad condition, and must give way to the new schools' (Figure 7.1).[8] The Board completed negotiations for the Frog Street site in 1879. No doubt as a consequence of Frog Street's reputation, the schools to be built on the corner of the junction with Rutland Street were to be called after the latter.[9] By the time they were completed, the expenditure was over £12,000, £3,000 more than the next most expensive school in Swansea. The school buildings can be seen in the foreground of Figure 7.2. The cost per head of £15 16s 9d was far ahead of other provided schools. The boys' school provided accommodation for 328. It comprised a big schoolroom, two large classrooms and two smaller classrooms, a remarkable advance on Goat Street. The different rooms were separated by glass sliding doors. Standards I and II formed the junior department under John Adams, and Standards III to VII the senior under Richard. There was an infants' but no girls' school on the site. *The Swansea and Glamorgan Herald* noted that the schools were 'constructed on the newest principles and specially adapted to meet the present requirements of teaching, and the great advantage is that 340 boys can be taught in one department, and be under immediate supervision'.[10]

The perceived lavishness of the School Board's provision at Rutland Street, locally far in advance of anything that had gone before, outraged ratepayer opinion. The editors of the local newspapers voiced conflicting feelings. The *Swansea Journal* was

Figure 7.1. Slum clearance, Frog Street, Swansea

euphoric, claiming that 'for internal arrangement and external decoration' the schools were second to none in Wales.

Parsimonious individuals are inclined to grumble at the comparatively small amount that has been expended in beautifying the facade of the edifice, entirely forgetting that 'A thing of beauty is a joy for ever', and also that ornamental buildings ... are erected for almost the same amount as would have to be spent on a 'house of correction' style of architecture ... all will now be able to gaze on and admire the noble edifice, which reflects credit on the architect and honour to the town.[11]

The *Swansea and Glamorgan Herald* was more restrained, guardedly supporting the initiative, but entering the caveat that 'active steps will be taken to prevent the costly buildings just opened from being used for the education of middle-class children at the expense of the poorest ratepayers'.[12].*The Cambrian* was altogether more critical.

This new schoolhouse ... is conceived on a scale of size, ornamentation and costliness which, however satisfactory it may be to the personnel of the Board, will ill accord with the feelings and pockets of the poorer tax-payers. We quite think that beauty ought to go hand in hand with utility, and that the community must be prepared to pay something extra for the

Figure 7.2.   Pre-war aerial photograph of Rutland Street Schools, Swansea

added gracefulness, but there is a vast difference between this and what we too often see accomplished by our local authorities.

It claimed that Church opinion was correct in protesting that the school was wrongly located, with inner area populations moving out, threatening that it would be impossible to fill the school from its heavily industrialised catchment area near the docks (Figure 7.3).[13] At the same time, he conjectured that the reputation which Mr Adams had gained 'would be enhanced owing to the new splendour with which his Department was surrounded'.[14]

As part of the widespread campaign against extravagance a columnist presented an account of the balances of each Swansea Board School. He noted that the Rutland Street schools had total receipts of £391 12s 11d and payments of £785 9s 7d, giving a debit balance of £393 16s 8d. The total deficiency for all the 17 board schools was £2,604 14s 6d. He argued this was 'another proof of the freedom with which our public boards deal with the public pocket.... We are afraid our School Board has launched into an excessive expenditure which, unless the pruning knife be applied, will make the ratepayers ask whether after all they are not paying too dearly for the advantages'.[15] Countering this *The Cambrian*

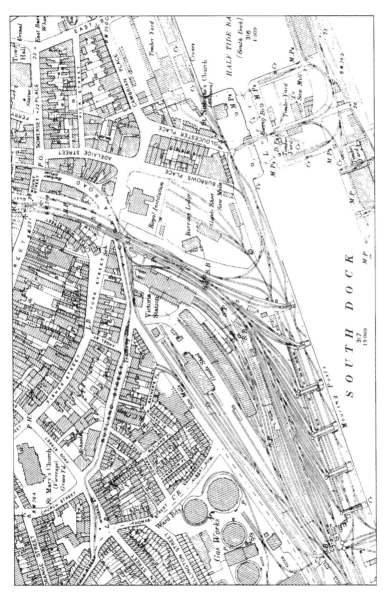

Figure 7.3. OS Map of Rutland Street area, 1890s

received an anonymous letter, signed 'L.V.', an erstwhile supporter of the Adams family and, it would seem, of the Board,
defending the construction of Rutland Street. He produced facts
and figures to suggest that in general the Swansea School Board
was not extravagant compared with counterparts such as Cardiff.
One of the problems in the Rutland Street case was the high cost
of land in the town centre, where the school was needed. In
addition, 'if a public building be erected, which has to stand in a
conspicuous part of the town for years, surely no one will object to
some form attempt at artistic display. If that be not so, then a
town would be noted for its unsightly buildings, and lose caste in
that respect'. He also defended the members of the School Board,
who had clearly no motive to squander ratepayers' money:
'Unasked their gains and martyrdom their price', he concluded.[16]

The Rutland Street issue rumbled on for many years as an
image of school board waste. In 1883, the Swansea Board was
again portrayed as matching London's in its extravagance. 'The
grand architectural structure and finely-carved walls of Rutland
Street School will ever remain a conspicuous monument to the
extravagance of those who legislate for the educational requirements of the people.' The correspondent trusted that the current
Board would soon retire into obscurity, and leave the way for
'some of Swansea's more honoured, intelligent and economical
sons, who know how to legislate in a thrifty manner for the people,
and to provide proper accommodation...'. Such opinions generally surfaced during School Board elections but more specifically
over the issue of providing higher grade schooling, criticised
locally as a 'mad experiment', designed to benefit not the working
but the 'shopkeepers and tradesmen class', thus subsidising the
education of 'higher caste' children. 'Fellow ratepayers! Will you
allow the bread to be taken out of your children's mouths to feed
the caprices or the interested acts of men ... who in their
arrogance and pride now deceive and defy you?'[17]

By 1884 the School Board rate had risen to 13 pence in the
pound, presented locally as one of the highest in Britain, and
characterised in *The Cambrian* as 'the modern education craze in is
most unreasonable and virulent form'. It reminded its readers how
Goat Street had done excellent work but had been replaced by an
expensive new schoolhouse.[18] The School Board in the following
year was said to have a majority of 'dissenters of aggressive princi-

ples, devoid of all kindly feeling for the voluntary schools'.[19] Complaints were also made about high salaries being paid to board school teachers.

The fears that Rutland Street schools would be colonised by middle-class children, or would fail to recruit enough children, both proved groundless. They were filled quickly from what was a downtrodden working-class area. Few middle-class parents would have thought of sending their children there. But the high local regard towards the Adams pair as good choices to head the new schools was at first dented by a poor initial HMI Report, the circumstances and consequences of which are recounted in Chapter 2. The situation was soon rescued, however. The percentage of passes in the three Rs for Rutland Street in 1881 had been 78.4, while the highest for any school was 85.1 per cent. In 1882, Rutland Street's figure was 85 per cent, the best in Swansea. In both these years the average for the town was just over 81 per cent. School fees over these two years increased from £155 19s 3d to £192 12s 4d, and government grant from £208 11s 0d to £269 18s 0d.[20]

Following the death of his father in 1883 Richard Adams (Figure 7.4) remained until at least the late 1880s at the Mansel Street residence, shown as it is today on Figure 7.5. Before the 1891 census, he had moved to an outer suburb of Swansea on the edge of the Gower peninsula, Mayals, at the time a scatter of residences detached from each other, still in a semi-rural setting. Here in 1891, aged 41, Adams was living with his aunt, aged 66, her husband, Stephen James, aged 57, described as a florist, and his cousin Jane James, described as 'living on her own means'. In 1893 he married this cousin, eleven years his junior, and during the 1900s moved to a new but modest terraced house in Parcwern Street (Figure 7.6), in the developing suburb of Sketty, on the west side of Swansea.

Meanwhile, the district round his school was in social decline. The rapid growth in population of the town, over 110,000 at the time of Richard Adams' death in 1910, an increase of over 20 per cent on 1901, was accompanied by environmental decay on its east side. As a general HMI Report on elementary education in Swansea noted, its surroundings were 'notoriously dreary and repellent, as the fumes from the works have deprived the naturally beautiful Tawe banks of almost all their verdure'.[21]

Figure 7.4.   Richard Adams, Headmaster of Rutland Street Boys' School

Teacher Salaries in Swansea

On the transfer of Goat Street to the Swansea School Board, Richard Adams' salary was fixed at £100 per annum. This was supplemented by night school work, for which he had to pay the Board for the use of heating and lighting of Goat Street school-room. In 1878 the Board approved a new scheme based in the usual formula of a fixed income proportionate to the responsibility. Opportunities to supplement this were given through evidence of diligence in the performance of duties, particularly in respect of securing good attendance and success in the collection for school grant, the latter having not been well accomplished under the old scheme.[22] Whether or not as a result of this scheme, the Board by

Figure 7.5.   John and Richard Adams' residence, 44 Mansel Street, Swansea

the 1880s had gained the reputation among lay people of being as extravagant over teachers' salaries as it was over buildings.

A sub-committee on salaries was appointed in 1886. In making a comparative review of payments to the headteachers of 32 school boards, it found that the average total salary bill for head-teachers was £4,866, as against £5,015 in Swansea. It recommended various reductions, particularly to the fixed rather than incentive element in the salary, which would reduce the bill by £465. By 1886 the Swansea range was from £240 to 250, as against an average, it was claimed, of £214 for England.[23] By the 1888 election, candidates were advocating new economies in School Board expenditure, including salary cuts. The incentive

Figure 7.6.   Richard Adams' residence, Parcwern Road, Sketty

one of these offered to voters was his support for 'the great scheme for the reduction of the high salaries paid to Head Teachers.... When it is remembered that many of our Head Teachers are paid over £1 per day, I think you will agree with me that the time has arrived when we should commence to cut down on such extravagance'.[24]

For the year ending September 1890, the accommodation in Richard Adams' department was 310, the average attendance was 257, and his net salary £224 15s 3d. The highest net salary, in a department of nearly 400, was £250. Yet another new scheme was proposed, to be based on average attendance rather than accommodation. This brought down the majority of the salaries of head-

teachers in Swansea. Adams' new remuneration was calculated at
£210, with a £5 bonus for obtaining the excellent merit grant,
though as that concession was not to be used in succeeding years,
it did not offer much compensation.[25] The scheme was contested
on the Board, some members feeling that old and valued servants
should not have their salaries reduced. A counter-argument was
that there was now much competition for the headships of schools,
and if they could get competent people for less, they should
reduce the amounts paid. One member argued for a £200 maximum for men and £100 for women. The scheme was agreed.[26]
Evidence was also gathered to indicate that Swansea was paying its
assistant teachers less than other boards. In 1896 it was shown
that trained assistants in London received a maximum of £155, in
Birmingham £125 and in many places £120, whereas in Swansea
the average maximum was £105. It was therefore difficult for
Swansea to attract good teachers.[27] Over the coming years there
were protests from both headteachers and assistants about the
scales paid in Swansea, always faced with resistance from a Board
on which ratepayer opinion was well represented.

During 1897 the National Union of Teachers' Annual Conference was held in Swansea.[28] Predictably, *The Schoolmaster* in its
reports on the conference drew attention to the salaries issue,
noting that Swansea School Board teachers fell lamentably below
the national average, though the Board ranked second to none in
its educational activity. The standard national scale was £80 to
£150 for certificated men teachers. In Swansea it was £70 to
£95.[29] Salaries did, however, increase. In 1904–5, for example,
Adams' two chief assistants were each receiving £130 per annum.

It is intriguing to compare the nature of the teaching provision
required by the old and new systems, as exemplified by Goat
Street in the mid-1850s and Rutland Street at the turn of the
century, and is illustrative of changing epochs of provision, as
categorised by J.F. Adams (pp. 175–6). In the earlier period, John
Adams was responsible for over 350 children with a pupil teacher
in charge of each section. In 1899, Richard Adams did not have a
single class under his control. Standards I and II, with 46 and 41
children respectively, were taught by two former pupil teachers,
both women. Standard III, with 53 children, was covered by a
third- and fourth-year pupil teacher, presumably supervised by
Adams. Standard IV, with 45 children, was in charge of another

ex-pupil teacher. Standard V with 57 pupils was taught by the most experienced assistant on the staff, who had been at Rutland Street from its opening, while Standards VI and VI, with 42 children together, were covered by another certified assistant. There was also a candidate teacher on probation. By old Goat Street standards, therefore, there was a very large teaching staff for less than 300 children. The ratepayers of Swansea, in which there remained many voluntary schools, were acutely conscious that the modern system of class teaching demanded greater financial support, as did the comparative approach which the NUT advocated. Teachers and their heads regularly drew the attention of the Board to the higher salaries paid in other places.

Curriculum Change

After its poor start, the Rutland Street Boys' School for a time continued to receive generally favourable HMI reports. That of 1883, for example, was again good, though weakness was pointed out in the elementary subjects in those classes which took specific subjects. 'The wisdom shown in burdening the staff with two of these extra subjects is thus open to question, especially when schools are feeling their way as regards the new regulations'.[30] The new regulations referred to were those of the Mundella Code of 1882, which instituted a complicated system of grants, basing the reckoning not on individual children but on the average attendance of the school, and offering a merit grant according to the HMI's judgement as to whether the school's overall performance was 'fair', 'good' or 'excellent'. A further grant was available on the basis of two class subjects assessed by group examination. The class subjects included one compulsory one, English, and a choice from geography, history, elementary science and (for girls) needlework. In addition grants could be achieved for individual passes in not more than two specific subjects, to be chosen from the 12 offered Code.

The HMI reports for 1884 to 1886 were again favourable, especially that of 1885, in which it was noted that the work of the two lower standards 'can scarcely be more highly praised',[31] justifying the excellent merit grant. At the same time, the school experienced the usual educational problems associated with teaching in a difficult and declining social area. It was accompanied by a gradual diminution in the enthusiasm of HMI reports. In 1887 Adams was warned by the Inspector not to strike boys' names off the registers before the facts of the case had been carefully established and the action shown as warranted, otherwise in future grants might be withheld.[32] The 1888 Report also suggested a falling off, 'due to inferior work in the elementary subjects and the rather noisy manner in which the school was carried on'.[33] At the end of the 1880s, of 350 children at the truant school at Bonymaen, 97 were from Rutland Street, the next highest number from a single school being 49. By 1894, Bonymaen had been opened for 12 years and of the 615 children sent there from Swansea schools, 117 were from Rutland Street, the next school being a poor Catholic school with 83, and the next Board School having sent 53. Between 1889 and 1891 the value of local prizes won by the boys' department declined from £14 6s 0d to £6 6s 0d, while grants for average attendance also declined, from £259 2s 10d in 1889 to £195 6s 0d, though that could have been explained by a fall in scholars from 342 to 295.[34] The HMI Report of 1890 indicated that the excellent merit grant had been awarded 'with some hesitation. . . . The general discipline is perhaps good in a military sense, but truer discipline could be more easily maintained by a less showy and noisy demonstration of authority'.[35]

The Reports of the early 1890s were generally less than enthusiastic. That of 1893 referred to an 'inferior set of boys in the first standard', in which order, recitation and reading were seen to be a 'little backward'. Adams wrote to the Board asking that the School Management Committee should have their attention drawn to this fact, affirming that the Report did not reflect in the slightest degree on the teaching imparted but on the 'indifferent class of boys admitted'. Thirty-three of them, in fact, had never attended an infant school.[36] In 1895, however, Rutland Street received the excellent merit grant and, though inspected, was exempted from examination in the following year.[37]

The 1890 Code abolished grants for the three Rs, and is generally recognised as putting an end to the worst aspects of the payment by results system. The fixed grant was raised, the merit grant was confined to discipline and organisation, and examinations controlled only the grants for specific subjects and those associated with the work of the Science and Art Department. There was general support for improving the status of elementary science, to be taken in Standards I to III under the label of object lessons, physical activities, and manual instruction, as well as technical subjects, grants being available for laundry work and cookery as well as needlework. Drawing became compulsory for boys in the upper departments. Singing and recitation could earn further grants. The Swansea School Board was caught up in the change. In 1890, for example, it appointed 'an able and experienced peripatetic demonstrator' of science, who took round his apparatus in a covered handcart. His lectures were supplemented by lessons given by senior assistants in the schools. Military drill, too, was being replaced by a range of physical education activities, including swimming, gymnastics and Swedish drill.[38]

Adams was discomfited by the broadening of the curriculum and relaxation of the Codes of the 1890s. He was evidently more at ease with the prescriptive nature of those of the Revised Code era, which gave prominence to the three Rs, introduced during his years as a pupil teacher. Though he was resistant to change, the power of government regulations meant that the curriculum of Rutland Street had to be broadened. During the 1890s he dutifully recorded in his log book the songs and recitations, geography and history schemes, and object lessons in elementary science to be used each year. The history programme for 1893, for example, focused on the great names and battles of British history. Gill's First and Second history books were used as texts.[39] Both geography and history followed the Code schedules. It may be conjectured that object lessons were not one of Adams' favourite curricular offerings. Under the label of elementary science they were taken as a class subject. The usual topics – domesticated animals, plants, foods, sources of energy, raw materials, natural phenomena, and the like – were included in the work of Rutland Street's Standards I to III. Object lessons had indeed raised considerable ire both in Swansea and further afield with the teaching profession, particularly when prescribed for junior departments. The National Union of Teachers ran a strong campaign against their introduction. They were regarded by *The Cambrian* as representing educational luxuries, resisted by all the schoolmasters. 'The masters were practical workers: the members of the Board were only theorists and faddists.' Some School Board members were critical. One queried whether his peers knew what object lessons were. He considered them almost useless – physical exercises and drill got better results. 'What children required was a sound, solid and thorough instruction, and not a smattering of everything, and of certain subjects which could prove of no earthly use to them.' Some argued they were a good basis for technical education. Most apparently thought not.[40] Richard Adams was publicly silent, though privately vitriolic about the changes.

After the 1902 Education Act, the school became Rutland Street Council School. Accommodation was a problem as this was a crowded area, with few free sites for building.[41] HMI Reports for the early years of the century were good, though the log book records difficult professional relationships with certain staff. Adams became irascible with his two senior colleagues whom he criticised for regularly leaving early, arriving late and being absent without explanation. One he accused of filling in the time book wrongly, and was told in turn he was making a fuss about nothing.[42] He was also angry that he had to assemble this teacher's class in the playground himself, and take them to prayers, which Adams regarded as not his responsibility.[43]

Adams' teaching philosophy and practice were increasingly seen as reactionary in the curriculum changes of the 1900s. The post-School Board codes for the first time gave expression to an official conception of what were the purposes of the elementary school: a set of aims and objectives. They demanded what for their time was a broad and balanced curriculum, covering most of the subjects demanded by the National Curriculum over 80 years on. Adams was by now too set in his ways to adapt successfully to the new ideas. The HMI Report for 1905 tersely commented that the teaching of arithmetic could be made more interesting – 'slates should be discarded'. But it agreed that the Headmaster was very successful in his main aim of achieving accuracy in the work.[44] Adams' final HMI Report, in 1909, was damning:

The school is in good order. The class teachers work steadily, and the periodical examinations are systematically carried out by the master. Unfortunately, however, the tests are of a somewhat mechanical nature and have a cramping effect upon the teaching, especially on the English side. The syllabus of instruction is meagre in most subjects and does not emphasise those modes of treatment which would develop the boys' intelligence, increase their powers of observation, and give them a livelier interest in what they are learning. It is believed that the teachers are capable of doing excellent work if a more liberally conceived programme was set before them.[45]

RICHARD ADAMS: THE VERDICTS OF HIS PEERS

Richard Adams died from a cerebral haemorrhage just short of his sixtieth birthday in April 1910, having suffered for some months from severe debility. He had been granted two months' leave of absence on full salary. Like his father and brothers, he died in harness. There is no doubt that following 40 years' service in the town, Richard Adams had acquired a distinctive reputation, as a local historian recounted, in writing about the legendary status of Goat Street.

> The personality of the last named gentleman (John Adams) was such that the school became known as Adams' School. When he closed it down in 1881, the boys marched straight from it to a new Board school, under the care of Richard Adams, his son Dick, a Bohemian character who would have been an 'acquisition' to the Savage Club, off-duty, (who) nevertheless presided over the education of junior males with flair, dedication and discipline for many years. He was one of those for whom school-mastering was not a job, but a vocation.[46]

The obituaries were much more revealing of his character and opinions than of the content of his work. He was a man who 'brought certain views and predispositions' to the work of education, wrote the editor of *The Cambrian*. Much was made of Richard Adams being a pioneer in popularising rugby football in South Wales, and of him standing on the touchline with notebook in hand, keeping a minute record of every match Swansea played.[47] A schoolmaster 'of the old type', but with 'a bright and breezy disposition', he was for many years a sports reporter for the *South Wales Daily Post* and *South Wales Echo*, and 'Dick' was noted in the press box for his 'ever proffered snuff-box'.[48] He was also well-known as an athlete and cricketer, excelling as a bowler of the 'lob' variety. Though interested in team games in general, he referred to cricket as 'the king of sports'.

The *Herald of Wales* noted that with Richard Adams' passing 'one of the very last links which connects Swansea's old educational system with the modern system snapped'. The association of the Adams name with Goat Street and Rutland Street for so many years gave Richard Adams a patriarchal status: 'people wondered when on earth he was going to finish'. He held a particular affection for Goat Street, mention of which would bring a sparkle to his eyes, and he recounted that he was the last to leave in the 'celebrated exodus' from the old school: 'the reverberating bang of the door as he closed it for the last time always rang clear in his memory'. His reactionary nature was not ignored in this obituary. 'Mr. Adams, at any rate in recent years, was a confirmed cynic, and was the possessor of a dry and caustic fund of humour. He was absolutely immovable in his likes and dislikes. . . . He detested cant and humbug, and the blunt outspoken manner in which he made his opinion of these things vocal often obtained him enemies.' He was convinced of the superiority of the country-bred over the 'anaemic and unreliable' town-bred. He was conservative in his ways, if not in his politics.

He abhorred changes of any kind, even in the school curriculum. One of his sayings was that teachers, guides and codes were generally compiled by scholastic failures. He was a remarkably strict disciplinarian and ... held very pronounced views on the efficacy of corporal punishment.... It will seem strange in the future to enter the porch of the school at any opening time, and not see the relentless figure awaiting the loiterers.... He did not like the modern system of education, and made no scruple in avowing the fact. In his view, better men were turned out under the old. As to the modern principle of 'moral 'suasion', it was to him a thing accursed.[49]

The editor of the *Cambrian Daily Leader* was notably supportive of Richard Adams' educational philosophy, again linking him with a better past, seeing the bald three Rs curriculum as linked with 'thoroughness in the instruction.... When, for instance, we contrast the beautiful handwriting of some of the old Goat Street scholars of fifty years ago with the slovenly calligraphy which is general today, the conclusion is forced upon the mind that the youngsters were not permitted to waste the time either of the teachers or of themselves'.[50]

This was an appropriate epitaph for the likes of Richard Adams, who was content with local respect, while his older brothers were achieving fame on the broader metropolitan and national stages. It was noted in Richard Adams' obituary that his eldest brother, Henry, had been a successful merchant in the United States, and had died recently in London. He 'was supposed to have left Richard a large fortune, the amount varying with the imagination of the particular retailer of the gossip'.[51] In fact at his death Richard's estate amounted to £639 6s 3d, well short of the legacies his two London teaching brothers passed on to their spouses. Both territorially and temperamentally he seems to have remained distant from them. Whether his demonstrably narrower educational outlook was a matter of personal ability and outlook, or whether it stemmed from the more restricted educational environment in which he passed his professional career, must be a matter for conjecture. Probably it was a reflection of both.

REFERENCES AND NOTES

1. *Swansea and Glamorgan Herald*, 25 Jan. 1868.
2. *Cambrian Daily Leader*, 5 July 1867.
3. *Educational Record*, Vol.8 (1870), p. 78.
4. *Swansea and Glamorgan Herald*, 21 Oct. 1874.
5. Ibid., 28 August 1878.
6. *Swansea Journal*, 9 April 1881.
7. *Swansea and Glamorgan Herald*, 6 April 1881.
8. Ibid., 20 Oct. 1875.
9. Ibid., 12 March 1879.
10. Ibid., 6 April 1881.
11. *Swansea Journal*, 9 April 1881.
12. *Swansea and Glamorgan Herald*, 6 April 1881.
13. *The Cambrian*, 1 April 1881.
14. Ibid., 15 April 1881.
15. Ibid., 17 May 1882.
16. Ibid., 1 Dec. 1882.
17. Ibid., 24 Aug. 1883.
18. Ibid., 28 Nov. 1884.
19. Ibid., 27 March 1885.
20. PRO ED16/397.
21. PRO ED91/6.
22. SSB *Triennial Report*, Nov. 1879.
23. *The Cambrian*, 29 July 1887.
24. Ibid., 23 Nov. 1888.
25. SSB *Minutes*, 3 Feb. 1890.
26. *The Cambrian*, 28 Feb. 1890.
27. SSB *Minutes*, 2 May 1896.
28. *The Schoolmaster*, 27 Feb. 1897.
29. Ibid., 10 April 1897.
30. Rutland Street Board School Log Book, 1883 insert.
31. Ibid., 1885 insert.
32. Ibid., 1887 insert.
33. Ibid., 1888 insert.
34. PRO ED 16/397.
35. Rutland Street Boys' Board School Log Book, 1890 insert.
36. SSB *Minutes*, 18 Oct. 1893.
37. Rutland Street Boys' Board School Log Book, 1895 insert.
38. J.A. Weaver, 'The Development of Education in Swansea, 1846–1902' (unpublished University of Wales, Swansea, MA Dissertation, 1957), pp. 220–30.

39. Rutland Street Boys' Board School Log Book, June 1892.
40. *The Cambrian*, 2 Dec. 1892.
41. PRO ED 16/398.
42. Rutland Street Boys' Board School Log Book, 28 Oct. 1903.
43. Ibid., 2 Nov. 1903.
44. Ibid., 1905 insert.
45. Ibid., 1909 insert.
46. W.C. Rogers, *A Pictorial History of Swansea* (Swansea: Gower Press, 1981), p.98. 'The Savage Club' in London included many literary figure, for example, Charles Dickens, and claimed to have in common being unfettered by society's conventions, believing in individual freedom of choice and expression.
47. *The Cambrian*, 15 April 1910.
48. *South Wales Daily Post*, 9 April 1910.
49. *Herald of Wales*, 16 April 1910.
50. *Cambrian Daily Leader*, 11 April 1910.
51. *Herald of Wales*, 16 April 1910.

Part 3
THE THIRD GENERATION

8

John William Bateman Adams in London and Pembrokeshire

EARLY YEARS

John William Bateman Adams was born in Finchley on 11 June 1868, the only child of William and Mary Adams. From the age of 11 he attended a middle-class school, Marylebone Philological School (later Marylebone Grammar School, and now an office building) (Figure 8.1), not far from the family home in Lorne Gardens. The school had been founded in 1792 for the sons of clergymen, army and navy officers, professional men, and others of similar class in reduced circumstances. In 1856 it moved into a new building in Gloucester Place, 'very handsome and appropriate', not least because at that time there was ample playground space, 'a means of physical education which, in our crowded metropolis, can hardly be too highly valued.'[1]

In 1868, D.R. Fearon described the Philological School to the Schools' Inquiry Commission (Taunton Commission) as one of the best examples of the second grade of middle-class day school in his district. A notable characteristic was the good discipline, achieved without the use of corporal punishment. Fearon also approved the stress on arithmetic and mathematics as part of a broader curriculum, which included Latin, Greek, French and German, as well as geography, history, drawing, chemistry, and elements of natural philosophy, giving a general education for boys until the ages of 16 or 17. He was particularly impressed by the annual examinations run by independent examiners, linked with public prizegivings. Every boy in the school was ranked by marks which reflected not only actual achievement in the examination,

Figure 8.1.   The former Marylebone Philological School

but also diligence and good conduct. Some boys went from the school to finish their secondary education at the City of London School.[2] It also provided a point of contact with the elementary system in that some of the London School Board's scholarship holders were able to take up places at the Philological School.[3]

The school was run on meritocratic principles. Thus the 1875 prizegiving was presided over by the famed Henry Fawcett, MP, formerly Professor of Political Economy at Cambridge, who testified to the value of examinations, on the grounds of educational merit 'superseding political jobbery and family patronage'.[4]

There were two groups of entrants to the school.[5] Foundation Scholars, who paid £3 per annum, were restricted to the sons of clergymen, naval and military officers, professional men, merchants, manufacturers, clerks in public offices, higher orders of tradesmen and other persons of an equally respectable class of society whose families had been in better circumstances, and were reduced by accident or misfortune. Secondly, contributory scholars paid 10 guineas per annum. The fees were regarded as sufficient to exclude lower middle-class parents, and appropriate to recruiting from the solid centre of the upper middle class. Each term the boys were ranked in form league tables. The rank was determined by the number of marks obtained as a reward for application, regular attendance and general good conduct. Detailed marks and rankings were printed and sent to parents at the end of each term. The summer term ranking was that of the annual examination.

John William Bateman Adams was not a high flier on the evidence of these records. He first appears in the Easter 1879 rankings, then aged 11. There were about 50 boys in each form up to the Fifth. In the first form, he came 14th in the annual examination in the autumn of 1879, with 6,645 marks (as against the 9,980 of the top boy). For much of the time in his second year he was not classified, but was noted as absent for a long period 'owing to illness or other necessary cause'. In the third year, his best termly position was 15th, but he came 25th in the annual examination of 1881, with 7,970 marks (against the top boy's 14,400). In his final examination in the summer of 1882, he matched his highest form position, 14th out of 46, with 10,760 marks (as against the 17,145 of the top boy and the 1,710 of the bottom).

Adams' career path did not follow the normal one of successful Philological School pupils, which was geared to eventual entrance to the City of London School. This might have been because his scholastic record was not then distinguished, or because the greater expense of the City of London School was forbidding. It may alternatively have been a case of positive parental choice, following the family's move to Hampstead. He was apprenticed as a pupil teacher at Fleet Road in October 1883, at the age of 15. Well publicised during his time there were his regular contributions to the school's musical entertainments, as a singer and as an accompanist. On completion of his apprenticeship he applied for entrance to Borough Road Training College. In a letter to the British and Foreign School Society, dated 25 February 1887, his father made it clear that he wished him to carry on the example of his grandparents, who had both, albeit very briefly, attended Borough Road.

In his application form W.B. Adams offered assurance that his son appreciated the importance of a teacher's work and was prepared to engage in it as a Christian service, training as well as teaching the children in his care, in ensuring their acquaintance with the Scriptures without using his influence to give a particular

denominational slant. He confirmed he had suffered no serious illness, had no reason to fear any constitutional disease and had no
bodily defect or deformity. He recorded that his conduct had been
satisfactory, that HM Inspector had reported favourably on his
work, and that he had shown skills as a teacher and a fondness and
general aptness for the work. The Minister of Elm Grove Congregational Church in Cricklewood also testified to the fact John
William Bateman attended regularly that place of worship, and
had been valued for his gratuitous services as organist.

J.W.B. Adams successfully completed his teacher training
course at Borough Road, being placed in the First Division, and
played with some distinction for its cricket team. Thus in a match
against Homerton College, Homerton were dismissed for 26 with
Adams taking 5 for 13. The Borough Road fielding was good, 'two
catches by Adams at slip being very brilliant'.[6] On completion of
his course at Borough Road, John William Bateman sat for the
Intermediate BA at the University of London, but did not do well,
to the chagrin of his father, as is evident in a confidential letter,
dated 7 September 1891, to the British and Foreign School
Society. 'He sat for the inter B.A. – against my wish – and is now
ashamed of his position in the 2nd division. The classical work at
Oxford is, as you know, heavy – but I have no doubt he will profit
by the lesson. He hopes you will not publish his name in any list,
but wait till he gets his honours degree at Oxford.'

The young Adams did gain an honours degree in modern
history, in 1894 at Pembroke College, and this achievement was of
course publicised. His Oxford BA became an MA in 1897, and he
went on to achieve a London BA in 1900.[7] At Pembroke College
he was President of the College Musical Society, captain of the
cricket team and a member of the football team. On completion of
his Oxford course, he was appointed as a tutor at Borough Road,
which by this stage had moved out to its new buildings in Isleworth. He taught history, literature and classics. On 5 November
1894, W.B. Adams, by this time on the Committee of the College
himself, wrote enthusiastically to the Secretary of the BFSS.

Both Mrs. Adams, and myself, rejoice to hear of our son's appointment
at Isleworth. We feel we are much indebted to you [the Secretary] in the
matter, and we trust, and believe, that you will never have any reason to
regret your kindness. P.S. May I ask you to kindly see that his name

appears in the next issue of the 'Educational Record' as having graduated B.A. in Honours at Oxford.

On his appointment, the Borough Road Magazine, *The B's Hum*, reminded its readers that J.W.B. Adams had been a 'B' at the old hive, and suggested his presence promised well for the success of the College cricket team.[8]

THE TENBY EXPERIENCE

Appointment

Adams' experience at Isleworth brought mixed fortunes on the probably one-sided evidence of a letter from W.B. Adams to the Secretary of the BFSS dated 26 August 1896, informing him of his son's new appointment at Tenby.

My son has been appointed Head Master of the Tenby Intermediate School, a most desirable appointment in every way. .... The shabby conduct of the Principal of Isleworth was a blessing in disguise. I happened to meet General Laurie, M.P. for Pembroke, and in the course of conversation told him my son's position. The question of the Tenby School then turned up, with the result most gratifying to us all. He had his opponents at the final election: a London M.A. (Hons) Teacher of Classics at Cardiff; and a 1st Class Oxford Hons. man, a grammar school assistant. Let me add that, with the exception I have noted, my son received the greatest possible kindness from every member of the staff at Isleworth, and we shall always remember your kindness.

This was followed by another exulting letter dated 25 September, W.B. Adams having attended the opening of the new Tenby school as an invited guest. 'The day was observed as a general holiday, and the greatest enthusiasm was displayed. I enclose cuttings giving all of the proceedings with my son's speech, which perhaps you will honour me by reading. P.S. Please note his appointment in the next "Record". The title is "Principal", and not "Head Master"'.

Adams' appointment at the school was supported by testimonials from five Oxford college luminaries, including the master of Pembroke College, and from influential contacts of his father, including Lyulph Stanley. The resumption of the link with Pembrokeshire was greatly to W.B. Adams' satisfaction. The family had taken holidays at Tenby in August 1894, staying for a fortnight in a town-centre boarding house with their Oxford undergraduate son.[9] They also came with him to Tenby at the time of his appointment two years later. Though his father's personal contacts were no doubt helpful in his appointment, John William Bateman Adams brought with him unusual and perhaps unique qualifications, having been trained under two systems: the elementary school/pupil teacher/training college, and the middle-class secondary school/university. He was thus fitted for high-level teaching employment on two types of accreditation. He made this double qualification explicit in his own entry in Tenby Intermediate School brochures.

The Aberdare Report of 1881 had opened the way for Welsh Intermediate Schools, which A.J. Mundella viewed as a kind of pilot experiment offering useful intelligence before embarking on secondary provision in England.[10] Nothing was done to implement the recommendations of the Report until the 1888 County Councils Act provided a mechanism for running such schools. This was followed by the Welsh Intermediate Education Act of 1889. J.W.B. Adams thus took over a new breed of school which offered a pioneering grant-aided secondary education in the branches of art and science covered by the Department of Science and Art, in various kinds of craftwork, in commercial subjects, and in other subjects applicable to the purposes of agriculture, trade and industry. Tenby Intermediate School was established and controlled by Pembrokeshire County Council.[10]

The Council's scheme for an Intermediate School in Tenby was first mooted in 1890.[11] Over the next six years there was much criticism in the local press over delays in deciding on a site, and in planning and opening the school. In 1893, for example, the Tenby Intermediate School Committee held a meeting at a house known as Green Hill, which had been used as a private school, with an extension being built for that purpose. It was agreed it would be suitable for a master's house, taking boarders.[12] A governing body was formally appointed in August 1894. By January 1895 complaints of great delays had been reported in carrying out the preliminary work, and regret was expressed that other Pembrokeshire towns such as Narberth and Pembroke Dock would succeed in opening their schools before Tenby.[13] Indeed, the Greenhill site was only finally approved in September 1895. The building still stands, as shown in Figure 8.2. The *Tenby Observer* denounced the affair in July 1896 as 'a glaring piece of jobbery', accusing the

Figure 8.2. The former Tenby Intermediate School

governing body of maladministration, negligence, bad management and bungling of a scandalous order, and of making themselves 'a lamentable exhibition'.[14]

As the time of the opening of the school approached, it was
agreed that the headmaster be paid a salary of over £200, on top
of which there would be tuition fees of £260 and indeed the
opportunity of earning approaching £500. This scheme never
came to pass. The reality was more parsimonious. J.W.B. Adams
was appointed in August 1896, a mere month before the school
opened. He argued for an early opening to form part of the commemoration of 60 years of Victoria's reign. His first Committee
meeting was acrimonious, tensions looming large on relationships
with the county governing body and on associated financial matters.
There was a heavy deficit on the schools.[15]

Notwithstanding the looming problems, the celebratory opening
of the schools clearly merited W.B. Adams' enthusiasm, with the
Mayor and Corporation meeting at the Town Hall and processing
to the schools. Speeches giving the background to the Welsh Intermediate Education movement, and to an extent justifying the
delays in the completion of the school as the fault of non-Tenby

forces, were followed by music from the Tenby Male Voice Party. Forty children had already applied to register at the schools. Nine scholarships of £6 each, five for boys and four for girls, had been provided. Following the opening, upwards of 50 guests were entertained at the local Cobourg Hotel, to which W.B. Adams, in his capacity as Chairman of the Pembroke County Club in London, was invited, and indeed responded to the toast offered to the Club.[16]

The keynote speech of the new 28-year-old Principal was nicely tuned to the occasion.

I may say that I do not commence my professional work in Tenby as a stranger; as the son and grandson of Pembrokeshire men, who commenced their careers as teachers in the County, I venture to think that there is some degree of appropriateness in my appointment as Principal of the Tenby Intermediate Schools. I will say nothing of my father, who is present, but of my grandfather I will remark that his work as one of the pioneers of popular education in Pembrokeshire is still held in high esteem by many Pembrokeshire people.... Gallant little Wales should utilise to the utmost the present advantage over England in having an organised system of intermediate education, and we wish Tenby to take a high place in the competition.

The 'lofty peroration' was greeted with loud cheers.[17]

Running the School

The brave new world of Tenby brought Adams (Figure 8.3) daunting problems. The *Tenby Observer* continued to scorn the internal divisions which it saw as likely to undermine the work of the governing body, and also accused it of underhand practices in contravening that element of the scheme which restricted the ages of scholars who could be registered. It condemned the dangerous precedent of the school in admitting both pupils over the age of 17 and under the age of 10. The prospectus was also cited as 'a discredit to the typographical art'.[18] There were to be later lapses. In 1898, for example, the Central Welsh Board found that one of the assistant masters, an ex-elementary teacher, literally had no qualifications, and demanded that the staffing be placed on a better footing.[19] Even so, the governors retained the master for a further six months.

The school had opened with 26 boys in the Michaelmas term of 1896. Ten more joined in the Easter and two in the summer term

Figure 8.3. J.W.B. Adams, Headmaster of Tenby Intermediate School

of 1897, giving a total of 38 by the end of the school year. Of these 13 came from Tenby Wesleyan School, seven from Tenby Parochial, four from Saundersfoot Board School, five from private schools, and the rest from other schools. It was clear that parents did not intend their children to stay too long. Of this first cohort eight left in 1897, ten in 1898, nine in 1899 and six in 1900. A similar number of girls, 36, was also recruited by the end of the inaugural year. Of these 13 came from private schools, 11 from Tenby Wesleyan School, and the rest from other schools. Of this group 14 had left by the end of 1897, and 11 more by the end of 1898. The reasons most given for the early leaving of the girls were being needed at home, moving out of town, or going to work. Only two of this first group proceeded to training college.

Of just over 150 entrants whose parents' occupations were recorded between 1901 and 1910, the most remarkable feature was that the largest single group were farmers, over 25 in all, whose children no doubt made up some of the boarders. Otherwise the intake was predictable, by far the largest majority coming from respectable lower middle and upper working-class families, and very few from either upper middle on the one hand or unskilled working-class groups on the other.[20] Indeed, apart from the farming children, the socio-economic groupings of the intake were remarkably similar to those for Fleet Road, his father's school in Hampstead. While the majority of pupils were from Tenby, not all those from outside were boarders. Harrison records that some walked to their local station to catch their train into Tenby, its station conveniently hard by the school, or even came in horse-drawn trap, on bicycle, or walked between one and seven miles, on dusty or muddy roads. In 1897 Adams persuaded the governors to pay £2 for coal for the fires of a drying room to take account of these travellers to school.[21]

After a stormy opening, matters settled down for a time. Adams was to enjoy a honeymoon period in so far as relationships with the local community and press were concerned. Like his grandfather and father before him, he was adept at public relations. At the prize-giving in 1897 the Mayor, C.W.R. Stokes, drew attention to the happy looks of the children and the kindly feeling existing between them, the Principal and the staff. Adams stated that his central purpose was not to cram scholars for examinations, but to 'teach them to use their brains and think for themselves'. It was also his aim to 'try and help the children to become not only clever but good and honourable men and women'.[22] Another honeymoon was soon to follow, for in August 1897 he returned to Hampstead to marry Pauline Alberta Frank, the daughter of a naturalist residing in prestigious Haverstock Hill, a wedding which excited 'considerable local interest' and was attended by a 'fashionable company'.[23] The honeymoon involved a sea crossing via Harwich to Holland, followed by a Rhine journey.[24]

The annual report of 1898 of the Central Welsh Board on Tenby Intermediate School was 'most satisfactory and encouraging', a tribute to Adams, 'to whose untiring energy and abilities this most gratifying success is in a great measure due'. In addition to those gained at the annual examinations of the Board, the scholars had achieved over 50 successes in other public examinations. The subjects taught were English grammar, composition and literature, scripture. history, geography, arithmetic, domestic economy, Latin and French, algebra, Euclid and trigonometry, physics, drawing, shorthand, and music. It was intended to introduce book-keeping as well.[25]

The school was subject to a series of inspections by both the Central Welsh Board and the Board of Education (Welsh Division). By 1900 numbers were at their lowest point with only 48 children in the school, seven of them under 12 years of age, 19 between 12 and 15 years, 16 between 15 and 17 years, and six over 17. In this and the following year there was a marked majority of boys. Twelve of these scholars received scholarships and three bursaries which together had an aggregate value of £57. Adams' salary was by then fixed at £120 with a capitation fee of £2 for each pupil, and a house free from taxes but with rent charged. His main assistant teachers received respectively £120 and £110, with some minor perks. The Report indicated a need for an assembly hall, a chemical laboratory and lecture room, a workshop and a kitchen, though it noted satisfactory physical apparatus and facilities for recreation, and the presence of a school library.

The academic element of the Report did not, however, support the uncritical praise accorded at the annual prizegivings.

Discipline and order were quite satisfactory. The teaching that came under my notice was, in the main, sound and effective. Some of the lessons were interesting and attractive, but the pupils, on the whole, lacked animation. ... The development of the School is greatly hampered through lack of funds. If the district could only be thoroughly roused to support the School, the existing debt on the building would be soon cleared off, and the Governors would then be in a position to consider such a scheme of extension as would enable them to place the scientific and technical work of the school on a satisfactory footing.[26]

Adams was keen, as his father and grandfather had been, to see that school achievements were given full publicity. The local newspapers regularly reported successes in the Science and Art, and Central Welsh Board examinations. A variety of others were taken also, including those of the Pharmaceutical Society, the Civil Service, for apprenticehips for HM Dockyard at Pembroke Dock, Queen's Scholarships, the College of Preceptors, Pitman's Shorthand, and matriculation to the Universities of Wales and London.[27]

The growing prestige of Adams by the turn of the century was reflected in local press report that Henry Thomas, son of the Rev.

J. Calvin Thomas, late of Tenby, had been appointed as assistant master at Ellesmere School under the Tottenham School Board (where Adams' uncle John was, of course, the Clerk). Thomas had been a Queen's Scholar, and had later matriculated at London, and had passed the first and second-year certificate examinations of the Education Department in London.[28] This was followed by a letter from a grateful J. Calvin Thomas, a former Tenby minister who recently had moved to Liverpool. He thanked the paper for the notice about his son, and mentioned the debt of gratitude he owed to the school and especially to Adams. Though in Liverpool, and despite the educational advantages available there, he had continued to send five of his children to Tenby for their higher education. He confirmed that the wisdom of the course he had adopted had been demonstrated. The cost of sending them as boarders had been repaid by their results. He concluded: 'Time proves that with fair educational advantages Tenby children give a good account of themselves, and with every success the name of Mr. Adams is most honourably associated.'[29]

Adams and his governing body were manifestly less convincing on the management than on the academic side of affairs. It was reported in 1902 that the school had been fined one tenth of its government grant, a loss of £9 9s 10d. The attention of the managers, it was said, had been 'frequently called to alleged irregularities in the staff without amendment'.[30] The resource base of the school was also sub-standard. The Central Welsh Board Inspector in 1903 condemned the buildings as 'quite inadequate for school purposes'. There was still no hall, gymnasium, cookery room, field for games, nor small room for the head to receive parents, and the school remained in deficit. 'The steady increase in indebtedness is a serious feature of the financial position of this school ... it must receive prompt and large assistance in the provision of new buildings.'[31] Because of its many deficiencies, the Board of Education refused at this stage to recognise Tenby as a secondary school, and continued for some time to comment critically on its inadequate facilities and financing from the local authority.[32]

By this stage Adams was clearly jaundiced about the state of affairs, for in 1903 he applied for the post of sub-Inspector with the London School Board, together with 500 others. But he failed to gain a place even on the long short list of 45.[33] The following year, however, brought an improvement in numbers at the school to

67, with 27 girls. In general, the Central Welsh Board Inspector's report was favourable though he found the children 'somewhat apathetic and listless' in class, with in some cases the teachers working harder than the scholars. Again there was a strong complaint over resourcing, reference being made to good work being done 'under depressing conditions', with 'very low salaries and no fund for repairs'. Science especially was pursued under great difficulties, with laboratory space for only six pupils.[34] By the end of the 1904–5 session the school had achieved recognition by the Board of Education as a Secondary School and Pupil Teacher centre. The latter responsibility in particular created great pressure on staff, and good staff could not be retained at the salary rate then in vogue.

Over the years, Adams' addresses at annual prizegivings, outlining his educational philosophy and management style, were regularly reported in the local press. In one he expounded a basic element in his preferred educational practice, namely that nothing could properly be learned by a pupil unless he had thought it over in his own mind. Information that was simply given to children, so that they did not think about it afterwards, was just so much useless lumber. The important point was to get children to understand what they were doing.[35]

In the quest to keep up numbers, Adams was not infrequently in trouble with the County authorities for admitting pupils who did not have the requisite Standard V qualification for entry. The correspondence between Adams and Haverfordwest was often marked by hand-written frustration on his part and starchy, typed, bureaucratic responses from the County. Apart from the question of admitting unqualified scholars, there were minor disputes as to who paid for what and appeals for loans. A not uncharacteristic exchange was when it was reported that Adams, having written to the Director of Education requesting further information in regard to the training of pupil teachers and monitors at the school, was told that the Education Committee declined to consider the letter, and resolved that all correspondence must come through the clerk of the school.[36]

Numbers improved, however, with 78 pupils (38 girls) in 1905, 84 (35 girls) in 1906, and 74 (34 girls) in 1907. Usually about six or seven of these were boarders, and a similar number was found approved lodgings. Round about half the children over this period

were between 12 and 15, and the large majority were recruited
from public elementary schools. Adams' basic salary was no
greater in 1907 than in the late 1890s, though he was receiving a
higher capitation fee for pupils. By 1907 the accommodation
situation had improved, with a new and excellent laboratory,
demonstration room and large hall. There was still a pressing need
for a larger maintenance allowance in order to offer higher
salaries.[37] A new workshop and kitchen were brought into operation in 1908, but there was still no staffroom for the mistresses
and the sanitary arrangements for girls remained poor.

Reports on the teaching of particular subjects were generally
good, if not uniformly so. In the 1909–10 triennial Welsh Board
Inspection Report, Adams' teaching of the upper school history
was praised as being 'most scholarly, combining a broad grasp of
principles with the essential details. The methods of instruction
are excellent, and include constant reference to historical and
other atlases, and the use of original documents; while wall
pictures and standard works convert the classroom into a real
history room'. In the lower forms, however, it was suggested that
a 'more modern method of instruction', basic work on local
Pembrokeshire history then social, constitutional and political
contexts, should be initiated. The science programme gave some
cause for concern, and the geography was criticised for not being
'sufficiently educational and scientific in character'. With the new
rooms in operation, the work in practical subjects was considered
favourably.[38] Adams himself indicated that he adopted a biographical approach to history, with some reference also to local history.

The Board of Education Welsh Department's Inspector remained dissatisfied despite the improvements in accommodation.
In a report on the Pupil Teacher Centre which formed part of the
school's provision, he made scathing comment about the salaries,
which he regarded as insufficient to retain qualified teachers.[39]
There seemed consistently to be at least two changes of staff per
annum, which made continuity of teaching difficult. For the third
time the Report commented on problems of poor County support
and the millstone of the school's £700 bank overdraft.[40] Matters
worsened from November 1909, when there was a complaint from
the Pembrokeshire authority that the governors of the school were
not making loan repayments regularly. Governors' meetings
became increasingly acrimonious. The local press was rigorously

excluded, though a good deal of information on the situation 'leaked out'.[41] The governors defended themselves to the authority on the grounds that the recent inspection had made yet more demands for equipment, which they could not finance. They queried whether they could afford to carry on the running of the schools, with an increasing overdraft and expenditure exceeding income by £150 per annum. They demanded a grant to wipe out the overdraft and to carry out the work demanded by the inspectors.[42]

Again, during this period of stress, the *Tenby Observer* was more than positive about the school's progress, writing of the already extensive modernisation of the school buildings at the opening of the new practical facilities in 1908. At the school's prizegiving Adams pointed out that in these new facilities the boys would learn how to make furniture and the girls to cook. The cookery room would be opened to the public for evening classes, but 'with reference to the laundry, they were not in a position to give any definite information as to whose washing they were prepared to take in ...' (Laughter). The former Mayor, C.W.R. Stokes, opined that the way to make a happy man was to cook well and iron his shirts without badly mangling them.[43]

The Writer of Textbooks

Like his grandfather, who had published some mathematical cards, and his father, who had produced a pair of history textbooks, John William Bateman Adams engaged even more enthusiastically in textbook-writing. During his Tenby period he wrote history textbooks about the Stuart and Hanoverian periods, and English texts on William Shakespeare and Sir Walter Scott. For his *Illustrative Histories,* as in that on the *Stuart Period,* the objective was to use the material to complement standard history textbooks, supplying fuller and more picturesque detail than was the norm, which Adams described as 'somewhat colourless and dry', making it difficult for the pupil to realise 'the actuality of persons and events'. The materials were also designed for private study, history being seen as a subject 'peculiarly adapted' to such an approach. The 'habit of consulting detailed works, and constantly verifying references' were regarded as precursors to taking part in discussions and writing essays. Other stated intentions were to lead the boys 'by degrees to take a real and active interest in their work and think it over in their minds for themselves', and to provide 'illuminating sidelights on character or social custom, which, properly subordinated, are absolutely essential for an intelligent interest in so human a study'.[44] Thus on the Stuart period he selected extracts not only from contemporary historical sources but also from novels and legends, the criteria of choice of documentation being qualities of narration and fine examples of English literature. As well as using extracts from Neal's *History of the Puritans*, and Stowe's *Chronicles*, his Tudor materials included Scott's *Fortunes of Nigel*. Visual illustrations were also inserted.

His English literature texts were contributions to a series entitled *Carmelite Classics*. In his commentary on Shakespeare's *King Henry IV, Part II*,[45] he stressed that it was intended for pupils and not for teachers. It was but 'lightly annotated', with notes only on such matters as would be unreasonable for the pupil to work out for himself. The publication included a glossary, an appendix and questions. That on Scott's *The Lay of the Last Minstrel*[46] included a biographical introduction, the text of the poem, a bibliography, an illustrative sketch map, a glossary of terms and words, and questions. The *Tenby Observer* also recorded other texts of Adams as including *Heroes of Mediaeval England* and *Historical Plays*.[47]

Extra-curricular Contributions

School Prizegivings and Entertainments

Jack (as he was known at this time) and Pauline Adams established their reputations in the town not only through their running of Tenby Intermediate School, but also in their extra-curricular contributions. Pauline Adams helped to run the residential accommodation. Soon after her arrival in Tenby she was noted in local newspaper accounts for the 'substantial and well-served' teas she provided at end-of-term entertainments and prizegivings.[48] These were built up into major public celebrations of the progress of the school under the patronage of the Mayor of Tenby. That in December 1898 was performed before an 'enthusiastic and appreciative audience', and was run 'without the slightest hitch of any kind'. The occasion was enhanced by 'the artistic decorations arranged by Mrs. J.W.B. Adams and her staff of willing helpers'. The entertainment consisted of songs, instrumental solos and recitations and, as the high spot of the occasion, a 'musical fairy extravaganza' entitled *The Ace of Hearts*, again managed by Pauline Adams, who was responsible for the designing and making of the costumes.[49]

The precedent was set and in the following year another public entertainment was held in the Royal Gatehouse Assembly Rooms. Equally well received, it was the occasion of a dramatic public demonstration when, in *The Jolly Sailor Boy*, a romantic play, the point at which the Union Jack was unfurled coincided with a report of a success in the Boer War, which moved the audience 'to the wildest enthusiasm ... a remarkable exhibition of patriotic feeling that interrupted the proceedings for some minutes'.[50] National fervour was indeed intense as vigorous recruiting was taking place for the Pembrokeshire Company of the Imperial Yeomanry, about to embark for service in the Boer War. Notably patriotic himself, Adams took part in a concert to raise funds for the war. He was also present at the farewell dinner for the Pembrokeshire troop.[51]

The Boer War victory was followed by a decade in which imperial sentiment rose to fever pitch. In 1908, the Tenby authorities invited 780 local children to an Empire Day ceremony at the Royal Gatehouse Assembly Rooms. Teachers marched their pupils through the streets to the town centre. The room was decorated with flags and slogans like 'Honour the Flag' and 'One King, One Flag, One Empire'. The Mayor gave the address, and reminded the children of their indebtedness to the Empire. Lord Meath, the founder of Empire Day, had forwarded a message to be read out. Each individual's action, he demanded, should help in 'elevating the British character, strengthening the British Empire, and consolidating the British race'.[52]

The dramatic entertainments offered by the Intermediate School continued through the Edwardian period until the end of Adams' tenure in Tenby. All were well reported in the local press, and Pauline Adams' contributions were praised, as in 1903, when a play and a short programme of music were followed by a repeat of *The Ace of Hearts*, which caused 'a constant ripple of laughter among the audience'.[53] One of the best received was that of 1908, which included two fairy plays, *The Dream Lady* and *Rumpelstiltzkin* (Figure 8.4), the performances of which were said to reflect 'the greatest credit on Mrs. Adams who was loudly cheered on the fall of the curtain'.[54]

Figure 8.4.   A Christmas entertainment at Tenby Intermediate School

Social Activities in Tenby
In addition to these school entertainments, Adams and his wife
occasionally took part in amateur theatricals in the town as well,
performances taking place also at the Royal Gatehouse Assembly
Rooms, before large and fashionable audiences. In a play entitled
Local Talent, about student life in Heidelberg, for example, Jack
Adams played the part of a celebrated baritone from the local
opera house, while Pauline was one of the peasant girls.[55] On
another occasion he starred as Hardcastle in *She Stoops to Conquer*
doing it 'the fullest possible justice'.[56]

Over time, the Adams had become accepted in Tenby high
society and participated in the annual January Tenby Hunt Week
celebrations, which, as in 1907,[57] included two balls, two meets of
hounds, a Hunt Breakfast, and theatrical entertainments. In 1908,
The Pirates of Penzance by Gilbert and Sullivan and a musical comedy, *Lady Selina of K*, were performed. In the former Adams was
the Pirate King, his execution of the part praised as 'very realistic
... making capital use of his voice in meeting the many demands
made on it'.[58] In the same year there were two meets of the
hounds which Pauline Adams attended, albeit 'not on horseback',
but with the party 'in carriages and motors'. At the Fancy Dress
Ball that year she came as 'La Cigalle', with Jack Adams in
evening dress. Over 200, including the Adams, attended the fol-

lowing Hunt Ball. Dancing began at 9.30 and extended into the early hours of the Saturday morning.[59] In their last years in Tenby one or both of the Adams were also recorded as in attendance at the customary Hunt Breakfast at Lydstep, the home of Lord and Lady St. David's.

Cricket was another leisure interest Adams brought with him to Pembrokeshire. He was a founder member of the Tenby Cricket Club. His first match, against the Royal Artillery, was his most successful of the inaugural 1900 season, for he scored 27 out of 95 in a victory which owed most to his 'very fine exhibition of batting'.[60] In 1903 he was proposed as Secretary but declined the responsibility, somewhat reluctantly agreeing to become Joint Secretary. He deplored the fact that the team still did not have a field fit to play on, nor a pavilion decent enough to keep its gear in. Visiting teams had complained about the lack of facilities. The grazing of sheep made playing almost impossible, while the lack of a proper scorer was another disadvantage.[61]. The following year Adams and his fellow joint secretary resigned, and in the absence of anyone willing to take over, the club was disbanded. The other Tenby team, the Wanderers, then renamed itself Tenby United.[62]

Adams was recruited by the new club which from 1905 joined the just-established Pembrokeshire Cricket League. Noting that he had played in the first match of the following 1906 season, the local reporter expressed his pleasure 'to see Mr Adams turning out to give us a hand. I have seen him pull many a match out of danger, and I hope his first taste of cricket this season will have the effect of making him hunger for more'.[63] One of his most successful days of the 1907 season occurred in the game against Narberth in May. Adams scored 23 not out in a total of 134 for 4 declared and took four wickets as the opponents were dismissed for 32. His innings was described as showing 'sound defence and only punishing the loose ones'. In bowling, the 'slow enticers' of Williams and Adams 'simply played havoc with the later batsmen'.[64]

After the end of the 1907 season, the *Tenby and County News* began to publish the Tenby club's seasonal averages. Adams had played eleven innings, was once not out, and scored 100 runs, making him second in the averages with 10. His highest score was 23 not out. He took 10 wickets for 44 runs, averaging 4.4, making him 4th in the team's averages, and 5th in the number of wickets. He was the joint top fielder with seven catches. The Tenby team won the county title for the first time.[65] He made a good start to the 1909 season also, during which he made his best-ever score, 'a magnificent 69 not out' out of a total of 177.[66] He ended up third in the team's batting and 11th in the bowling.[67] Tenby again won the Pembrokeshire Cricket League The Chairman at the annual dinner was G. Lort Stokes, Town Clerk and son of the former Mayor, who was destined to become the second husband of Pauline Adams. Adams himself was there to offer one of the toasts.[68]

Another initiative of Adams was an attempt to establish lectures in Tenby as part of the University Extension Movement. In November 1902 he was asked to organise a free 'pioneer' lecture to whet local appetites for a full course after Christmas.[69] The first sessions, illustrated by magic lantern slides, was entitled 'Animal Life in Relation to its Surroundings'.[70] Audiences were described as appreciative but not as large as was needed, and by February 1904 Adams was reporting a deficit on the season's lectures.[71] As part of his Extension work Adams was also involved for a time as Honorary Secretary of a sub-committee to form a Natural History Society, to arrange winter indoor meetings and summer outdoor excursions. One of the latter was to the geologically outstanding south Pembrokeshire coast at Skrinkle Haven.[72] Later in the year University Extension lectures in geography, and Natural History Society lectures were reported. At the end of the former series regret was expressed that audiences had not been larger.[73] The Annual Report suggested that they averaged between 60 and 70. The associated Library was said to be much in demand. But Adams complained that on the evidence of two years it did not seem that Tenby residents were enthusiastic about the lectures. He was reappointed as Honorary Secretary,[74] but the initiative was to be short-lived.

Leaving Tenby

Adams resigned his Tenby post in December 1910, having been appointed as headmaster of a new secondary school in the growing suburb of Ashford, Middlesex. The *Tenby Observer* described the lavish – by Tenby standards – provision of the Ashford school, located in 'the centre of a very populous district, with a fine climate, a sandy soil and excellent golf links'.[75] Adams expressed his regret at leaving, but stated firmly that 'if I am ever to obtain preferment, I must perforce do so now, as before long my age will begin to tell against me in my application for higher posts'.[76] He returned with Pauline in May 1911 for his official presentation, before staff, pupils, parents and friends of the school at the Royal Gatehouse Assembly Rooms. The former Mayor and a member of the school governors, C.W.R. Stokes, presided, and paid lavish tribute to Adams' dedication and skill, and determination to inculcate good principles, 'most ably supported by his dear wife', who had 'a marvellous power with children'. Both of them he claimed had a deep appreciation for Tenby, though he agreed the school did not offer full scope for Adams' abilities. He had 'encouraged cricket, football, hockey and many other games which created manliness. There was nothing, in the speaker's mind, so disgraceful as an effeminate boy . . .' (Applause).

The speeches on this occasion hardly went beyond conventional public plaudits, and do not give a true feel of the Tenby experience of John William Bateman and Pauline Adams, nor of how they were seen by their pupils and others. More helpful are the oral records of old pupils who knew John William Bateman and his wife, which can be found in Wilfred Harrison's book. Among other things they provide interesting insight into the boarding arrangements in the Adams' household. Though the school house offered fairly commodious accommodation, a former boarder wondered

... how two sensitive adults could have put up with the invasion of their privacy by half a dozen somewhat obnoxious stranger boys who, although to some extent segregated, even used their bathroom ... We had lunch, and were on our best behaviour, at the Head Master's table, but the other meals were judiciously timed so that we were kept out of sight. As to that bathroom – the regime prescribed for us was a cold bath every morning and it was difficult to evade, since the bathroom adjoined the Head Master's bedroom.[77]

Other former pupils had clear recollections of Adams himself, one as

... a man of considerable stature. He was an Oxford man. I do not know his origins but he certainly regarded himself as 'county' and was so regarded by the town in general. His associations were with the 'quality'.

I remember him as a very well groomed man of polished manners. He had an aristocratic manner and somehow impressed one as a man of character and culture in whose presence anything shabby or mean wilted at once ... He was kindly but strict. He maintained discipline without any difficulty.... Of an evening he would get some of the elder boys to bowl at him on the school playing field. He would place a threepenny bit on his middle stump as a bait for the bowlers. Normally, this did not cost him much....'[78]

Another remembered his music lessons:

He was a very patriotic man and constantly reproached the times in which we lived for their lack of patriotism. He strove to correct this deficiency by teaching us songs, mostly of a patriotic nature. Prominent among them were the *Songs of the Fatherland*. He feared the then increasing militarism of Germany and had, I think, little but conservative scorn for the liberalism and pacifism – and even republicanism, which at that time had gained impetus as a reaction from the Boer War.[79]

Like the rest of his family, Adams was a meritocrat, but possibly of a more elitist disposition than the others. One of his maxims was that there would always be 'hewers of wood and drawers of water'. He sought in his school to imitate the public school spirit, as his father had done at Fleet Road. The school photograph of 1897 shows the boys wearing mortar boards (Figure 8.5). He introduced the practice of pupils saying *adsum* when their names were called at registration. When rebuking pupils, he did not call them by name, but might refer to 'that silly fellow in the corner over there'. One pupil recalled that 'he taught us to love poetry. He was rather romantic and became dreamy'.[80]

On the other hand, Pauline Adams was less well liked. One old boarder remembered her 'extremely economical and inadequate catering', causing the pupils to be 'perpetually hungry'. This led to some 'fearful and risky enterprises' aimed at meeting their schoolboy famishment, including clandestine trips to the first local fish and chip shop and a local temperance hotel kept by one of the parents. Another ally was the school cook, who would make a meal of the cheap fish they bought down at the harbour, and supply them with left-overs from the day's meals. He thought that Adams was aware of his wife's miserliness, but feared scenes before the boys in the light of her 'overbearing manner'. He saw Mrs Adams as John William Bateman's 'Achilles' heel'. By contrast, another old pupil spoke warmly of Mrs Adams. 'But for her

Figure 8.5.   Tenby Intermediate School, staff and pupils, 1897

he would have been in hot water much oftener than he was, and he now apologised for all the trouble he had given her.' Yet another witness indicated that the tradesmen of Tenby were sorry that she was going, because she always gave them the first opportunity of providing supplies for the school.[81] Adams timed his leaving shrewdly. The pressure brought by poor resourcing would seem to have dimmed his enthusiasm, although his social life on the face of it still flourished. He was poorly paid. The school photograph of 1910 shows him as silver-haired, looking older than his 42 years (Figure 8.6). It was also reported that while his successor, the science master at the school, would have same fixed salary of £120 p.a. as Adams, the capitation grant of £1 10s 0d for each scholar would be reduced by 10s 0d.[82]

The Adams retained some contact for a time with Tenby, for in October 1912, on the death of C.J. Williams, a former member of the Town Council and Chairman of Governors of Tenby County School, a wreath was sent 'in loving memory' from Pauline and Jack Adams.[83] Pauline, but not her husband, was also present at one of the meets during the 1913 Hunt Week.[84] There was, however, a powerful sting in the tail of the Adams' Tenby experience. In April 1914 a Major Price Lewes, formerly of Tenby, obtained a divorce from his wife on the grounds of her misconduct with

STAFF c. 1910
back row, left to right: Mr. J. R. Roberts, Mrs. J. W. B. Adams, Messrs. J. T. Griffith and
E. J. Head, in front: Miss Gaynor R. Jones, Mr. J. W. B. Adams, Miss Gore Lindsay
photo: H. Mortimer Allen

Figure 8.6.   Tenby Intermediate School staff, about 1910

J.W.B. Adams. The pair had first met in Tenby and had subsequently, it was revealed in the divorce court, frequently committed adultery in a flat in West Kensington, London. This was at the time when Adams and his wife were residing at Hyde Park Mansions in Marylebone, and he was teaching in Ashford. Following the Lewes divorce case, Adams left his wife, even though she agreed to overlook his 'moral lapse'. But he rejected any possible reconciliation. The following exchange of letters was published in the *Tenby Observer*:

Dear Jack,
I cannot think why I have not heard from you since you left. Surely you will let me know what you intend to do. I think after all I have gone through, you might consider me a little.

His response was abrupt and unbending.

Dear Pauline,
After what has happened it is quite impossible for us to live happily together again. Since I left I have made up my mind not to return to you in any circumstances.[85]

The letters were read at Pauline's appeal for restitution of conjugal rights. Jack Adams did not defend the case and was therefore triply accused: of non-compliance, of desertion and of committing adultery. His whereabouts were apparently not known. He had either joined or was soon to join the army. A decree nisi was granted in October 1914 and the final decree in May 1915.[86]. While still recorded at her London address in a 1915 Directory, Pauline Adams returned to Tenby and was living there with her mother later that year[87] when in November she married the Town Clerk, G. Lort Stokes. It was a quiet wedding. The warmth with which it was received suggested that she was regarded in Tenby as the innocent party.[88] Wilfred Harrison, however, biographer of Tenby Intermediate School, in correspondence indicated that in his files he had information that 'Mrs. Adams was friendly with George Stokes and it was this which caused the trouble between her and Mr. Adams'. Her second marriage lasted twelve years, Stokes dying suddenly in 1927.

REFERENCES AND NOTES

1. *Illustrated London News*, 15 Nov. 1856, p. 499.
2. *School Inquiry Commission (Taunton Commission)*, Vol. 7 (1868), pp. 347–8.
3. M. Bryant, *The London Experience of Secondary Education* (London: The Athlone Press, 1986), p. 436.
4. *Borough of Marylebone Mercury*, 31 July 1875.
5. The details which follow are taken from the archives of the former Marylebone Philological School (later Marylebone Grammar School), now housed in the Westminster Record Office. A list of them can be found in E.G.B. McNeal, *St. Marylebone Grammar School: A Brief History till 1954* (1979), Appendix 7. It should be noted that the initials for Adams in the school records varied and were never given fully as J.W.B.Adams. But the chronology is correct, the family history record tells us that he attended the Philological School, so that can be assumed with some safety, if not absolute certainty, that the boy concerned was W.B.Adams' son.
6. *The Schoolmaster*, 7 Sept. 1889, pp. 307–8.
7. *Educational Record*, Vol. 14 (1897), p. 444; and University of London, *The Historical Record, 1836–1912* (University of London Press, 1912), p. 198.
8. *The B's Hum*, Vol. 5 (1894), p.2.
9. *Tenby and County News*, 8 Aug. 1894.
10. For fuller background, see W. Davies, *The Curriculum and Organization of the County Intermediate Schools, 1880–1926* (Cardiff: University of Wales Press, 1989). See also K.D. Evans, 'The Development of Secondary Education in South Pembrokeshire 1889–1939' (unpublished University of Wales (Aberystwyth) MA, 1970).
11. For fuller background, see W. Harrison, *Greenhill School, Tenby, 1896–1964: An Educational and Social History* (Cardiff: University of Wales Press, 1979), on which sections of this chapter draw heavily.
12. *Tenby and County News*, 1 Nov. 1893.

13. *Tenby Observer*, 31 Jan. 1895.
14. Ibid., 23 July 1896.
15. Ibid., 27 Aug. 1896.
16. Ibid., 24 Sept. 1896.
17. Harrison, op.cit. (1979), pp. 89–90.
18. *Tenby Observer*, 8 Oct. 1896.
19. Harrison, op.cit. (1979), p. 152.
20. Tenby County School *Admissions Register*, 1896–1910.
21. Harrison, op.cit. (1879), pp. 106–7.
22. *Tenby Observer*, 28 Dec. 1897.
23. *Hampstead and Highgate Express*, 7 Aug. 1897.
24. *Tenby Observer*, 5 Aug. 1897.
25. Ibid., 6 Oct. 1898.
26. Tenby County School, Central Welsh Board Annual Inspection *Report*, 1900.
27. *Tenby and County News*, 18 Oct. 1899.
28. Ibid., 19 Sept. 1900.
29. Ibid., 26 Sept. 1900.
30. Ibid., 26 Feb. 1902.
31. Ibid., 25 May 1903.
32. PRO ED 35/3401.
33. SBL 795, 1 May 1903.
34. Tenby County School, Central Welsh Board Annual Inspection *Report*, 1904.
35. *Tenby and County News*, 26 Dec. 1906.
36. Ibid., 9 Nov. 1904.
37. Tenby County School, Central Welsh Board Anuual Inspection *Report*, 1907.
38. Tenby County School, Central Welsh Board Triennial Inspection *Report*, 1909–10.
39. Board of Education (Welsh Division) Annual Inspection *Report*, 1908.
40. Ibid., 1909.
41. *Tenby Observer*, 14 July 1910.
42. Dyfed Record Office *Archives*, ED/2/511.
43. *Tenby Observer*, 26 March 1908.
44. J.W.B. Adams, *Illustrative History: Stuart Period* (London: Horace Marshall and Son, 1905), p.v-vii.
45. J.W.B. Adams, *Shakespeare: King Henry IV, Part II* (London: Horace Marshall and Son, 1906).
46. J.W.B. Adams, *Sir Walter Scott: The Lay of the Last Minstrel* (London: Horace Marshall and Son, 1905).
47. *Tenby Observer*, 19 Jan. 1911. These texts are not recorded in the British Library Catalogue.
48. Ibid., 28 April and 4 Aug. 1898.
49. Ibid., 15 Dec. 1898.
50. Ibid., 14 Dec. 1899.
51. Ibid., 8 Feb. and 1 March 1900.
52. *Tenby and County News*, 27 May 1908.
53. Ibid., 29 April 1903.
54. Ibid., 4 March 1908.
55. *Tenby Observer*, 18 Dec. 1902.
56. *Tenby and County News*, 22 Dec. 1904.
57. Ibid., 16 Jan. 1907.
58. Ibid., 15 Jan. 1908.
59. Ibid., 22 Jan. 1908.

60. *Tenby Observer*, 24 May 1900.
61. Ibid., 30 April 1903.
62. Ibid., 10 March and 21 April 1904.
63. *Tenby and County News*, 23 May 1906.
64. Ibid., 29 May 1907.
65. Ibid., 2 Oct. 1907.
66. Ibid., 19 May 1909.
67. Ibid., 24 Nov. 1909.
68. *Tenby Observer*, 4 Nov. 1909.
69. Ibid., 27 Nov. 1902.
70. Ibid., 22 Jan. 1903.
71. Ibid., 4 Feb. 1904.
72. *Tenby and County News*, 29 July 1903.
73. Ibid., 23 Dec. 1903.
74. Ibid., 3 Feb. 1904.
75. *Tenby Observer*, 19 Jan. 1911.
76. Harrison, op.cit. (1979), p. 172.
77. Ibid., p. 112.
78. *Tenby Observer*, pp. 114–5.
79. Ibid., p. 115.
80. Ibid., p. 159.
81. *Tenby and County News*, 3 May 1911.
82. Ibid., 11 Jan. 1911.
83. Ibid., 9 Oct. 1912.
84. Ibid., 15 Jan. 1913.
85. *Tenby Observer*, 30 April 1914.
86. PRO J77 1159/5213.
87. *Tenby and County News*, 24 Nov. 1915.
88. *Tenby Observer*, 25 Nov. and 2 Dec. 1915.

9

J.W.B. Adams: Return to England

THE ASHFORD EXPERIENCE

The new school at Ashford (Figure 9.1) was built by Middlesex County Council to supply secondary places for pupils from Ashford and the adjacent districts of Feltham, Shepperton and Staines. The school was close to Ashford station, giving good access. It was designed for 200 boys and girls. The yearly tuition fees were £6 7s 6d. The eight classrooms were built not round a central hall, but a quadrangle, with each ventilated from both sides. There was also a large hall, two science laboratories with a preparation room and dark room, a Principal's room, staff rooms and spacious playing fields.[1] (Figure 9.1) Forty-six pupils were enrolled on the first day, in January 1911, and there were 94 by the beginning of the following term, 112 by the January 1912, and 194 by July 1912. Most of the children were in the 11–16 age range, with 33 under 11, and only seven 16 and over.

According to an initial HMI Report of February 1911 the start was satisfactory, but provision was lacking for manual work for the boys and housecraft for the girls. There was also a 'grave defect' of no special dining arrangements, in circumstances in which large numbers of pupils needed to stay for a midday meal. With these provisos, the school was recommended for recognition. The social background of the parents was recorded and included 22 per cent from the professional classes, 61 per cent from the lower middle classes, and 15 per cent from unskilled occupations, with 2 per cent not given. The July HMI Report paid 'great credit' to Adams and his staff for an excellent beginning.[2] Adams quickly established a school magazine, a debating society, form libraries, a chess club, school gardens, a nature study group, and a house system. The

Figure 9.1. Pre-war aerial photograph of Ashford Secondary School, Middlesex

houses, Ashford, Feltham and Staines, were each made up pupils from the area in which they resided. Adams was described in a school history as 'tall, slim, silver-haired and blue suited with a pleasant voice and a pleasant personality.'[3] He had gained significant financial advantage from his move from Tenby. In 1913 his salary was £320 per annum, on an incremental scale of from £300 to £400, though living and travelling expenses would have been much greater in London than in Tenby. He had a regular staff of seven graduates, and two other certificated teachers, with occasional provision for physical education, art, housecraft and manual work.

Adams' stay at Ashford was to be brief. In a letter to his governors dated 13 October 1913 he resigned.

I deeply regret to inform you that in view of a nervous breakdown I am unable to continue my school duties, and in consequence am compelled to ask you to accept my resignation. I need hardly say that it is a great grief to me to have to relinquish my work here, and sever my connection with the school which I began and to which I am devoted.[4]

It would be fair to assume that the breakdown was connected with the stress associated with the divorce proceedings in which he had been named as co-respondent. There may possibly have been another reason, bound up with the report of the first major inspection in July 1913. This indicated that Adams was well liked by the pupils and had gained the confidence of the governing body. The staff were hard-working, but they were also young, adding to the headmaster's responsibilities. The 'corporate life of the school' had received careful consideration. The sting was not in the published report, however, for the governing body, in Adams' absence, was informed that the inspection team was 'not greatly impressed by the organising and teaching abilities of the Head Master, but he evidently possessed other qualities and it was necessary to take into account the great difficulties he had overcome in building up a new School with a new Staff ... the Governors at the Conference assured the Inspectors that they were well satisfied with him, and they seemed to suggest that he was a better Head Master than the Inspectors thought he was....'[5]

It may be that his governors were sensitive to the personal travail that Adams was experiencing at the time. Moving back to London from the quiet backwater of Tenby, together the travelling burden, may, too, have added to the tensions of a personal life marred by the breakdown of his marriage to Pauline, and the complications of visits to his mistress in West Kensington. On his return to London, Adams lived from 1912 to 1914 in the prestigious Hyde Park Mansions (classified earlier by Booth as in the 'yellow' or wealthy residential category), by Edgware Road Station in Marylebone. The entrance to his part of the buildings is shown as it is today in Figure 9.2. The location was not entirely convenient for his journey to school. An obvious route would have been first via the Bakerloo line, opened in 1906, from Baker Street to Waterloo, then proceeding by train from Waterloo Station. At best, the journey each way would have been at least one hour and a half.

WAR SERVICE AND AFTER

Less than a year after his nervous breakdown J.W.B. Adams enrolled for war service. A later autobiographical account of his

Figure 9.2. J.W.B. Adams' residence at 7 Hyde Park Mansions

army experience entitled *A Pedagogue's Fatigues*, which included a quote on the title page 'Most Lamentable Comedy', at least implies that he began in the ranks, enlisting in the 'fateful August' of 1914. He was at pains to stress his great impracticality, being self-confessedly 'hopeless' with his hands, stating that it had been 'extremely fortunate for my small family that it was not necessary for them to rely on my capabilities in the Mechanical Arts'.[6] He refers to either as 'hidden mysteries' or as 'inglorious experiences' or as 'boring beyond expression' activities such as hut-washing, quarrying, road mending, machine cleaning, and sewing on buttons. The implications of the later chapters are that he saw active service and was wounded at some stage in France. He describes the bitingly cold weather and the death of a private. The whole

87–page book is, however, nostalgic, whimsical and lacking in chronological detail.

There are discrepancies as between the autobiographical account and the official record. Adams states that he rose to the status of 'acting sergeant', though at his mother's death in 1918 he is recorded as a Temporary Second Lieutenant. In fact he was promoted to this rank in March 1918 and became a Temporary Lieutenant in September 1919. At a later stage he described himself as having been an Army Education Officer. The army lists reveal, however, that he was a member of the Royal Army Service Corps. The last Army List in which he was recorded was January 1922.

SARISBURY COURT

On the title page of his textbook, *School Certificate French Composition* (1932), J.W.B.Adams noted that he had been a tutor at Sarisbury Court Training College, though this is the only firm evidence of this appointment. In anticipation of the demobilisation process at the end of the First World War, a Ministry of Labour Memorandum of November 1917 specified that priority would be given as a 'pivotal class' to officers and men on the teaching staff of universities and institutions engaged in training of students over 18, before the general demobilisation of students serving in the forces.[7] Apart from the need to deal with disabled servicemen, there was also a pressing demand to engineer the huge demobilisation, vocational retraining and resettlement of millions of men and women who had served in the war.[8] The *Times Educational Supplement* noted the great dissatisfaction from all grades over the employment situation and cited the demand for adult education. The Editor argued for the establishment of links between LEAs, with responsibilities for adult education through the 1918 Act, the Army scheme for training teachers, and the Ministry of Labour scheme.[9]

In June 1918 Sarisbury Court, an imposing nineteenth- century mansion on the banks of the River Hamble, was taken over and adapted as a 400-bed American Military Hospital.[10] In October 1919 it passed from the American Red Cross to the British government, to be used for the training of disabled soldiers in agriculture. The Director of Education for Hampshire was to direct the studies.[11] By April 1920 there were 47 government instructional factories, of which Sarisbury Court was one.[12] The industrial training offered was mostly manual, but included also higher training for professional and managerial posts.[13] An element in the Sarisbury Court provision was the training college for teachers. It opened in September 1920 with 150 places, and was said to be 'well planned, equipped, and working under really good conditions for what is after all a temporary scheme'.[14]

The mature students at Sarisbury Court were generally regarded as better than the general run of training college students. There is little record of its professional activities in the local press, but some glimpse is given of the social. Sarisbury Court was well known for its large theatre and concert parties, one of its entertainments being described as 'of the highest order' with 'all tastes catered for.'[15] The students' 'high jinks ... led by a jazz band in costumes of every description' to the local village green for fireworks on a bonfire night followed by a large crowd, were tolerantly reported.[16] The following week 200 of the ex-servicemen students 'invaded' Southampton, again dressed in various costumes, collecting for the remembrance day poppy fund.[17] In the following year, it was reported that the students had a fortnight's leave to go home and undertake some teaching practice in their own neighbourhoods.[18] In March 1923 the Director of Education reported that 140 men would be released that Easter, and enquired whether any could be retained under the service of the Education Committee.[19] By 1924 the training college facility at Sarisbury Court had closed.[20]

Adams was certainly not on the first group of tutors appointed in 1920, clearly, because he was still in the army. It would seem therefore, though there is no formal record of appointment, that he could have been in the second cohort of staff appointed on the extension of the training college, occupying the buildings of the agricultural college, closed down in 1921. He possibly filled an advertised post for an English instructor.

THE CHRISTCHURCH EXPERIENCE

How J.W. B. Adams was employed between the closure of Sarisbury Court Training College in 1924 and his appointment in June 1925 at Christchurch is not documented. The old Christchurch Congregational School building was located in the centre of the town (Figure 9.3). It was something of a time-warp situation for Adams, for he was returning to a Congregational institution, the denomination in which he was brought up, and to an architectural style that predated the board school. On the face of it, it represented a considerable demotion for an Oxford graduate who had been the headmaster of two secondary schools and an army officer. No doubt he had to tailor his ambitions to the exigencies of the time, for he was re-entering teaching in a notably cost-conscious period, and one in which teaching posts, and particularly head teaching posts, were difficult to secure.

Adams' time at Christchurch was, however, for the most part to be a fruitful and indeed culminating professional experience. He had presumably been made aware at the time of his appointment that the old school was not to remain a mere elementary school. As early as 1922, the Hampshire LEA had indicated to the Board of Education that the Congregational managers had notified that the school was to be discontinued in approximately 18 months as the buildings were required them for church uses. Hampshire also reminded the Board of its existing plans to erect a council school for 300 children. The Board challenged the need, citing over 350 spare places in and around Christchurch, but acknowledged there was a religious complication to be considered. Some of the spare places were in a Roman Catholic school and others were

Figure 9.3.   Christchurch Congregational School, front elevation

inaccessible. The local HMI, in a memorandum to the Board, confirmed that in the event of forcing Nonconformist children into church schools the 'slumbering embers of religious discord would be fanned immediately into the fiercest conflagration.'

Somewhat reluctantly, the Board allowed Hampshire to proceed to build a school for 300 pupils, so long as the plans were on 'the most economical lines'. By the end of 1922 it was suggesting that while a new school was 'not unnecessary', it might in the first place be built for 200, with the possibility of a later increase to 300. It was as late as March 1924, however, that the LEA applied for final approval for a replacement council school. Further delays ensued, and by the following year the Board of Education, having recognised a pending problem, was critical that plans had still not been received and went to far as to state that the current position amounted 'almost to a public scandal'. The organisation of the existing schools, awaiting a new headmaster, was also deemed

Figure 9.4. Pre-war aerial photograph of Christchurch

unsatisfactory. When the plans were finally approved in April 1925, they were for not more than 345 children.[21]

Adams began his duties as Headmaster of Christchurch Congregational School, which he described in his log book as Christchurch Council School, on 30 June 1925. His entries were thin, but he noted the introduction of a school magazine, and the fact that the Chairman of the Managers had called to congratulate him on a Shakespearean production at the school.[22] The local newspaper was also impressed with this production, and congratulated Adams on instilling the spirit of the school song, 'Follow up, Follow up'.[23] On breaking-up day in July, the chairman addressed the scholars on the 'historic occasion' of its imminent transfer to new buildings.[24]

The move to the new school in Clarendon Road, on the northern outskirts of the town, brought the most heated controversy in its wake. Parents had learned before the opening that there was the possibility of the exclusion of children because of pressure on places. The County Council was challenged also by the Bournemouth and Christchurch Board of Guardians, having been told there was no room for Cottage Homes children (67 in number) at the new school. The *Christchurch Times* suggested that the doors for such children appeared to be 'barred, bolted, and, indeed, fortified'. There was a hint that there was a stigma attached to Poor Law children, though the guardians were anxious they should not be regarded as such and should be mixed in ordinary schools. It was alleged that the opening of the school had been kept very quiet and, though it was advertised as elementary, some of the school was to be set aside for higher education. This would be to the detriment of younger children. One local JP claimed that the Education Committee was 'trying to make this new elementary school into a university like Southampton'.[25] The County Council confirmed that it had always had the intention to upgrade the school quickly to a Central School.

About 93 children were unable to gain entry to the new school. Adams claimed that this was because economies had meant that places had been provided for only 305 and not for 345. But it was the science-dedicated rooms that reduced the new accommodation from 345 to 305. Notwithstanding the deficiency, Adams had, as was planned, reserved 80 places for the higher education of boys and girls. The Cottage Homes children who arrived were assembled in the empty science room but were debarred from admission. Most children refused were between five and eight years of age. Preference had to be given to pupils from the old Congregational School, and Adams pointed out that there were 335 of these, of whom 308 wanted to attend the new school. The newspaper report added that local church schools were still half empty, having accommodation for over 500, with only 318 in attendance.[26] The Editor of the *Christchurch Times* divulged that Adams had been summoned to Winchester and told by the Director of Education that all the classrooms must be occupied forthwith. It was understood that one room, set aside as science laboratory, had been 'sealed up', pending arrival of equipment, which might not be until Christmas. Its use would allow 32 more children to be admitted.[27]

The protests continued, and in late October it was reported that Christchurch's magistrates had declined to convict seven parents whose children had been kept at home as a result of not being admitted to Clarendon Road. In one case the two elder children of a family had been admitted but the infant sibling not. In another case the infant would have had to walk one and three-eighths of a mile four times a day – that is, nearly six miles. In fact the statutory maximum was one and a half miles.[28] Court cases continued, and aroused extra-parochial interest in reports in the *Bournemouth Times and Directory.*[29]

In the following year the Board of Education gave permission for a change of name from Christchurch New Council School to Christchurch Senior School.[30] To cope with space problems, it was agreed that a nearby Drill Hall could be opened as a junior annexe.[31] The LEA explained to the Board that the hall was 'a very suitable light building' which would offer 60–80 places, needed urgently because parents had refused to send their children to occupy the spare places at the Church of England School. The Board made it clear that the Drill Hall was not suitable, but agreed to its use as a 'strictly temporary arrangement'. It was also unhappy about the principle that the headmaster of a senior school would be responsible for the organisation of infants.

In 1928 Hampshire County Council followed the proposals of the Board of Education. The Clarendon Road building was to become Christchurch Junior Council School, accommodating

elementary age children, and a new senior school was to be built
on a site in Soper's Lane, taking only 11+ pupils,[32] basically following the lines recommended by the 1926 Hadow Report on *The
Education of the Adolescent*.[33] The progress of the Council was
again too sluggish for the Board of Education, which described the
situation of overcrowding at the Clarendon Road and the Drill
Hall as causing local feeling to become increasingly 'strong and
embittered'. The accommodation of 140 at the latter was exceeded
by the average attendance. With four classes in one room conditions were described as prejudicial to health: 'On a hot day the
place is an inferno'. Even so, children were still being refused
admission. At the Senior School there were approaching 50 more
pupils on the books than accommodation was provided for. The
Headmaster had to teach groups in the staff room. The LEA was
urged to proceed very rapidly with the Soper's Lane site. The
Board approved the new plans in July 1930 and the new school
was opened in September 1931, with accommodation for 520 boys
and girls.[34] It can be seen in the left middle ground of Figure 9.4.

The staff, apart from Adams himself, included a senior assistant,
taking history and economics, a London science graduate who
taught science and mathematics, a sports master, an art master, a
woodwork and metalwork master, and a senior assistant mistress
(Muriel Gossling). An unusual and even illegitimate feature was
the use of two school monitors who were learning the theory and
practice of teaching, and being prepared for public examinations
to go to training college. The accommodation included ten classrooms, plus a science laboratory, a science lecture room, a wood-
work and metalwork room, a cookery and laundry room, and two
art rooms. Hot lunches were provided at moderate charge for
children coming from a distance. The commodious central hall
was well suited for entertainments. The school was to be referred
to as Christchurch Senior (Central) School. Its motto was to be
Non Scholae sed Vitae. The Town Council vetoed Adams' idea of
using the borough coat of arms on the badges of the school caps.[35]

Sports

Adams was keen to emphasise the sporting prowess of his school.
The *Christchurch Times* reported on the first competition of the
Christchurch Elementary Schools' Sports League, and noted that

Christchurch Council School had secured the challenge cup for cricket and had came second in the total number of points for all boys' athletic events.[36] In future years the school continued to compete strongly in these events and vied with the local Priory School for sporting pre-eminence.

More singular was Adams' initiative to promote a school boxing tournament, referred to in the local press as a 'great stunt at the Senior School', and as one of the Headmaster's 'latest innovations'. A specially constructed ring was made for an inter-school context against Bournemouth Collegiate School.[37] The *Christchurch Times* reported that those who liked boxing were more than delighted with the contest. 'The plucky way in which the boys fought, especially the smaller ones, aroused the enthusiasm of the audience.' The boxers went at it in an 'all-out spirit', and 'the claret flowed freely'. It was stressed that boxing was not compulsory at the school and the written permission of parents had to be obtained before it was taken up. A doctor attended, but was not called upon. 'Several ladies were present, but there were no squeals.'[38] The *Bournemouth Times and Directory* also reported on the tourney, and congratulated the 'more aggressive boys' of Christchurch Senior School on their win. It quoted part of the Deputy Mayor's homily, which claimed that boxing was 'an aid to sportsmanship when properly organised ... it taught both men and boys to curb their tempers'.[39]

The schoolboy pugilism provoked local controversy, however. One correspondent protested that it was degrading. During the tournament, one boy's face was covered in blood and he collapsed afterwards. He demanded that schoolboy boxing should be prohibited by the Education Committee.[40] In response, there was a supportive letter from an ex-military man arguing in favour of anything that would 'beget manliness in our lads'. The problem of otherwise good recruits in the late war had been that they were nauseated at the first contact with flowing blood. Boys needed to have an early acquaintance with 'claret'.[41] In the contest the following year, the Christchurch boys again beat their Bournemouth Collegiate opponents before a large audience of parents and boys. The Deputy Mayor congratulated Adams for an excellently organised event, which he claimed 'had been very sporting and dispelled the criticism which was levelled at the tournament last year'.[42]

School Entertainments

The local newspaper generally offered copious space for accounts of Adams' school entertainments. The report on the December 1926 entertainment, for example, was headed 'Scholars' Wonderful Performance', describing an overflowing house at the Lecture Hall in Millhams Street. The programme included the trial scene from William Shakespeare's *Merchant of Venice* and an adaptation of Hans Andersen's *The Tinder Box*. The following day there was a prizegiving at the new Council School in Clarendon Road, again attended by the Mayor and Mayoress.[43]

The Christchurch Senior School pupils' 1928 entertainment was described as the best they had produced to date. It included a pantomime, *The Forty Thieves*. The reporter suggested that Adams and his staff must have experienced 'a thrill of pride at the faultless manner in which the children performed ... the children looked radiant in their gorgeously coloured and resplendent costumes, while the scenery was enchanting'. Adams played the piano accompaniment while the choir performed the school song and other choruses and sea shanties. The proceeds were to be donated to the 'Christmas Cheer' programme for the locally unemployed.[44] The pantomime was performed twice in Christchurch and repeated at East Cliff, Bournemouth, where the audience was reported to be even more enthusiastic than those in Christchurch.[45]

The following year's entertainment, in January 1930, took place in the Town Hall instead of Millhams Street lecture hall, as the popularity of the performances made it necessary to move into a larger auditorium. Despite accommodating 400 people, 50 to 100 were still turned away. The *Christchurch Times* described it as the best children's performance ever given in the town, with two and a half hours of solid entertainment. The key items were a fairy play, *Rumpelstilzkin* (was it the same as that performed in Tenby?), and a pantomime, *Aladdin*. The performance was in aid of school funds. At the special request of the Countess of Malmesbury, a repeat performance in the Town Hall was arranged, with proceeds in aid of local nursing organisations. Tickets were priced at 2s, 1s 6d and 1s[46] and raised £17. An Australian town councillor from the Melbourne area who was present contrasted the programme favourably with other forms of current entertainment.

'Instead of jazz music, motion pictures with their film heroes and heroines of artificial make-up, I heard the spoken words and singing voices of your own boys and girls.... I will indeed carry away with me to Australia – a part of your Greater Britain beyond the seas – a very kindly recollection of a dramatic and musical treat.'[47]

The 1931 entertainment included an abridged version of *A Midsummer Night's Dream* and *Dick Whittington*,[48] while the 1932 show, the first to be held in the new senior school, was again reported as surpassing any that had gone before. The hall had the great advantage of accommodating 350 in the audience with 45 performers, and having good technical facilities and acoustics. The programme included scenes from Shakespeare's *King John*, an adaptation of Dickens' *A Christmas Carol*, and one of Hans Andersen's *The Tinder Box*.[49] *The Bournemouth Times and Directory* was especially impressed by the 'home industry' effort, the only outside help being given by parents in making the costumes.[50] In November 1932, the *Christchurch Times* reported on the pantomime rehearsals. It was noted that the school had the only raked stage in Christchurch, and 'master craftsmen' aged nine to 13 were making all the fitments, including the lighting, and also producing the scenery. Elsewhere 'young ladies' in the costume department were designing and making the costumes. 'There can be no finer media for the youngsters, no wider scope for their budding talents, and no finer vent for the display of all the arts than this playing at theatres.... It is at once an inspiration and an antidote to the sex-cum-gangster entertainments of this American-ised age. In many ways the "Theatre Royal, Central Schools" is absolutely unique.'[51]

The *Bournemouth Times and Directory* was equally excited by the array of handicrafts at the school's first public exhibition in the same month (see Figure 9.5). The work, all produced as part of the normal activity of the school, included paintings and drawings, needlework, embroidery (including a school flag) and rug-making (the contribution of the retarded class), jams, cakes and bottled fruits. Many articles were sold. Pride of place went to the wood-work exhibits, not least the large stage which had been constructed for school plays, together with stage sets and lighting.[52] Adams' final pantomime production took place at the end of 1933. The preparations again were said to have surpassed the previous year in

Figure 9.5.   Christchurch Senior School: Exhibition of children's handiwork

this 'school of dreams'. Once more 'budding electricians were obtaining their first interest in their work by studding the cavern walls with living flame, and side by side with them, youngsters wielded the brush or saw, all intently engaged upon the lure of the pre-holiday show'. The girls had been equally heavily involved on the costumes: 'industrious needles plied with fashioning and jewelling turban, fez or robber's cloak'. Four scenes from Elizabeth Gaskell's novel *Cranford* were enacted. There was also a musical entertainment, and finally the pantomime *Ali Baba and the Forty*

Thieves. The quality of the staging and lighting were commented upon in what was regarded as a 'definite and well-marked milestone in the history of things theatrical of the school'.[53]

Extra-mural Activity

John William Bateman Adams lived in a modern high quality residence in Hurn Way, on the northern outskirts of Christchurch. His social life outside the school was more restricted than it had been in Tenby. In 1926 he gave a lecture before an 'appreciative audience' on 'Dickens' Schools and Schoolmasters' at Christchurch Congregational Guild which, taken at face value, provides some insights into his educational philosophy at that time. He pointed out that Dickens painted a picture of unrelieved gloom in the scholastic profession. He concluded:

We hear much nowadays of the want of discipline among children; parents are the chief grumblers and tell of lack of respect, disobedience, laziness and so forth ... Can it be that the pendulum has swung back too far, in reaction from the old brutal days? Some people seem to think so. Well, manifold and obvious as their shortcomings may have been, the schoolmasters of Dickens one and all kept strict discipline.... But this essential is now attained by far different and infinitely better methods. Poor Mr. Squeers had never heard that 'blessed word', psycho-analysis. ... We cannot do without discipline, despite the views of certain famous modern novelists, who are also, apparently, ex -officio educationists![54]

Adams was also the organising headmaster of the classes and evening school which were run at the new senior school. These covered commercial, technical and recreative subjects. The old classes had been held at the Town Hall, also under Adams, who by 1930 had placed them on a more 'result-yielding basis'. He stressed the value of entering for appropriate examinations, like those of the Royal Society of Arts for commercial subjects.[55]

Still a staunch patriot, Adams made sure his school wholeheartedly celebrated Empire Day, and indeed supported associated imperial promotion in the school. In 1927, he arranged a programme which included Kipling's 'Recessional' and Elgar's 'Land of Hope and Glory'. The address was delivered by Brigadier-General Sloman of the local barracks. Fifty to sixty parents attended.[56] The following month Sloman visited the school again to give the senior scholars a talk on the origins and the history of the British Empire.[57] On Empire Day in 1928, the children were reminded in a 'splendid Empire address', that their headmaster had served in the war. The speaker, a former colonel of artillery and now the minister of Charminster Congregational Church, Bournemouth, informed them that Europe stood for justice, and that coloured people, members of the Empire, should not be made fun of. As pupils and future citizens, they should be honest, straightforward and truthful, and supportive of an Empire for Christ, who lived in every part of it. The imperial story was recounted – how 'this little country of ours was one of the smallest in the world, yet it was one of the most powerful'. He extolled the work of adventurous forefathers, pioneer settlers and famous soldiers. One of the managers proposed a vote of thanks, and advised the children that if they followed in the footsteps of their fathers and mothers of the old days there would be no need to worry about red and yellow perils.[58]

Adams as Author

At Christchurch Adams became more involved with modern language promotion. He returned to textbook writing, in 1932 producing *School Certificate French Composition*. This was of a less liberal bent than the textbooks of his Tenby years, in being exclusively geared to Oxford Board Senior French Composition questions. The content included 'helpful notes' and model answers, not readily available in grammars and dictionaries. It was based on 'the solution of difficulties which have actually been raised and discussed by intelligent pupils in group work'. The model solutions of the answers were given on the left-hand page to discourage direct copying of the answer. These solutions were straight translations, with significant points numbered and explained in footnotes. The front cover of this text selectively revealed the career details of its writer. Adams noted his experience as a Tutor at Borough Road, as Headmaster at Ashford, as an Army Education Officer and as a Tutor at Sarisbury Court Training College. But reference to his most extended and important appointment, at Tenby Intermediate School, was expunged.[59]

Adams' *A Pedagogue's Fatigues* appeared in the same year and was reviewed in the *Christchurch Times*, which praised it for the 'rich and succulent humour' with which the 'now strange days' of wartime experience were recalled. In fact there was virtually no direct address to the horrors of the First World War in France. It was in the opinion of the reviewer, a 'little volume of laughs and chuckles', of army humour recounted in 'inimitable style ... The whole is good reading indeed ... the fact that it is the work of a local author adds interest'.[60]

The Apotheosis

After Christchurch Senior school was inspected in 1932, HM Inspector referred back to its situation in the late 1920s:

This school ... has had a chequered career. It was originally housed in a new building in Clarendon Road which was soon found to be insufficient for the purposes of a Senior School. During this period it suffered from all sorts and varieties of inconvenience. Changes in the staff took place ... with embarrassing frequency; overcrowding was the rule rather than the exception, and drafts from the Infants' Department ... gravely interfered with classification and organisation. The school knew no rest.... Nevertheless, preparations for the future were made and a definite line of policy was evolved.

The Report was full of enthusiasm for the work of the school. The new accommodation was approved: 'the arrangements made for the comfort of the Head Master and his staff leave nothing to be desired'. There were still too frequent staff changes as neighbouring authorities paid higher salaries, but good substitutes had been found. Though the teachers themselves would be 'the first to disclaim any pretensions to brilliance', they were well above the average in technical skill and efficiency. The inspectors found a well co-ordinated staff, with a 'unanimity of aim and purpose'.

To have secured this is the greatest of all the many achievements of the Head Master, and he has secured this by the example of his burning enthusiasm for the School. No appeals by him for carrying out extraneous duties are necessary. Offers of help are spontaneously given by each and every member of his staff, and all are actuated by the simple desire to promote in all directions the activities and welfare of the whole school.' Among the tenets of his very definite creed the Head Master believes in a liberal education (with a pardonable bias in favour of the value of language training), and the encouragement of some sort of test in the form of a public examination – the latter to provide a definite objective at which to aim.

Pupils were entered for examinations of the College of Preceptors and Royal Society of Arts, the Cambridge School Certificate and the Royal Air Force entrance examination. In preparation for the successes in these examinations, there was not the slightest suspicion of 'cramming'. They had been achieved 'entirely by means of intelligent instruction and a happy process of stimulating intellectual ambitions'. The Inspectors praised the work organised for 'slow-moving' children. Particular praise was lavished on the teacher of Form 1(f) which consisted 'of very retarded children who stand on the edge of mental deficiency'. In view of Adams' previous special interest in history and music, however, it was curious that the Inspectors were critical of the provision in history, which they found 'not a flourishing subject', with too little time found for it, and a syllabus 'rather out of touch with the most recent developments', while music was seen as going through a bad patch, owing to a 'fortuitous shortage' of musicians on the staff. Most other subject tuition was praised as was the extra-curricular work of the school, both in sports and in cultural activities. In sum

... the school plays a very important part in the intellectual, social and civic life of the town. No claim to novelty or originality is put forward. No attempt has been made to pour new wine into old bottles. On the contrary all that is taking place is the refreshment of the old vintage. The two great principles, which lie at the root of the success of the school, are easily discerned. The first is that progress and achievement depend mainly upon the industry and enthusiasm of the children themselves and upon the extent to which these can be cultivated and stimulated by the teachers. And the second is that the education of the child, so far from being confined to the four walls of the classroom, is of small account unless it envisages life in a broader aspect and keeps in touch with the outside world. That the school has succeeded in putting these principles into practice there can be no doubt, and both the Local Authority and the Managers are to be congratulated in having secured the services of a Head Master who has succeeded in assimilating high ideals with practical accomplishments.

The Report did find, however, 'a very abnormal, possibly an unconstitutional, feature' in the employment of promising monitors whom Adams had trained himself. They were, however, judged to be exceptionally capable uncertificated teachers, two of whom were now taking the University of London Intermediate Examination.[61]

A major innovation, also approved in the Report, was the choice of Spanish rather than French as the main foreign language, on the grounds that it was less difficult to acquire and had more commercial value. Adams himself was proficient in both tongues, and had made his decision personally on the grounds of conviction and experience. During the 1920s there had been a surge of interest in promoting the subject. Professor Alison Peers of the University of Liverpool had been commissioned to write a Report on the matter by the Board of Education. This showed a pronounced growth in Spanish teaching since the First World War, which Peers regarded as justified by the importance of commerce with the Spanish-speaking world. Indeed his initiatives were supported by the Central and South American Trade Section of the Liverpool Chamber of Commerce.[62] From the early 1920s Peers regularly publicised the conferences for Spanish teachers held at the University of Liverpool and its summer schools at Santander in Spain. These led to a Certificate qualification for would-be teachers of Spanish. One of Peers' objectives was to establish at least one school in every large town in which Spanish was taught as the first foreign language. He claimed, at an inaugural meeting of the Institute of Hispanic Studies at Liverpool in 1934, that over 300 secondary schools were now offering Spanish.[63] Another pressure group was the Anglo-Spanish Society, based in Cavendish Square, London, which offered prizes for secondary school essays in Spanish. There was also a Society for Spanish Studies, with its headquarters in Liverpool.

Adams was clearly a national figure in the promotion of Spanish education. A colleague of Professor Peers, Victoria de Lara, confirms that his work in this field at Christchurch was well-known in Liverpool, though no surviving record exists of his actually attending the courses arranged there. In Christchurch, Adams ensured that the school's Spanish provision was brought to the fore on speech days. The striking advance in Spanish teaching in preferment to French was, for example, demonstrated in a dialogue in that language between two children as part of the programme of 1930.[64] Another occasion was the school speech day and prize-giving of 1933, Adams' last, when the Chairman referred to the recent HMI report as one of the best he had ever seen. Particular point was made of the recitations in costume by the Spanish scholars on that occasion. 'With fluency and ease the pupils spoke in the Spanish tongue some delightful verse.' The reporter commented that these scholars were 'going out into the world armed with a language which plays increasingly an important part in the world of commerce'.[65] Once more Adams may well have been influenced by his formative years as a pupil teacher at Fleet Road school, where commercial education was held to be so important, and for which now Spanish was regarded as so valuable an instrument.

In an editorial account under the heading 'An Ambassador of Christchurch', it was stated that Adams was at present on his third visit to Spain 'in the interest of educational matters'. He had covered 3,000 miles to Andalusia, visiting Cordova, Seville and Madrid en route. He was said to find Spanish people 'most kind and hospitable' and his associations with them were 'of the happiest order'. He had called upon the Spanish Ambassador in London. The editor concluded that Spanish people appreciated 'the educational activities of Mr. Adams as much as we do'.[66]

In 1933 it was reported that Adams had been awarded the MBE in the New Year's Honours List,[67] variously claimed to be for his services to education[68] and to the Foreign Office.[69] The *Times Educational Supplement*, however, specifically commented that 'those interested in the Hadow scheme will be glad that it has been recognised in the person of Mr. J.W.B. Adams...'.[70] Certainly Adams is recorded in an appendix to the Hadow Report as having sent memoranda, statistics or other data for the use of the Committee.[71] It would seem likely that either his work in promoting Hadow principles in working out the concept of a Central School which combined both liberal and vocational principles, or his promotion of Spanish teaching, or both, had brought him some official recognition. He had also travelled widely to military educational centres to gain wider knowledge of the working of their entrance examination systems, in which his boys were very successful, again gaining some public visibility.

Adams should have retired in 1933, but the County Council secured the permission of the Board of Education to extend his services to 31 March 1934.[72] The reporting of his retirement read oddly in the light of the *Christchurch Times'* previous praise of the work of Adams and his. It was merely recorded that there had been a pleasant occasion at which the retiring headmaster was thanked for all he had done for the school, and was presented with an armchair, a smoker's cabinet and a casket of cigarettes.[73]

BATEMAN ADAMS' IMPACT ON CHRISTCHURCH CENTRAL SCHOOL: ORAL EVIDENCE

At the time of the preparation of this book, it was found possible to gain valuable oral evidence from a former member of Adams' staff, Muriel Gossling, his senior assistant mistress who, aged 93, agreed to be interviewed in August 1995. She was trained at Basingstoke Pupil Teacher Centre and Brighton Training College. After a short spell of teaching in Wednesbury in the Midlands, she was one of Adams' first appointments. She taught English, botany, mathematics and needlework, but saw her special strength as geography. She remained at the same school until her retirement in the early 1960s.

Muriel Gossling recalled Adams as something of a man of mystery. She and the staff did not know whence he came or where he went after his retirement. At Christchurch his extraprofessional image was that of a private man. She thought he lived with a housekeeper. He did not appear to take much part in local social life. He made trips abroad. He was a tall man who looked well for his age. He was intensely polite to women. Miss Gossling felt he was more at ease with men and not least with officer types.

Miss Gossling could hardly have been more supportive of Adams as a person or of his achievements at the school. In her view, he was totally devoted to his work, and a happy person when engaged in it. His image was that of an authentic officer and gentleman, reflecting his Oxford and military experiences: a public school type in fact, though he had never been to one. His external reputation gave the staff a lift. He was revered at County Hall, where the administrative staff were said to stand in awe of him. He built up the school into something Christchurch had not seen before. In his Christchurch years he was referred to by the name Bateman-Adams, which had become his preferred term of address. Adams was affectionately regarded by the staff as a character who was somewhat unpredictable, erratic and eccentric. He continually spawned bright ideas and, having had one, rushed around the school in mortar-board and flowing gown, informing the class-teachers there was to be an end-of-day school staff meeting to discuss it. Some dubbed him 'the vision'. He taught English and history. He was keen on promoting good diction, and was himself an excellent public speaker. Assembly speeches were given with much expression.

He was regarded as generous and supportive towards the staff, and took them out for an annual Christmas meal at a Bournemouth hotel. Outings were arranged to the Winter Gardens in Bournemouth to hear the famous Municipal Orchestra. Miss Gossling remembered the excitement generated by the school entertainments, on which Adams worked with the music teacher and others. He remained an enthusiast for cricket, especially Oxford and Cambridge games. He took boys to cricket matches and older children on visits to places of historic interest. She confirmed he was a convinced patriot. The lessons of the First World War were regularly recalled, and he was particularly keen on boys training for the forces. He travelled around forces' colleges to identify what was required to advance the career prospects of his pupils. Like his father, he was a stickler for cleanliness and tidiness. Pupils were taught the things they should respect and the things they should do for their country. In sum, Miss Gossling judged that his mind was always on innovation, but introduced according to its worth and whether he valued it.

There is some slighter, but still useful, corroborative detail from a pupil of 1932, Mrs R. Topp. Like Muriel Gossling, she retained an image of Adams as headmaster 'floating by' in mortar-board and black gown. He took a great interest in commercial French and encouraged her to take the Junior College of Preceptors' examination. Her aunt paid the fee required, but she did not find the qualification very useful in getting work in the depression period. She recalled taking part in the successful production of *Cinderella* in 1932. She helped with other senior girls to provide lunches for senior staff as part of domestic science, a fascinating glimpse again of the influence of Fleet Road, where Adams' father used the senior girls in the same way. Overall, Mrs Topp wrote of spending 20 or so happy months at the school, which she attributed to the positive atmosphere prevailing.

There is in addition a more detailed insight into pupil views of Adams' time. In September 1931 the *Christchurch Times* ran an essay competition, offering prizes of 2s 6d each for the best essays from a boy and a girl on what they thought of the new Senior School. There were 57 entries. Among general perceptions were the quality of the school hall, the size of the dining hall, the specialist teaching rooms, the extensive playing fields and gymnasium, the room for the staff and the one for the headmaster, the arrangement of the school into four houses, the use of class monitors and prefects, the central heating instead of smoky stoves, and the special bus service for children living at a distance.

After judging the essays, the newspaper first printed the best entries received.[74] In the following week it published brief extracts from the rest, in the original spelling.[75] Some of the more revealing contributions follow:

> While you are walking down the corridor you have to be strictly silence because there will be a tremendous echo. The classrooms are emensely big and will hold 50 children fairly easy. Mr. Adams is our headmaster and he rules us justily.
>
> Our headmaster Mr Adams spoke to us and told us how to help the staff, also how to make everyone as happy as possible and how to enjoy the school.
>
> The headmaster has a very nice study for himself and there is a waiting room for anybody who wants an interview with him.
>
> The playground waste paper baskets are very good ideas. There didnt ought to be any rubbish in the playgrounds if the boys and girls keep the rules.
>
> In the porches there are looking glasses shaped like a lifebuoy with 'Am I clean and tidy on them' which I think is good idea.
>
> I think it is up to all the boys at the school to keep it in perfect order. We have excellent teachers and a very nice headmaster.
>
> We are strictly forbidden to cross the quadrangles or speak in the corridors because the sound echoes so.
>
> I think the new school is built splendid and the architect was a man of brains to plan such a building. ... And we are very gratful to Mr.Adams and the Educational of Winchester for our wonderful school.

POSTSCRIPT

Following Adams' departure there was some surprisingly disdainful comment on his regime in the *Christchurch Times*. In referring to the 'new and popular headmaster', the correspondent observed that he had replaced the entertainment and speech days, with their 'preening, specially decked and trained groups of scholars', with open days. The heading of the article was 'A Sane School at Last'.[76] The newspaper also reported that Adams had taken a part-share in a preparatory grammar school at Horsmonden in Kent,[77] but no further documentation on this has been found.

What is known is that J.W.B. Adams, MBE, MA, as a former Pembroke College graduate was admitted to membership of the

United University Club in 1934. Founded in 1821, the club was located at 1 Suffolk Street, Pall Mall, London. Membership in 1934 was restricted to 1,100 persons, but was increased on its amalgamation with the New University Club in 1938. Ordinary members included 'any gentleman who has regularly proceeded to a degree at Oxford or Cambridge'. Extraordinary members were qualified by being Princes of the Blood Royal, Cabinet Ministers, Bishops, Judges, Speakers of the House of Commons, the Lord Chancellor, and Governor Generals of the Dominions or Colonies. Adams had clearly retained a taste for mixing with the elite. The entrance fee was 10 guineas and the annual subscription 15 guineas. The facilities included a coffee room, smoking room, library, card room, billiard room, ladies room and squash court, and bedrooms were available on payment for short stays of members.[78] The former club building is now occupied by the British School of Osteopathy (Figure 9.6)

It can reasonably be inferred that Adams was unable to afford the cost of membership of the club, at least during his final years. He made his will at the club in 1940, but by the end of the Second World War was residing with six other lodgers in quite modest

Figure 9.6.   Former United University Club, Suffolk Street, Pall Mall

circumstances at 7 Denning Road, Hampstead (Figure 9.7). The back bedrooms on his side of the street overlooked the houses of the parallel street to the north-Willow Road, where his family had lived between the early 1880s and 1918. John William Bateman Adams died from heart trouble in Hampstead Hospital on 12 January 1946, aged 77.[79] In attendance at his death was one of the Jannaways, his mother's family. There appear to have been no other relatives. The last of the dynasty, he was buried by his father's grave in Hampstead cemetery. In 1918 he had been bequeathed £1,743 14s 6d by his mother. In his own will he left a mere £225 5s 0d, to a Mrs O'Hea, described as a 'married woman'.

Figure 9.7. J.W.B. Adams' final lodgings, Denning Road, Hampstead

REFERENCES AND NOTES

1. *Middlesex Chronicle*, 28 Jan. 1911.
2. PRO ED 35/1822.
3. R.J. Clapp, *A Short History of Ashford County School, Middlesex, 1911–1961* (Ashford, 1960), p.11.
4. Greater London Record Office, E.Mx 4/1, Ashford County School *Minutes*, Oct. 1913.
5. PRO ED 35/1822.
6. J.W.B. Adams, *A Pedagogue's Fatigues* (London: Ocean Publishing Company, 1932), p.7.
7. PRO ED 10/76.
8. *Labour Gazette*, Vol. 26 (1918), pp. 436–7.
9. *Times Educational Supplement*, 13 Feb. 1919, p. 79.
10. *Hampshire Independent*, 29 June 1918.
11. *Hampshire Telegraph and Post*, 31 Oct. 1919.
12. *Labour Gazette*, 28 April 1920, p. 173.
13. Ibid., 28 Oct. 1920, p. 540.
14. PRO LAB 2/631/198/1919/Part 1.
15. *Hampshire Independent*, 13 Nov. 1920.
16. Ibid., 11 Nov. 1921.
17. Ibid., 18 Nov. 1921.
18. Ibid., 23 June 1922.
19. Reports and Proceedings of Hampshire County Council, *Minutes*, 7 March 1923.
20. *Hampshire Advertiser and Independent*, 19 April 1924.
21. PRO ED 21/29298.
22. Christchurch Congregational School Log Book, 23 March 1926.
23. *Christchurch Times*, 3 April 1926.
24. Ibid., 29 July 1926.
25. Ibid., 21 Aug. 1926.
26. Ibid., 4 Sept. 1926.
27. Ibid., 18 Sept. 1926.
28. Ibid., 30 Oct. 1926.
29. *Bournemouth Times and Directory*, 4 Dec. 1926.
30. *Christchurch Times*, 16 April 1927.
31. Ibid., 15 Oct. 1927.
32. Ibid., 26 May 1928.
33. PRO ED 21/29298.
34. PRO ED 21/29299.
35. *Christchurch Times*, 12 and 19 Sept. 1931.
36. Ibid., 24 July 1926.
37. Ibid., 5 March 1932.
38. Ibid., 26 March 1932.
39. *Bournemouth Times and Directory*, 18 March 1932.
40. *Christchurch Times*, 19 March 1932.
41. Ibid., 2 April 1932.
42. *Bournemouth Times and Directory*, 7 April 1933.
43. *Christchurch Times*, 1 Jan. 1927.
44. Ibid., 15 Dec. 1928.
45. Ibid., 9 Feb. 1929.
46. Ibid., 25 Jan. 1930.

47. Ibid., 8 Feb. 1930.
48. Ibid., 31 Jan. 1931.
49. Ibid., 6 Feb. 1932.
50. *Bournemouth Times and Directory*, 5 Feb. 1932.
51. *Christchurch Times*, 12 Nov. 1932.
52. *Bournemouth Times and Directory*, 4 Nov. 1932.
53. *Christchurch Times*, 2 Dec. 1933.
54. Ibid., 26 Nov. 1926.
55. Ibid., 10 Sept. 1932.
56. Ibid., 8 May 1927.
57. Ibid., 4 June 1927.
58. Ibid., 26 May 1928.
59. J.W.B.Adams, *School Certificate French Composition* (London: Herbert Russell, 1932), pp. 5–6.
60. *Christchurch Times*, 3 Dec. 1932.
61. PRO ED 21/29299.
62. *Times Educational Supplement*, 17 Aug. 1929, p. 364.
63. Ibid., 15 Oct. 1932, p. 394, and 13 Oct. 1934, p. 348.
64. *Christchurch Times*, 30 July 1930.
65. Ibid., 5 Aug. 1933.
66. Ibid., 15 April 1933.
67. *London Gazette Supplement*, 2 Jan. 1933, p. 10; *Times Educational Supplement*, 7 Jan. 1933, p.5.
68. *Christchurch Times*, 7 Jan. 1933.
69. Clapp, op.cit. (1960), p.11.
70. *Times Educational Supplement*, 7 Jan. 1933, p.5.
71. Board of Education, *Report of the Consultative Committee on the Education of the Adolescent (Hadow Report)* (London: HMSO, 1926), p. 252.
72. Hampshire County Council Elementary Education Sub-committee *Minutes*, 8 March 1933.
73. *Christchurch Times*, 24 March 1934.
74. Ibid., 5 Sept. 1931.
75. Ibid., 12 Sept. 1931.
76. Ibid., 24 Nov. 1934.
77. Ibid., 7 April 1934.
78. United University Club, *Rules, Byelaws and List of Members* (1944).
79. *Hampstead and Highgate Record and Chronicle*, 18 Jan. 1946.

Conclusion

This biographical excursion into the professional experiences of a Victorian teaching dynasty is, so far as I am aware, the first published attempt at such a cross-generational study in the British historiography of education.[1] As Ruth Jennings pointed out in her book on three Victorian schoolmasters[2], the tracking of teachers' lives of that time 'opens a window on to a wider and far more complex scene' than can be envisioned from the less well differentiated portrayals 'from above' of popular schooling that have more often been handed down. The biographical approach generates insights into a professional culture that became increasingly rich and heterogeneous as the Victorian period progressed, and brings to light a nexus of small-scale interpersonal and inter-group working and social relationships from within the actual world of teaching and learning, which co-existed with the broader legislative and organisational frameworks.

The title of Ruth Jennings' book is interesting, drawing as it does on a quotation from a Liverpool School Board Inspectress, whose watchword for elementary school teachers was *Lofty Aims and Lowly Duties*. This limited and somewhat sinister concept of course derived from an earlier hierarchical set of social principles designed to humble elementary schoolteachers and mock their aspirations. Even though the attempt was unsuccessful, the resulting downbeat stereotype became enshrined in later academic studies of the profession, in part perhaps because of the nature of the source materials they relied on, such as influential but prejudiced newspapers and journals targeted at the upper and middle classes; in part through taking at face value the complaints of early schoolteachers who were understandably taking advantage of this negative image in their broadsheets to drum up support in their campaigning for improvement; and in part through limiting the contextual focus to macro-structures and to population aggregates, whether of children, parents or teachers. Most accounts draw little on the actual experience of teachers.

There is little feel, therefore, for the 'lived realities' and the 'human consciousness'[3] of teachers as normal working and living beings. They were part of the growing Victorian respectable lower middle-class cohort, obsessed with status, striving to keep up appearances and keep out of debt on the one hand, and to achieve more secure and comfortable futures for their families on the other. Its individuals had family rows, confrontations with their peers and professional superiors, and indeed in some cases with their servants. In the family sphere they fell in love, conceived children before marriage, had extramarital affairs and suffered the traumas of divorce, shopped for clothes and for Christmas, rented or bought houses, while in the social world they attended theatres, football and cricket matches, enjoyed domestic musical evenings, joined churches, social clubs and professional associations, travelled to conferences, and engaged in many other activities. Most of these 'lived realities' were exemplified at one point or another in the lives of members of the Adams teaching dynasty.

This study has drawn attention to the power of human agency. The story of the Adams family illustrates the range of career opportunities available during their times, and the capacity, within reason, to make personal choices and exploit those opportunities. Why did John Adams elect to switch from the National to the British system, for example? We cannot be sure of his motivation, but it would seem likely that he saw a prospect of career advancement in the change. It may also have fitted more comfortably with a liberal, nonconformist conscience. Similarly, William Bateman Adams overcame early setbacks to pursue single-mindedly the career path he had mapped out for himself in the metropolis, his mind increasingly set on being appointed to the headship of a London Board School. He was able to take advantage of the favourable starting point provided by influential mentors and family contacts, but his achievement was in essence earned by his own considerable prowess.

His brother John Frederick also achieved national visibility, again after a devastating preliminary setback in Wales. He had shown at an early stage political and communication skills, and like his elder brother took advantage of family connection to move to the metropolis. Then their paths diverged, J.F. Adams deciding to seek his niche in educational administration, and in national union and association activity. Richard Adams took the less ambitious career trajectory of returning to his father's school and remaining in his home town for the 40 years of his teaching career. Once more the choice was his.

The representative of the third generation, John William Bateman Adams, came nearest to being born with a silver spoon in his mouth. He enjoyed the unusual experience of a professional training along two pathways: the pupil teacher/training college, and the prestigious university system. The support of influential personal connections was again much to his advantage, but he would not have achieved so much without the benefit of the professional and personal skills he had developed for himself, and the choices these made possible. He rose to upper middle- class status, and became a member of a prestigious London club. In all his posts he exuded the image of the public school man, though he was not such. Where his career was set back was not through any professional failure, but through a personal life choice of which the external world must have disapproved and which caused a nervous breakdown. When he returned to teaching in the 1920s, the demand–supply equation was less propitious, and he had to accept a post of lower status than those to which he had been accustomed before the war. But he made the most of this opportunity, greatly raised the reputation of his school, and ended his career to his own evident professional satisfaction, and with an MBE gained for his services to education.

A continuing feature of the Adams family history was the presence of both similarities and differences as between generations. All three broadly accepted and worked to the respectable social and professional values of their time. They shared the competitive will to get on in the world, an unrelenting belief that education was a civilising and improving influence, and a wide range of leisure interests. Their professional lives varied, however. William Bateman achieved eminence as one of the most successful headmasters of his era, like his father before him. He propounded and translated into practice a broad and liberal view of the curriculum, while not neglecting the more utilitarian and vocational elements that the more reactionary forces of his time would have preferred to see dominant. John Frederick Adams shared William Bateman's progressive views, but found his métier in educational administration. The youngest son Richard, however, held fast and even more opinionatedly to a much narrower set of educational purposes, and ended as an unashamed reactionary.

What is fascinating about the career of the representative of the third generation, John William Bateman Adams, is the extent to which, in later and different circumstances, he adapted so many of his father's ideas in his work: within the curriculum in his interests in history and literature, modern languages and the commercial subjects, and outside it in a range of extra curricular activities. He was also brought up in the heyday of Empire and fought in a war, which might explain his more obvious concern for the national interest than that shown by grandfather, father and uncles, patriots though they were too.

The family's socio-economic progress quintessentially illustrated the ladders of meritocratic advance. Choice of residence clearly reflected aspirations and the capacity to realise them. Had Charles Booth's colour categories been applied to the family's Swansea residences, for example, John Adams' first choice near the town centre would probably have been in purple, signifying mixed comfort and poverty. His later residences in Swansea, and indeed W.B. and J.F. Adams' first homes in the metropolitan area, would have been classified in the pink of respectable comfort. W.B. Adams' choice of dwellings in Regent's Park and in Hampstead, and J.F. Adams' in Tottenham, were securely in the red of the well-to-do. This represented clear social advance, whereas Richard Adams' Sketty residence just maintained his position in the pink of comfort. By contrast, in his brief sojourn back in London just before the First World War, J.W.B. Adams resided in prestigious apartments categorised by Booth in the yellow of wealth.

In three generations of professional experience, the family witnessed many evolutionary transitions and also more radical educational changes. As already noted, J.F. Adams observed in one of his speeches that, whether as pupil, pupil teacher, certificated assistant or school board administrator, he had been through four epochs of school organisation. The first was the monitorial system, in which his grandfather spent his formative years. This evolved into the pupil teacher system, under which he and his brothers grew up. By the time they were teachers themselves, as demonstrated at Fleet Road and Rutland Street, they had moved into the classroom or Prussian system, operated largely by a headteacher and certificated assistants. Adams looked forward to the fourth epoch: an all-graduate profession. Fleet Road, and the schools at which John William Bateman Adams taught, had by 1903 moved some way in this direction.

The two members of the Adams family who begat children, John Adams and William Bateman Adams, were preoccupied with one of the most endemic anxieties of lower middle-class existence, the need to attend to the prospects of their offspring and particularly to protect them from social descent. Here they were helped by the socio-economic changes which guaranteed at least widening opportunities for the coming generation. Of course there were limitations on what could be achieved in the period before the Newcastle and Taunton Commissions. But these Commissions at long last recognised the demands of the third middle force in British society, to which the Adams' belonged.

While the family believed in the formative powers of education, they were also realists as to what could be achieved, and externalised their particular circumstances in advocating a broader set of social strategies. They believed in a graded system of schooling. Both W.B. Adams to the Cross Commission, and J.F. Adams at his conferences, spoke strongly in favour of the idea of basic schools for the under-privileged, a second group for the average, and a third group, as exemplified in the Fleet Road Senior Mixed Department, or the Tottenham Higher Grade School, serving more favoured social areas, charging higher fees, and taking pupils until they reached their early teens, helped by a scholarship system. Both of them considered that the standard of teacher-training needed to be raised to meet with the requirements of this last group, which led them to support the idea of employing graduates and specialists or semi-specialists in their upper forms. They therefore appreciated the link between social class variation, residential segregation and school gradation, as part of their philosophy of improvement.

Another major transition was one with which the Adams family, especially John Adams, found hard to come to terms. Although all were ostensibly meritocrats, we have seen that they were not averse to taking advantage of older types of career advancement, based on family and church connection. The Adams inevitably relied heavily on the patronage of their sponsoring organisation, the British and Foreign School Society. They took care to keep on good terms with the Society, and were keen to publicise their successes precisely in its journal, the *Educational Record*. They were materially helped by the good reports of the Inspectorate, including the BFSS's own Inspector in South Wales. While comfortable with this system, John Adams was seriously irritated by the more formal, bureaucratised administrative approach of the Swansea School Board, and it was only W.B. Adams' huge reputation with influential members of the London School Board, it might also be conjectured, that prevented confrontations with its administrators, for he too was an independent spirit, disliking imposition from above. So was his brother J.F. Adams, who caused offence to those on the Tottenham School Board who insisted on following formal committee procedures, rather than acting in what he claimed to be a common-sense and effective way by pressing on with business through prior personal arrangement with the Chairman. J.W.B. Adams also fell foul of the bureaucratic formalities of Pembrokeshire County Council during his Tenby period.

At the same time, once more reflecting a change from the pre- to the post-Revised Code arrangements, John Adams and his two older teaching sons were studiously deferential to those they considered their superiors. While not kowtowing to the socially or politically privileged, they at the same time revered those they viewed as persons of culture, who became valued role models. These included members of the pre-Revised Code inspectorate, and influential members of their school boards. J.F. Adams' furious denunciation of the judgments of the sub-inspector condemning his Llanelly school, and his early response to the praise of the Tottenham School Board, both used the word 'gentleman', meaning a person of refinement. The family were climbing socially and this culminated in J.W.B. Adams' convincing presentation of himself to his contemporaries as a scholar and the gentleman.

Another trend of the second half of the nineteenth century was the secularisation of society. This had a strong impact on the educational system. The Adams family members were active in these changes, not least in their dedication to school prizegivings and associated entertainments through the three generations. It is hard to judge how intrinsically religious the family was. John Adams was accused of being a turncoat, having moved from a National to a British School. Though proclaiming vigorously his

Nonconformist lineage, and not being allowed to attend an Anglican training college, William Bateman Adams was none the less married in a parish church. Though his son was in turn a Congregational church organist, he too was married in an Anglican church. When J.F. Adams died, his local vicar publicly drew a veil over his religious leanings, or presumably the lack of them. It would seem doubtful whether any of the family was deeply religious, though some at least were practising church or chapel goers.

One factor the first and second generations had in common was that they died in harness, in their late fifties or early sixties. Not one of them reached retirement age, though Mary Adams retired early, as a result of nervous debility. The pressure on teachers at the time was exceptionally heavy. The argument then on the size of classes was whether they should be of 50 or 60 children, not 20 or 30, as J.F. Adams reflected in one of his conference speeches. On ethnic and gender issues, the family, as one of Anglo-Welsh origin, faced tensions. We noted how William and Mary Adams' sojourn at Cefn Coed was undermined by concerns over their lack of Welsh. Even though his early experiences in the principality were not propitious, W.B. Adams in later life made great play of his pride in his Welsh origins, as reflected in his founding membership of London's Pembroke County Club, and in his welcome of London's Welsh-origin Lord Mayor to the Fleet Road school. In gender terms, both John and W.B. Adams' families benefited financially from the difficulties of teacher supply in their respective generations, for both Eliza and Mary Adams found it relatively easy to obtain posts. William and Mary Adams were one of many London School Board headteacher partnerships, their two incomes ensuring true middle class socio-economic status. Certainly such as Mary Adams took advantage of the opportunities women had to advance themselves. And if they were still also expected to be devoted wives and mothers, they had the advantage over many of their counterparts today of being able to employ servants. W.B. Adams was also a notable exponent of co-education, and there is no doubt that the expectations he and his colleague Louisa Walker generated in their girls were beyond the norm for their time.

Major elements of continuity over the generations were also revealed. One of the most positive aspects of the Adams teaching dynasty was the high expectations its members had of the efficacy of universal schooling in improving the prospects of children and enhancing social cohesion. For example, J. F. Adams from an early age expressed his view that the utilitarian Revised Code was a grave handicap for working-class children. W.B. Adams' Fleet Road curriculum challenged a large percentage of its pupils to achieve high standards. Both J.F. Adams and later his nephew extolled the virtues of extending educational horizons, the former in letters to the press and in his speeches at School Board Clerks' Conferences, and the latter in his homilies at school prizegivings. These were not just rhetorical aspirations. The Adams, as part of the same social cohort, fully empathised with the demands of the parents whose children attended schools such as Fleet Road. Similarly at Tenby and at Christchurch, J.W.B. Adams successfully convinced managers and parents that an education that combined liberal concepts, that was competitive and demanding on the pupils, and kept vocational ends in view, was what their children needed.

Another involvement of the family was with the broader infrastructure of education. The first and second generations of the dynasty were all members of local teacher associations, which provided professional support and the benefits of social contact. W.B. Adams had an ambivalent attitude towards unions, supporting the local branch but criticising the national executive. On the other hand, J.F. Adams was a long-standing contributor to the work of the National Union of Elementary Teachers in the first place, and later to the conferences of the School Board Clerks' Association and of the Association of School Boards.

In a biographical study such as this, there are significant problems in interpreting the available historical material. In a number of cases there are discrepancies, some inadvertent and some deliberate, as between personal recollection and corroborative documentation. Local newspaper accounts in themselves are often lacking in balance, and are very selective in what they offer. Thus some years they might give a full account of a particular occasion, in other years a more limited one, and in others perhaps none at all. But in general sufficient supportive evidence has been found to allow the claim that the story has not been substantially distorted through wrong leads or gaps in the historical record of the family.

There are also the perennial problems of making and justifying generalisations from particular cases. To an extent these have been attempted above, but that was not the prime purpose of the study, which was, essentially, to provide a narrative of actual historic educational experience. It has, I hope, offered an appraisal of these people of the past that is also tinged with respect and admiration. It may be that many readers will not warm to the personalities of the Adams teaching dynasty. But in their enthusiasm for their cause, their vision and their translation of high expectations into achievement they surely offer role models for later times, as well as timely correctives to the view that schooling during the period under review was limited in outlook, undifferentiated and fixed in a low estate.

The death of Fleet Road as a Board School can be interpreted as symbolic of a policy which critically hindered the future progress of English education. The problem was not so much the collapse of the school boards as the rejection of the qualities the best of their schools demonstrated. The lower middle classes over the three decades following the 1870 Act increasingly recognised the superiority of the higher grade schools over the third grade schools identified by the Schools' Inquiry Commission, which by the end of the School Board period were more or less obsolete. It is ironic that Fleet Road inadvertently played so significant a part in the collapse of the system. It was certainly true that W.B. Adams played fast and loose with the strict provisions of the 1870 Act, a far too narrowly circumscribed piece of legislation for the aspirations of the middling groups in society of the 1880s and 1890s, as he well understood. His Senior Mixed Department was essentially of a middle rather than an elementary phase of schooling. Nevertheless, he and others like him evolved a liberal, practical and forward-looking organisational framework for the twentieth century that was supplanted, as a deliberate political strategy, by the more elitist patterns and procedures of the first and second grades of grammar school, with all their ancestral trimmings.[4]

REFERENCES AND NOTES

1. But see G. Bartle, 'George Bedloe: a London Board School Headmaster', *Journal of Educational Administration and History*, 11 (1979), pp. 13–21; and N. Pole, 'A Victorian Teaching Family', in R. Lowe (ed.) *Biography and Education: Some Eighteenth and Nineteenth Century Studies* (History of Education Society Occasional Publication No.5 1980), pp. 51–8.
2. R. Jennings, *Lofty Aims and Lowly Duties: Three Victorian Schoolmasters* (Sheffield Academic Press, 1994), p. 247.

3. B. Finkelstein, 'Redoing Urban Educational History', in R.K. Goodenow and W.E. Marsden (eds), *The City and Education in Four Nations* (Cambridge University Press, 1992), p.185.
4. See W.E. Marsden, 'Schools for the Urban Lower Middle Class: Third Grade or Higher Grade?', in P. Searby (ed.), *Educating the Victorian Middle Class* (Leicester: History of Education Society, 1979), pp.45–56.

Index

www.ingramcontent.com/pod-product-compliance
Ingram Content Group UK Ltd.
Pitfield, Milton Keynes, MK11 3LW, UK
UKHW041840280225
455677UK00010B/270